า\ร

TRAVELS WITH MACY

After a 35-year career as a vet, columnist, broadcaster and author, Bruce Fogle—the world's bestselling pet-care writer—decided to take a journey with his young dog Macy. Travelling in the footsteps of the great American novelist John Steinbeck, Fogle set off to see if the North America of his youth still existed. Would he, after living most of his life in Britain, feel at home in the land of his birth? Would he find the welcoming, peaceful backwaters of his upbringing unchanged?

Together with Macy, Fogle retraced Steinbeck's steps through the length and breadth of North America, travelling over 12,000 miles, meeting people, listening to their tales, sharing their homes and their generosity, and indulging in some of the world's most exciting dog-walking territory. At a point in history when all eyes are on America, what Bruce found in the changed heartlands surprised and delighted him. What Macy found—oceans, deserts and thousands of miles of unspoilt wilderness—made her very excited. And very bold.

TRAVELS WITH MACY

One man and his dog take a journey through
North America in search of home

Bruce Fogle

BBC
LARGE
PRINT

First published 2005
by
Ebury Press
This Large Print edition published 2006
by
BBC Audiobooks Ltd
by arrangement with
Ebury Press,
a division of The Random House Group Ltd

UK Hardcover   ISBN 1 4056 4813 9
UK Softcover   ISBN 1 4056 4814 7

British Library Cataloguing in Publication Data available

Printed and bound in Great Britain by
Antony Rowe Ltd., Chippenham, Wiltshire

CONTENTS

ACKNOWLEDGEMENTS   vii

THE ROUTE   x-xi

PREAMBLE   xiii

CHAPTER ONE
HEADING FOR SAG HARBOR   1

CHAPTER TWO
NORTH THROUGH NEW ENGLAND   53

CHAPTER THREE
EASTERN CANADA AND VERMONT   89

CHAPTER FOUR
NEW YORK AND ONTARIO   113

CHAPTER FIVE
THE MIDWEST   149

CHAPTER SIX
THE TRUE WEST   197

CHAPTER SEVEN
THE PACIFIC NORTH-WEST   247

CHAPTER EIGHT
SOUTHERN CALIFORNIA   285

CHAPTER NINE
ROUTE 66   315

CHAPTER TEN
INTO TEXAS   343

CHAPTER ELEVEN
THE DEEP SOUTH   367

CHAPTER TWELVE
GOING HOME   409

EPILOGUE   419

BIBLIOGRAPHY   428

ACKNOWLEDGEMENTS

The best editor I've ever had was my first one. Robert MacDonald simply left me alone to get on with my writing. After I'd completed *Pets and their People*, he showed me how, by breaking up large chapters into more containable smaller ones, by combining elements from different sections of a book into unified themes, a read could become more readable.

After I'd completed the draft manuscript for this book I met with my present editor. She gave me the best editorial advice I've had for over twenty years and I told her how grateful I was. I explained that her suggestions reminded me of the sound suggestions my first editor had given me. She asked what his name was and where he worked and I replied that Robert MacDonald worked at William Collins Sons Ltd. There was a pause and then Hannah smiled quietly and said calmly, 'That was my father.' Hannah remained very British, very composed, but her eyes were dancing. First and foremost, thanks to Hannah MacDonald, for commissioning this book and for her enthusiasm, and to the late Robert, for producing Hannah.

Needless to say, you can't leave work for several months unless those you work with take on more responsibilities. My veterinary colleague, Bas Hagreis, did the work of two vets, joined by Simon Lewi just before I returned. My veterinary nurses, Hester Small, Ashley McManus, Hilary Hayward and Suzi Gray all lived the trip with me, keeping a map at the veterinary clinic, tracking where Macy and I were.

I appreciate Buddy Bethune going beyond the call of commerce. He matched me up with the right GMC motorhome but he also helped with all the associated trivia, and has continued to help as the GMC has remained in storage in North Carolina.

The journey itself was made memorable by the people who opened their homes to me, Judy and Gib Krohn, the Wheelers, the Langford family, the Breslin family, Barb and Doug Bodine, Al and Carol Scott and Bob Hustler. In Stockholm, Wisconsin, I mentioned to Lucy Elliot, the local antique dealer, that I'd bought a Norwegian tankard from the son of the man who wrote *A Treasury of Norwegian Folk Art in America*. I couldn't find a copy, even on www.abebooks.com, but when Lucy visited London, she gave me her own copy.

I very much appreciate Professor Tom Loebel from York University in Toronto, giving me advice on how to transliterate regional American vernacular and Claire Kingston at Ebury Press for gently reminding me that I'd forgotten about planned meetings. The completion of *Travels with Macy* took on a family feel. I've always been impressed by Richard Evans's work as a book designer. (I know him, both through his dog Arthur and through the books he designs for Dorling Kindersley). Richard shares a studio with Don Grant, who has illustrated two of my previous books. It was simply fun to work with them and I'm grateful for their excellent contributions.

She had no say in the matter but she was my excuse, my non-judgemental travelling companion, sometimes even my bed-warmer. It would be great if dogs understood gratitude but I value Mace's benign acceptance of her role in our travels. Julia my wife did have a say and I love her for letting me travel for so long with another gorgeous blonde.

BRUCE FOGLE'S
Travels with Macy

PREAMBLE

Some time back, to prepare for a dog care book I was writing, I went to Burlington, Vermont, to a conference of the American Holistic Veterinary Medical Association. It was a wonderful three-day meeting—'groovy' is probably the way most attendees would have described it. Unreconstructed, laconic, ponytailed 1960s hippies, almost all of them men looking at ease with life and with themselves, gathered with 1990s veterinary graduates, almost all women, more intense, deeply, seriously—who knows, even religiously—concerned with our influence on the natural world and the direction technological medicine is going in. I listened to an elegant grey-haired vet, a New England brahmin, a perfect Establishment figure, explain how he determined where to place his acupuncture needles when he couldn't make a well-defined diagnosis. What my colleague did was to listen to the dog's heart rate as he passed small filter bottles of pure amino acids by one of the dog's ears. When the dog's heart rate increased he checked which amino acid was in the bottle. If, for example, it were lysine, it meant that it was the kidneys that were problematic and he placed his needles at the base of the spine.

I have no problems with using acupuncture needles to control chronic pain but his method of diagnosing other medical conditions such as kidney disease had me stumped. After the talk I approached this tall, pinstripe-suited New Englander and explained I was finding it difficult to rationalise what he'd just lectured on.

'Bruce', he explained, putting his hand on my shoulder, calmly, benignly, looking me straight in the eye. 'You just have to move yourself to a different plane.'

*   *   *

For years I'd thought it would be fun someday to retrace John Steinbeck's travels around America with Charley, his standard poodle, but in a curious way the word 'someday' also existed in a different plane. 'Someday' was irrational, aspirational, beyond practical reach. I'd love to climb the hidden plateau to the Lost World in Venezuela, someday. I'd love to trek to the South Pole, someday. I've love to go into space, someday. I'd love to ride a Harley in the Paris–Dakar rally, someday. I'd love to spend a few months vagabonding around North America, with my dog for company, someday.

Packing my dog Macy into a motorhome and taking her on a leisurely trip around North America seems easy compared to most of the other things I'd like to accomplish, 'someday', but until now it's been just as unattainable. Like most people with 2.3 kids, a dog and a mortgage, there have always been other priorities. But of late those are easing up, and, most important, the UK Pet Travel Scheme now includes North America. That means Macy doesn't have to go into quarantine on her return to Britain from the United States or Canada.

Why travel with Macy? Why not with someone I can more safely share the driving with? Let me be frank. I'm very comfy with my dog. Actually, it's worse. I feel absolutely contented with dogs—the plural. It's worrying because for over 25 years I've lectured internationally on our relationship with companion animals. If anyone should be able to rationalise this relationship dispassionately, it's me! With Macy in particular, rationally I know she's not the brightest canine spark I've shared my home with. Macy's a good-looker, a three-year-old golden retriever. She has the typical dual personality of a working retriever, calm as a mirror-like lake at dawn when she's indoors and as frenetic as a March hare when outdoors. Macy's not a thinker. I've just come back from exercising her in the park. She jumped out of the car and with a spring in her gait, nonchalantly trotted through the open front door of the house, then back out again 30 seconds later, tail proud and swishing, up our neighbour's front path, round the hedge down our front path and through her front door. She's a dumb blonde and I just love her.

Let me be even franker. I'm not one who talks much about emotions or feelings but I should explain that I don't feel claustrophobic. I don't feel male menopausal. I don't feel I need to escape. I don't feel no one understands me. I'm really comfortable, enviously so. My wife Julia and I spend a whole lot of time together. We relax and enjoy each other's company. We don't particularly like being separated for any length of time. So why have I chosen one ditsy blonde over the other as my preferred travelling companion?

Well, to begin with, Macy doesn't shop. While one of the blondes I sleep with is an unreconstructed city chick, the other's a country girl at heart, a true muck lover. Mace belly-flops in muddy puddles, just because. There's no more reason. Macy's not bothered by bugs, or sand or waves or crapping in the woods. Macy doesn't mind if I don't shower for a week or if I don't shave. The fact is, Mace *prefers* if I don't shower or shave for a week. Makes me more one of her family. As for me, I love watching her pretend she's a dog, watching her muscles tense and her gaze focus as she raises a pheasant in a field. Her enthusiasm for outdoor activities is infectious. Her gentle snoring indoors is endearing and curiously reassuring. I'm very content to share a bed with her.

What I'm planning on doing is really simple. I'm going to travel counter-clockwise around the United States and parts of Canada. There's no destination, no hallowed religious place I'm making a pilgrimage to. I'm just going to travel on. Like life, this isn't going to be a straight journey, it'll be a circumnavigation, back to the beginning. I'm not leaving anything behind because I'm coming back to everything.

OK, I lie. There's a bit more but it's personal stuff. I'm going back to the beginning in a physical but also a metaphysical sense, back to my roots, back to where I was born, raised, educated; back home. The thing is, I really don't know whether it's home any more. After so long in Britain I don't know who is 'them', who is 'us', or which one I am.

I want to return to see what North America is like now, while I still have the ability to do so and the choice of where to spend the rest of my life. I haven't travelled much in America during the last 35 years. How much has it changed? More to the point, what's happened to these people since 9/11?

What's happening right now, with troops in Iraq? Have Americans lost their innocence? What's happened to the land I left, where women drove around with curlers in their hair and you waved at passing cars on rural roads? Are the people I'm going to meet in the heartland of America (in what the former Dean of Tufts University's vet school, Frank Loew, calls 'The Empty Quarter'), people I can still feel at home with? After more than three decades living in Britain, I have the feeling everything in America is going to be kitsch and sappy and sentimental and naive and embarrassingly, patriotically parochial. I've got the feeling that America can't do irony at all, let alone do it well. Will I still feel at home, after living in a pragmatic and hugely ironic culture for 35 years?

John Steinbeck's *Travels with Charley* is my excuse and gives me a preferred route. He embarked on his travels because he felt he was losing touch with the heartland of his homeland. I read his book in the mid 1960s, during the Vietnam War, when I was a veterinary student. Why that book's stuck in my mind for so long is a real stumper, but since then I've thought I'd like to do the same, someday. In the mid-sixties I did drive East Coast to West Coast and back, but shortly after I took a trip to Britain and unexpectedly stayed. Steinbeck travelled in 'Rocinante', a ¾-ton pick-up truck, with a purpose-built cabin mounted on the back containing a bed, stove, heater, fridge, lights, butane, chemical toilet, screened windows, closet and storage. Macy and I plan to travel in a reconditioned 1977 GMC motorhome I found on the Internet. It looks like it once belonged to Elvis and is a seriously glamourous retro mode of transport. It has a shower room, flush toilet, three air-conditioning units, a microwave, fridge, freezer, oven and TV. I'm not going to give it a pretentious name.

Steinbeck's travelling companion in the 1960s was Charley, a big 'blue' standard poodle born just outside Paris, France. My pal Macy, a lean, lithe, athletic golden retriever was born in Cornwall in south-west England. Steinbeck wore a blue serge British naval cap, half-Wellington rubber boots with cork inner soles, army surplus khaki trousers, a hunting coat with corduroy cuffs and collar and a rear game pocket. I'll get most of my stuff at Gap and L.L. Bean. Macy'll wear natural fur.

For me, planning a trip is usually as exciting as the journey itself, but one particular part of planning this time has been truly, inspiringly rewarding. As Steinbeck travelled through Minnesota he wrote:

> If there had been room in Rocinante I would have packed the *W.P.A. Guides* to the States, all forty-eight volumes of them . . . If I had carried my guides along, for example, I would have looked up Detroit Lakes, Minnesota, where I stopped, and would have known why it is called Detroit Lakes, who named it, when and why. I stopped near there late at night and so did Charley, and I don't know any more about it than he does.

A quick visit to Google revealed what a national treasure the WPA Federal Writers' Project— American Guide Series is! The WPA, an acronym for what was first called the Works Progress

Administration, but which in the course of production of the American Guide Series changed its name to the Work Projects Administration, was set up to provide federally funded jobs for unemployed Americans during the great 1930s Depression. Most of these jobs involved physical labour—building dams, laying electrical lines into isolated valleys—but an inconspicuous clause in the congressional act that created the WPA, permitting 'useful employment for artists, musicians, actors, entertainers, writers . . . and others in these cultural fields', led to the Federal Writers' Project. The American Guide Series gave out-of-work journalists employment writing about the states they lived in. Each volume, written between 1935 and 1941, describes the state's history, geology, geography, culture, population, villages, towns, cities and roads. Each book is like a time-capsule, capturing the America that once was, just before I was born. In 1960, when John Steinbeck travelled with Charley, he considered them still the most relevant and informative state guides. I now have all 48 editions and several more besides—city guides, waterway guides—and I'm taking mine with me. (Yes, the *Minnesota Guide* does explain why Detroit Lakes is called Detroit Lakes.) I'll be using the American Guide Series as my reference texts, travelling the pre-interstate highway routes described in each book.

Tens of thousands of people travel across America in motorhomes each year and I'm pretty sure some use Steinbeck's *Travels with Charley* as their guide. I'm using his route as my template and Macy as my excuse. When I talk about how much Macy will enjoy the experience, all Julia sees are ticks the size of Portabella mushrooms, carnivorous fleas, fierce colonies of fire ants, killer bees, deadly scorpions, stealthy rattlesnakes, hungry alligators, brazen mountain lions and mean grizzlies. 'And those American hunters? Don't they shoot anything that moves in the woods? If you're going to take my Macy into American woods you make sure she wears fluorescent body armour—and a flashing collar—and a beeper—and satellite monitoring—and always has her mobile phone with her—and she's never, ever, ever off her leash.' I promise.

Bruce Fogle
London
August 2003

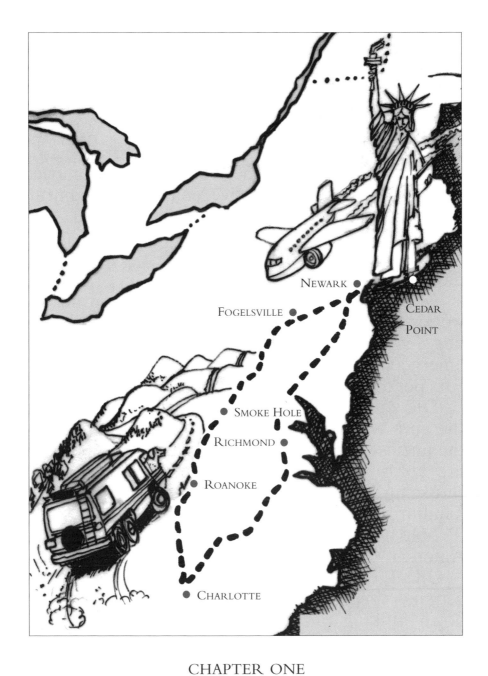

CHAPTER ONE

HEADING FOR SAG HARBOR

I lost her. The second I slid the SUV's door open at the New Jersey Turnpike rest area she bulleted off like a greyhound out of its trap. Dusk. Dark woods. Chronic turnpike traffic a hundred yards away. And Macy was gone. We'd been in America for less than five hours, five emotionally painful, exasperating, irritating, agonising, I-want-to-kill-someone hours, and I didn't know where Macy was. In fact for most of those first five hours I didn't know where Macy was.

'MACE!' I shouted. 'COME!' From within the woods beside the parking lot I heard thundering dog feet pounding through fallen leaves. Macy emerged, strutting like a lean Lippinzaner horse, ears perked, tail high.

'Did you see that humungous squirrel sitting on the curb when you slid open the door? That was the juiciest, fattest and slowest squirrel I've seen in my entire life!' She looked around at people returning to their cars with their mega-hamburgers, donuts and drinks. 'Hey,' she said, 'People here. They're just like that squirrel. I love America.'

OK, I embellish. I exaggerate. Macy doesn't actually speak. But you get to know what your dog's thinking and I could see in her eyes that she was on a high. Chasing a corpulent squirrel that spends its life pigging out on rest-area fast food cleansed her mind of what she had just endured. I wish it could have been as easy for me. I felt dreadful. I'd just put my innocent dog through hell

2

and wanted to sweet talk, lie or bribe my way back onto a plane, this time with Macy at my feet, and return home to London.

I'd worried a little about the long flight from London to New York, but had concluded that being caged for nine hours shouldn't be any more stressful for Macy than it is for any patient of mine dropped off at the veterinary clinic first thing in the morning and picked up at the end of the day. Sometimes it's necessary to endure a little unpleasantness so that life in future is better. Think positive, I told myself. Macy may be discombobulated for a few hours but think of what she gets in return—dog-paddling in the Great Lakes, mountain-climbing in the Rockies, beachcombing on the Gulf of Mexico. The two of us were embarking on the best sabbatical ever.

Everything had gone smoothly at departure. Julia, my wife, couldn't bear to see Macy crated for cargo, so our son Ben took Macy and me to the airport. Ben and I laid her blanket in the transport crate, put Macy in and gave her one of the soft toys she likes to have in her mouth when she falls asleep, a seal Ben had brought back for her from one of his trips to the Falkland Islands. I know it's sad but we buy each other's dogs stuffed toys when we travel abroad. Macy behaved in her typically benign way, with stoic resignation. She sat in the crate simply looking morose and concerned. At funereal speed the forklift driver drove into the small cargo warehouse, while two attendants with hands on the crate on both sides talked to her as they walked her away.

The flight itself was easy, almost no turbulence, but I must have looked troubled because a flight attendant, a warm, pink woman whose short sleeves cut like tourniquets into her fleshy arms, asked if I was OK. 'My dog's down below,' I replied. 'God, I wouldn't do that to my dog,' she responded. Did she know something I didn't?

She returned with a colleague. 'His puppy is in cargo,' she explained.

'Actually, she's a three-year-old golden retriever,' I replied.

'Oh, poor little puppy,' said the sidekick, not listening to what I'd just said. 'I have a cockerpoo. I'd never put her in cargo. Would you like a beverage?'

The well-meaning flight attendants did know something, though they didn't know they knew it. Their airline's airport personnel do not understand international pet transport. There. That's me being very British, very polite. Let me please revert to my origins for a second. They're a pack of rat-tailed ill-informed assholes! That's better. I got through Customs pretty fast, picked up my two very heavy bags and asked airline staff where I should go to get Macy. I won't dwell on this because my blood still boils when I think about it, but put simply, I was sent to four wrong places. Two hours later I decided she must have been taken to Continental's off-airport warehouse and asked airline staff where it was. No one knew this either! A porter eventually gave me instructions; I took the monorail to the car rental location, picked up an SUV which I needed to transport the large crate, then went searching through road construction for the warehouse.

Macy was there but I couldn't see her and she wouldn't be released from her crate until I paid the

4

airline an additional handling fee, and took the receipt elsewhere to US Customs for their stamp. I drove to Customs and, needless to say, it was shut. Do you get why I was feeling the way I was feeling? Then Julia phoned and with concern in her voice asked, 'Why haven't you telephoned? How's Macy? Are you being good to her?' I can't say I was very civil.

Other folks were hanging around Customs, waiting for their paperwork to be reviewed. The place wasn't supposed to be shut. After twenty minutes a black sedan arrived and two Customs officers nonchalantly returned. The throng let me go first. I'd told them about Mace. And so, over four hours after landing and after more than thirteen hours in her crate, Macy was free to go. The cargo warehouse reminded me of that last scene in *Raiders of the Lost Ark*—unending corridors of crate-filled shelves. Among all of this Macy was found and forklifted by a Michael Schumacher wannabee to the loading bay where I'd been told to wait. Macy looked up at me from inside her crate. 'Please! Help! Out!' she pleaded with her eyes. I opened her crate and wanted to get her outdoors as quickly as possible. There are, after all, physiological limits to what her magnificent bladder is capable of. Now Macy's not a demonstrative dog. She's very British, like I've become. Like me, she contains her emotions, but all she wanted to do was whimper high-pitched cries, lick any bit of me she could get her tongue on and dance for joy. Activity in the warehouse stopped. Forklift drivers, paper shifters, security, they all turned, looked, watched and smiled as Macy joyously greeted the bastard who'd put her in the crate in the first place. Dogs are forgiving. My guilt endures.

I didn't time Macy's first pee on American soil, but if I had it probably would have entered the *Guinness Book of Records*. I loaded the crate in the back of the SUV, put Macy on her blanket on the back seat, phoned Julia, apologised for my curtness, let her know that Mace was well, and headed for the New Jersey Turnpike. We were driving south to Charlotte, North Carolina, where a vintage motorhome I'd bought via the Internet was waiting for us.

At the rest area I got out her heavy ceramic water bowl I'd brought with me and filled it with 'microfiltered, UV-treated, naturally sodium-free, true, certified, spring water product'. She lapped while I marvelled at how many adjectives can be used to describe water. We sat on the curb and shared bites from a Roy Rogers quarter-pounder, some chicken nuggets and a couple of glazed Krispy Kreme donuts.

'You never let me eat this stuff,' her body language said.

'Take advantage, sweetheart,' I told her. 'How I feel right now might not last forever.'

So she did. In her deliciously delicate and gentle way, using her lips rather than her teeth, she took each morsel I gave her, chewed carefully and thoroughly. I tossed the remainder of our first American meal into her food bowl and she licked it clean, then licked the ground around the bowl clean. As we walked back to the car Macy's eyes lit upon another squirrel, sitting on the curb between two parked cars, eating a donut. She turned into the food police once more, but this time she

6

responded immediately to my verbal command and returned to the car. We set off down the turnpike. I wanted to put some miles behind me before we stopped for the night.

I enjoy driving and, although it was dark, traffic was dense, and my body clock was five hours ahead of local time, I felt comfortable and we drove south past Trenton, New Jersey, Philadelphia, Pennsylvania, then Wilmington, Delaware. Near Baltimore, Maryland, I checked into a sleepy seventies strip motel. 'Ten bucks extra fer yer dawg,' the night attendant droned. I backed up to the door to our room, opened the tailgate, unzipped a bag and Macy's bed decompressed out of it, springing back into a large soft rectangle. I left it to air while I gave her another small meal and took her across the parking lot to a grassy area.

'What a perty dawg,' a bottle blonde proclaimed, disengaging herself from the guy she was with and coming over to me. 'Will you breed her?'

Yes, I know, dogs are babe magnets but I was too tired for conversation. I took Macy's bed into the motel room, turned off the lights and both of us hit our respective sacks. Almost immediately there was a knock on the door. Macy went into German shepherd mode. Her woof is basso, profundo and magnifico. I love her territorial guard-bark.

The knocking persisted and I looked through the peephole. It wasn't the bottle blonde. Outside were two twelve-year-old kids sucking on Coke cans.

'Yah?' I uttered, rather eloquently.

7

'You left all the doors of your car open,' a kid replied.

I had. Driver's door, passenger door, back seat door, tailgate, they were all open. In the car were my suitcases, driver's licence, passport, money, laptop, camera, everything, the whole shebang, at a motel that had three locks on the bedroom door. This isn't how I planned our trip would begin.

*   *   *

By rights I should have headed north-east from Newark Airport, to Sag Harbor, Long Island, where Steinbeck started his travels with Charley, but my chariot, my vintage, 27-foot motorhome was awaiting me 700 miles south-west, in Cornelius, North Carolina.

Beyond Richmond, Virginia, I joined US 1, the old road my parents travelled on annually each winter, from Toronto, Ontario, to Miami, Florida. It may be that I've inherited my love of travel—my need to travel—from my parents. They've had a compatibly incompatible marriage for over 65 years now, during which they travelled to every continent but always headed to Florida each winter. My father, now in his late nineties—once a tall, muscular, ox of a man—still fiercely distinguished-looking—is a 'doer'. It doesn't enter his mind he can't do anything—repair a watch, plumb a house, raise a wharf. He's a quiet man and I get a kick, even now, when people turn and look when he walks past. Natural dignity. Natural presence. Leaving the cinema one evening after watching the Tom Hanks/Paul Newman film *Road to Perdition*, I said to my kids, 'Did you see what I saw?' 'It's amazing,' my daughter Tamara replied. 'Paul Newman is Grandpa!'

My mother is as opposite to him as a physique and temperament can be; small, blonde, warm, voluble, effusive, a bit histrionic, touchy-feely, mother-earthy, and although she never recognised it in herself, but every man she ever met did, deeply sexy. For a kid growing up, they made quite decent role-models: a handsome father who I knew could kick the shit out of anyone else's father and a mother loved by everyone who met her.

In their prime, my parents had a common love for travel. They drove frequently along this road I was now on, until it was replaced by the faster and more direct I-75. And as they drove they argued. And argued. My father's aim was to get where he was going as fast as possible. My mother preferred to soak in the countryside. She would have been enchanted if she had had with her the American Guide Series (AGS), *Guide to U.S. One*, as I now had, published the year they married. Like all the AGS books, this guide wanders from subject to subject as US 1 meanders from state to state and town to town. Here in southern Virginia, for example, the guide explains that ham was from peanut-fed porkers, cured by months of exposure to hardwood smoke then covered in a brown sugar and sherry paste. This region I was driving through was also the home of fried apple pie, baked corn pones and fried corn dodgers. While corn pones and corn dodgers are now gastronomically extinct, any visitor to a McDonald's restaurant knows that fried apple pie left the depths of Virginia and went international when it was added to that fast-food chain's range of desserts.

9

If you drive through Brunswick County, as I now was, the *Guide* recommends trying Brunswick Stew, giving a recipe that begins, 'First catch yourself a hare . . .' Tomatoes, onions, okra, carrots, celery, cabbage, potatoes, butter beans, red peppers, corn, bacon, everything went into Brunswick Stew. I looked for a local diner but lucked out. Macy and I stopped for lunch, sat on a grassy knoll, and in the clear, warm, penetrating sunshine we shared a box of Bojangles chicken and muffins from the adjacent fast-food outlet. 'Still feeling guilty?' she asked.

*　　　*　　　*

In North Carolina, US 1 passes through gently rolling farm land, studded with pine and oak woods. From their still-evident grandeur some of the abandoned farm houses once belonged to wealthy landowners. Two storeys high and surrounded by verandahs, some were almost totally hidden by the overgrown dogwood, tulip poplar and sweetgum trees that surrounded them. Behind one of these buildings I saw a line of four ivy-covered humps. Macy disappeared into the overgrowth covering one. I pulled the vegetation aside and found piles of rough-hewn planks and tar paper. The AGS *North Carolina Guide* says that in 1941 this northern part of Warren County was part of the State's 'black belt', predominantly inhabited by slave descendants. Three local families owned over a thousand slaves each. These tumbled piles of split logs and pine slabs may once have been slave quarters. Think about that. It's still possible today to wander off a highway in the Southern states and chance upon buildings that slaves lived in. Not in a museum. Not in a re-creation. For real. That's truly exciting.

We didn't see a single person, let alone meet anyone on this stretch of US 1, but did when I drove into nearby Kerr Lake Recreation Area. No slave descendants here. The parking area was filled with young white families, unloading everything from picnics to bicycles to fishing boats. While Macy bounded through the surrounding loblolly pines, beachcombed on the coral-coloured muddy shore and cantered up welcomingly to park visitors, I read the posted park regulations. 'People under age 16 must wear a helmet while riding a bicycle. Persons unable to maintain an erect, seated position cannot be bicycle passengers. Pets must be kept on a leash no longer than six feet.' Damn. We were both here to explore and investigate. There's no way I was going to restrict my dog's freedom.

At Durham we turned west onto I-40, past Greensboro and Winston-Salem, then onto I-77, south towards Cornelius, just north of Charlotte, where our vintage home awaited. The interstates were tedious and boring. I hadn't even begun to retrace John Steinbeck's route but already I was thinking back to his journey. In *Travels with Charley*, Steinbeck wrote:

> When we get these thruways across the whole country, as we will and must, it will be possible to drive from New York to California without seeing a single thing.

Prescient, that.

Dawn and dusk are my dog's favourite times of day. A dog's dawn world is accentuated by the intoxicating aromas embedded in morning dew. A dog reads these odours like the daily news; who passed by; how long ago. Dusk is almost as exciting. Dogs see well in dim light, far better than we do. It was dark when I took Mace for a walk on the forest-bordered lawn to the north of the motel we were staying in. She darted after a rabbit into a wild raspberry thicket and I heard her thundering through the underbrush. 'Mace,' I shouted in a whisper, remembering I was in America. I didn't want other motel residents to wonder why I was calling for pepper spray. 'Mace!' After a few minutes, during which I always knew where she was because I could hear her rummaging around in the humid, leafy compost, she reappeared, raced past me and leapt in the air. She stopped, trying her hardest to stand her ears up. She concentrated. She looked quizzical.

Mace was stymied and I was enchanted for we were surrounded by hundreds upon hundreds of luminescent fireflies all sending out slow pulsating green flashes. I'd never seen so many. As kids in Ontario we used to capture and bottle fireflies to act as lanterns. They kept flashing in the jam jars because they were so annoyed. What we were seeing were males flashing for females in the grass at our feet. They also use their amazing bioluminescence to illuminate the ground when landing. Here's some biological trivia. Do you know that some females of a related species flash back at guys looking for sex, deceive them into approaching, then eat them? This species's appropriate scientific name ends in *femmes fatales*. I stood mesmerised, watching the slow single flashes all around me turn on and off. It was gorgeous. The air was filled with green fairy lights and at one point it seemed as if they were synchronising, all going on at the same time, then off for around five seconds, then on again. It was scintillating, the perfect way to begin the trip. Macy didn't know what to think. She stared incredulously. I put her leash on and walked her back to the motel, making sure not to step on any flashes in the grass.

*   *   *

Macy and I both slept soundly, but at 4.30 a.m. we got up and walked up the hill to the all-night gas station-convenience store for some breakfast.

'Sir. We serve dawgs. Ya cain't come in,' I heard as I pushed the door open. I must have looked puzzled as I stood there, so she continued, 'Can ya leave yoare dawg atside?'

Only after I'd bought us a box of Krispy Kreme donuts did I see the hot dogs rotating on their rollers.

Munching breakfast we walked through the grounds of a pristine, luxury, gated condominium complex to a hill topped by a communications transmission tower. Macy darted through the unkempt overgrowth chasing whatever she was chasing and, following her, I found myself in a grassy field dotted eccentrically with low tombstones. Some stones were pink granite

13

engraved with names like Euphemia and Thelonious. Other graves had only concrete block markers. There was a fresh pine branch stuck in the ground at the top of a new mound of red earth, dug since the last rainfall. Macy has a habit of digging in fresh earth so I made sure she avoided that one. Beyond the field was a road, lined on one side by a row of luxury homes in the final stages of construction and on the other by old, decrepit, low-built wooden shacks, each with piles of clutter on the porches and lawns. Grass grew high around rusting cars.

Early risers, all African-American, were walking towards the main road. 'Mornin.' 'Mornin to ya.' 'That's some perty dawg.' At one unpainted clapboard home with an old wringer washing machine and piles of off-cut wood on the porch, there was a sun-bleached silver 1986 Buick Regal parked in the grass, with a Stars & Stripes sunscreen in the front window that read, 'Proud to be an American'. The juxtaposition of poverty and wealth surprised me, although it shouldn't have. When I grew up in aspirational North America, a big, new home was everyone's seemingly obtainable target. It didn't symbolise 'how that other half lives' but rather 'how I'll live one day'. Remembering that, my surprise turned to satisfaction.

At the Holiday Inn an elderly couple from Massachusetts, both lean and tall and looking as if they'd just stepped out of a Normal Rockwell *Saturday Evening Post* cover, checked out of the motel. Leaning heavily on his cane as his wife put their bags in their car, the man looked at Macy, then stared ahead avoiding any eye contact with me.

'My Jenny just died.' He paused and his jaws chewed. 'She was a good part of the family.' He paused again and now his jaws clenched. 'She just ran and ran and ran . . .' and his voice trailed off. Then, supporting himself on his cane, he reached down to touch Macy and as he did so she stretched her head towards him and pressed it deep into his hand. They stood there for perhaps a minute, the old man with the palm of his hand on Macy's head, Macy standing statue-still. 'She thought she was human,' he said, still staring into the parking lot.

As I've mentioned, I've lived in Britain for the last 35 years. You don't pry. You don't meddle. You don't get involved. But I asked anyhow, 'How old was she?' And the question seemed to bring him back from his reverie. He explained that Jenny was a standard poodle who lived until she was 17 years old.

'Have you ever had a chance to read *Travels with Charley*, John Steinbeck's story of his trip with his standard poodle?' I asked. 'Macy and I are setting off today to retrace his route.' Now, I'm not superstitious; I don't believe in omens. So why was it that this man—the first person I met to whom I'd mentioned what we're doing—pulled a new Penguin paperback copy of *Travels with Charley* out of his coat pocket and replied, 'Got it right here. It's my reading material'?

*   *   *

I'd spoken with Buddy Bethune, the dealer I'd bought my motorhome from, countless times on the phone, discussing the type of vehicle I wanted and what I proposed to put it through. On these twice-weekly calls I got an impression of the man. He answered his phone in a droll, laconic, lilting voice. 'B'thune Motah Sales, Buddah speak'n'.' I expected a wiry, 40-year-old rural farmer-turned-vintage-GMC motorhome enthusiast, dressed in oil-covered bib overalls over a dirty white T-shirt. The man who met me spoke in Buddy's voice but was my age, dressed in designer-casual clothes, with tasselled leather slip-on shoes, a gold watch and gold bracelet, and had a perfectly trimmed soup-strainer of a moustache. His razor-cut, thick, dark blond hair showed only the faintest hint it might ever go grey. Buddy walked me through his meticulous workshop-showroom and there, under spotlights and a flashing pink neon sign saying 'Bruce. It's yours!'—with Aaron Copland's *Fanfare for the Common Man* being played live by the Charlotte Philharmonic Orchestra around it (Leonard Bernstein conducting)—was my home: a sparkling, charcoal, silver and burgundy-coloured 1977 GMC Royale motorhome. I was seriously chuffed.

Buddy drove me to the vehicle records office in nearby Monroeville where I bought my North Carolina licence plates. The office had the ambience and user-friendliness of a high security prison. Credit cards? This was a branch of State government. Of course they didn't accept credit card payments. You pay sales tax and vehicle registration with inch-thick piles of cash or, if you're a local boy, with prearranged personal cheques. I offered traveller's cheques. 'They're the same as cash,' I volunteered.

'Da we accept these, honey?' my clerk asked

MY NEW HOME BACKING OUT OF BUDDY BETHUNE'S
WORKSHOP, SOUTH CAROLINA

another. It took a phone call to get a positive answer.

'What county?' my clerk asked me.

I explained to her she'd just recorded all the details from my Ontario driver's licence, that Toronto, the address on my licence, was a metropolitan region and no longer part of a county. 'What county?' she repeated in a monotone that government employees seem to use universally.

'Well, I don't have a county in Canada any longer, but I also live in the county of West Sussex in England. Will that do?'

'No, sir, I cain't give ya yoare tag unless you name me a local county.'

So this was a local history test. In the history chapter of the AGS *North Carolina Guide* I'd been intrigued by the story of the Mecklenburg Declaration, a declaration of independence drawn up in Charlotte on 20 May 1775, a date still commemorated on the State flag and State seal. Locals say that the Mecklenburg Declaration was the first true declaration of independence.

'Mecklenburg!' I said, eyeing her unblinkingly.

'Thank ya, sir,' she replied.

She took my traveller's cheques and handed me my motorhome licence plates, RZH 6357.

Buddy seemed pleased and I think surprised that the transaction had gone so well. He drove me back through Davison, a charming, quintessential college town where elegant Georgian homes have been converted into college offices. This was the site of perhaps the first X-ray vacuum tube in America, built here shortly after Konrad Roentgen discovered X-rays while experimenting in Wurzburg, Germany, in 1895.

I had an urge to stop at the Soda Shop in downtown Davison. From the outside it reminded me of the drug store soda fountains of my childhood. But Buddy was driving, Macy was on the back seat and I didn't want to inconvenience either of them, so we returned to Cornelius where Buddy took me item by item, facet by facet, through the motorhome, the furnace, the levelling system, air conditioning, fresh water, soiled water, oil changes, reserve battery. I loved it. This was exactly what I wanted, a vehicle with class, with style, with distinction, not some anonymous box tacked onto a truck chassis. It looked a million.

By the time Buddy backed the motorhome out of the workshop it was swelteringly hot, 90 degrees, 90 per cent humidity, but I was itching to drive. I left the generator on to run both roof air-conditioning units for Macy, climbed into the driver's seat and eased onto State 21.

*   *   *

I'd like to pretend driving it was fun, but it wasn't. It drove like a tanker-truck. On the merest of road bends it swayed into the bend as if I was riding the outside giraffe on a merry-go-round. Going over bumps I wouldn't feel in a car, it pretended it was a teeter-totter and rocked on for the next 17 miles. Instead of a modern, safe vehicle I was stuck with a Sherman tank on sponges, all because I thought it would look cool. Much as I hated it, Macy hated it even more. Between the noise from the air conditioners and the cork-on-the-ocean ride, Macy couldn't settle. She lay beside the sofa, got up and lay beside the steps up to the driver's level; then

19

she stepped up and lay beside me, went back and lay by the bedroom section. If she got comfortable or secure, I found a pothole or turned the steering wheel half a degree. 'I wanna go home. Now! Where's that woman who kisses me smack on my schnoz when I feel insecure?'

I'd passed the North Mecklenburg Animal Hospital yesterday, so we stopped there to arrange for the necessary US Department of Agriculture 'tick and worm treatment' paperwork I needed to pick up just before we returned to Britain in November.

I stopped too at the local Wal-Mart for sheets, towels and kitchen utensils, then headed north, past well-kept homes with freshly manicured lawns. Yellow finches darted from the trees and monarch butterflies drifted beside the road. I drove through Hamptonville, past a hand-painted 'puppies for free' sign and then past a just killed Beagle, with a pool of dried, caked blood around her nostrils. That distressed me. The first road-kill I saw was a beautiful young dog.

Beyond Roaring Gap, State 21 ascends a scary hairpin road into the Blue Ridge Mountains. The giant sponge I was driving swayed nauseatingly into each bend. Macy rolled from east to west, from north to south. And behind me was some bugger in a 48-foot, fire-engine-red, over-chromed Mack flatbed with Steven Spielberg whispering in his ear, 'Get closer, so all he sees in his rearview mirror are those pointed teeth you've painted on the grill. Tailgate him round the tightest bends. Scare the living shit out of him.' I was concentrating so much on this guy trying to climb up my tailpipe I missed the exit to the Blue Ridge

Parkway.

Just past the Eastern Continental Divide, where waters now flowed towards the Atlantic rather than the Gulf of Mexico, I pulled off the road, both to let this jackass pass and to give Macy a chance to stretch her legs. Back in the bitch, Macy tried lying under my feet. I'd moved her bed up beside me, between the driver's and passenger's seats, and she settled on it as we crossed into Virginia and, at Independence, turned north-east onto US 221 and through Galax. The word 'galax' was familiar to me because my father, a florist, used round, glossy, evergreen galax leaves in his floral arrangements. They seemed to last for ever, although it never crossed my mind they were harvested wild from this part of the southern Appalachians.

*   *   *

At Roanoke Mountain campground, marked on a map I'd been given at the Blue Ridge Parkway entrance by a Scandinavian-blonde National Parks Officer who, incidentally, should be on the cover of all their publications, I drove a circuit round the wooded campground, not knowing exactly what I was supposed to do, and returned to back into the largest of the very tight spaces that were available. There was a bicyclist camping nearby. I turned off the generator so there was no noise but for the birds, and instantly started to sweat. I stripped off, put shorts on, and took Mace for a long walk in the woods following one of the Roanoke Valley trails. An hour later, back at the motorhome, Macy lay in the grass, rolled and kicked sky while I made myself a meal of sliced beefsteak tomatoes, green leaf salad, olive oil and balsamic vinegar, followed by slices of seedless watermelon. As I sat on the ground beside Macy, an attractive, healthy, vigorous-looking couple, probably in their late sixties, volunteer park wardens, dropped by.

'Did you restore it yourself?' I was asked.

I took the husband for a tour inside, while his wife tossed a stick for Macy to retrieve until she remembered she was a park warden and asked or stated, 'You have a leash for her.' She handed me Blue Ridge Parkway Regulations, a pamphlet that listed regulations but also, in a polite, almost British way, explained the reason for each one.

Picking flowers is prohibited. It might seem a small matter to let your child pick a handful of daisies, but if everyone did this, soon there would be no daisies to enjoy. The same rule applies to gathering chestnuts, since the chestnut is an endangered species. The cutting of ginseng and pollonia is also illegal, but other edible plants may be collected for personal consumption only.

Keep your pet on a leash. This is as much to protect your pet as the wildlife. When a loose pet chases a squirrel or racoon, the wild animal's ability to survive is threatened, and when it is threatened, it may react aggressively.

It was quite obvious, now. In the wilds of America's woods, dogs are expected to act like extensions of their owners, not like dogs. This was going to be an ongoing problem for Macy and me.

The night was warm and humid. We both fell asleep to a cacophony of cicadas and crickets, awakening the following day to still, warm sunshine and the song of buntings, cardinals and chickadees.

*   *   *

Those crickets and cicadas and katydids last night were positively thunderous. The noise was louder than any city noise I've ever heard. The sound of male crickets rubbing their wings, looking for sex, was simply strident, but the way cicadas can amplify their vibrations is positively stupendous. How something so small can make such a loud noise is truly amazing. Incidentally, do you know that entomologists use an acronym for the quiet male crickets who hang out near loud wing rubbers, then sneak in and mate with females attracted to the male's song? They're called 'SFs', sneaker fuckers!

Past Roanoke I joined US 11, latching on for the first time to the route John Steinbeck took but one of which he wrote nothing.

> Near Abingdon, in the dogleg of Virginia, at four o'clock of a windy afternoon, without warning or good-bye or kiss my foot, my journey went away and left me stranded far from home.

He said the countryside through Virginia and West Virginia must be beautiful, which it is, but he bulldozed blindly through, into Pennsylvania, onto its great turnpike, through New Jersey on another

23

turnpike and finally to the Holland Tunnel, Manhattan, and home. That great swathe of America was covered in less than four pages of text.

Although Steinbeck whizzed through Appalachia I wanted to spend time in the Virginias. At one point I joined I-81, US 11's interstate successor, at one of the frequent criss-crosses these highways make.

'Thank you. Thank you. Thank you,' Macy said with her eyes and her body language as the road smoothed and straightened and she relaxed into deep dog dreams. Seeing her sleep soundly by my feet, I relaxed too and found a local blue grass country music station on the radio to listen to.

* * *

The mountains of West Virginia were once inhabited by the Sioux, Shawnee, Delaware, Catawba and Tuscarora tribes. Later Scots and Irish settlers arrived, followed by Germans. They cleared the land, cut the forests to feed their iron smelting furnaces or for timber for East Coast construction. By the beginning of the twentieth century most of the forests were gone. Today the land is almost primeval in its luxurious regrowth. This is a fascinating part of America where plant species from north, south, east and west all uniquely mingle. Driving through George Washington National Forest I turned off to a picnic area, a mile from the road, called Braley Pond.

Macy and I were the only visitors. We walked the circumference of small Braley Pond, Macy intrigued by the bluegills she could see in the shallows. She splashed up a creek lined with a profusion of scarlet cardinal flowers, vibrant yellow ragweed, white waterleaf, flowering wild mint and others I didn't recognise. Macy stuck her tongue in the water and almost jumped for joy. She raced circuits up and down the shale-bottomed creek, drinking the cool clear water at each end of her circuit. 'It's drinkable!' It only then dawned on me that she had never tasted sweet running water. Her experience of water was the English Channel and the tidal rivers flowing into it. She eyed minnows and apple-bobbed for them, and I sat there and watched and looked around me and saw only beauty and solitude and Disney World for dogs, and decided to stay.

While Macy followed scent trails and chose which sticks to pull the bark from, I went back to the motorhome, got out my laptop, sat down at one of the picnic tables by the pond and caught up on note-taking. Midnight blue admiral butterflies fluttered around me. Suddenly Macy stopped and went into alert mode. Soon I too heard a truck in the distance. When it arrived, Macy greeted its passengers with a proprietorial woof.

'Hello, big boy. How ah ya?' asked the driver, a tall, erect, big-bellied septuagenarian in bib overalls and an International Harvester baseball cap. He and his passenger of similar appearance and vintage had arrived for an early lunch. Soon after, two more vehicles arrived. More elderly men got out of their trucks. One of them, shorter, younger and dressed by Sears rather than Wal-Mart, looked at the motorhome, walked over to where I was sitting and said, 'Restore her yourself? She's sure a beauty.'

As we talked two more men joined us, one of them lean and sinewy wearing a plain dark green baseball cap, jeans, duck boots and a snow-white T-shirt printed with the Stars & Stripes backing the twin towers, and the words 'Memory of the World Trade Center' at the top and 'People of America United' at the bottom. As he approached, he simply stated, 'Yo a writah.' He'd probably seen my laptop and made an accurate assumption. 'But yo sump'n' else too.'

'You're right. I'm a veterinarian.'

'You know who George Washington Carver was?' he responded. 'He was the fust man t'say that animals get the raht med'cin from herbs. We kin too. That's why a'm so healthy.' He smiled a gold-toothed grin.

As he spoke, the first man, the Sears man—round-faced, rounder-bellied and with an engaging gentle smile—asked how much the motorhome cost.

'Thirty-five thasand dollahs,' answered the tall, wiry guy. He was pretty close.

'This guy's good,' I said to the trio.

'Don't tell him that,' said the third man, an unhappy-looking individual, my age, who walked stiffly and had a heavy growth of thick dark blond hair under his baseball cap.

'He's the foreman,' said wiry guy, whose name was Arthur, 'but we don't take no shit from him. Writ'n' someth'n'?' he asked, nodding towards the books and laptop on the picnic table. I told him about my trip, Steinbeck's travels and my belated discovery of the Federal Writers' Project.

'The books are good but what the Fed'ral Artists done was the best,' he replied. 'You ever see 'em at

26

the Smithsonian?' Before I could answer that I hadn't, Arthur continued. 'You read the Fed'ral Writahs' book *The Nigrahs of Nebraska*? Buffalo soljahs. When the civil war ended, the gov'ment didn't want the Nigrah soljahs stay'n' where they were so they sent them to Injun territory to protect the settlahs. That's how the Nigrahs ended up in Nebraska.'

While Macy chewed sticks we continued to chew the fat. The Sears man's wife bred Pomeranians, shih tzus and Yorkshire terriers. He and his wife had visited London last year. 'Piccadilly Square, Harrods, the white cliffs of Dover, we saw everything. I tried to have lunch with the Queen but she was out,' he chuckled.

'Yah, that's because she was at my place,' interjected the foreman. His stilted walk was the result of a neck injury in a traffic accident in Toronto. 'I was up there in North York, Ontario, picking up a load of peanut butter. They were real nice to me, but when I got back home and went to the doctor I had compression fractures at C5, C6 and C7. That's why I gave up driving my rig after twenty-five years and walk like this.'

It's common for people to tell me about their medical conditions. Because I'm a working veterinarian they know I'll understand what they're saying and sometimes want to know if I have anything to add to their stories. What startled me about this man's story was why on earth peanut butter was being delivered from Canada to the American South.

Sears man asked more about the motorhome. He was enamoured by it and I showed him around, explaining that I'd be staying in campsites each night. 'If you can't find a campsite, you can always park at a Wal-Mart as long as you're well away from the store. They're open twenty-four hours a day and have clean rest rooms. They like it if you park there 'cause you'll buy there too.'

While Sears man and the foreman and I talked, Arthur set about preparing what they were there for. The Department of Labor employs low-income retirees at five dollars an hour, the minimum wage, to attend to the grounds in National Parks. They were there to cut the grass.

Arthur came back to the group of us as the foreman was telling me, 'We're all veterans. We defended this land so that foreign people like you can come here and visit us safely. Enjoy your stay in the United States of America.' He said this with such an intensity and seriousness that all I could say was, 'Thank you.'

Arthur asked, 'Know who laid out these roads and trails and built the picnic tables and fire towers? The CCC did. The Civilian Conservation Corps. They were like the Fed'ral Writahs' Project 'cept they were local people with no ejication and no jobs. In fact the very fust CCC camp was right here in George Washington National Forest. From 1933 to 1942 they built almost everyth'n' ya see today in these mount'ns and on the Blue Ridge Parkway. Young people think consavash'n's a new idea. They were conserv'n' here before them youngstahs' parents were born. Whe'a ya head'n'?' he asked. I told Arthur I was going to Smoke Hole, West Virginia. The AGS *Virginia Guide* made it sound fascinating. 'The likkah maykahs,' he replied. 'It was a real war over there. George Washington outlawed moonshan in 1791 and

28

started tax'n' likkah. Fed'ral troops were needed, the fight'n' was so bad. They still mak'n' it. Sometimes, deep in them mountains you smell the air and it smells lak ev'yone in the neibah-hood's bakin' bread.'

Arthur was sharp and he was also knowledgeable. I was curious how, cutting grass with a work gang of retirees, he was so obviously much more savvy and perceptive. I asked him what he did before he retired.

'Fust ah was a trash man and a hustlah,' he explained. 'It was good work 'cause you could find fine things in trash. Ah worked 'n Washin'ton and collected gov'ment trash and ah read some of it. Ah had no ejication but the stuff was int'rest'n'. Some of it was 'bout hist'ry an' that was real int'rest'n'. You know, the most int'rest'n' thing 'bout hist'ry is who the people are who made America. It's the British and the French and the Spanish and others too, like the Dutch and the Swedes and the Afric'ns.'

Arthur explained that with graft, hard work and luck on his side he eventually became a licensed Washington DC tour guide. 'Ah learned that if yo- are con-fi-dent, you git ahead. Most people aren't con-fi-dent. Ah loved my job 'cause all the people ah met were happy. They were all on vacation. If anyone ever complained I just said, "A'm sorry you didn't appreciate the tour. Here's your money back and here's a little extra for mah wast'n' yer time."

'You know what ah learned? People don't like to read. They want ta hear. Ah can learn hist'ry from any book. Ah became a hist'ry broadcaster. Not many people were int'rested in Afric'n-Americ'n hist'ry then, but ah had to make sure what ah said

29

was absolutely raght 'cause someone list'nin' was bound to know if ah was wrong. After ah retired, ah came back home to Virginia. My family always lived here, for hundreds of years.'

We talked some more but Arthur wanted to get back to work, so as he and his crew raked, mowed and 'weed-wacked', Macy and I got back in the motorhome. Before we left, I got out the AGS *Virginia Guide* and flicking through it chanced upon this:

> Virginia was the Negro's first home in the British Colonies of North America. Anthony, one of the Negroes in the shipload that arrived in 1619, married Isabella, and the son born to them in 1624, of whom there is record, was the first native Negro of Virginia . . . After 1808, when Negroes could no longer be legally imported from Africa, Virginia became a breeding place for slaves needed in the cotton country . . . No matter how carefree the outward appearance of Negroes may be, behind their happy dispositions is the imprint of poverty, disease, and suffering— birthmarks of a people living precariously, but of a people wholly Virginian.

*   *   *

'Smoke Hole.' Doesn't that sound as uniquely American as Chattanooga—Abilene—Dolly Parton? How can you drive through the Appalachians without turning off the highway when you see a direction sign to Smoke Hole. This is hillbilly country; mountain music and moonshine.

Smoke Hole country lies on both sides of a rugged and isolated canyon in West Virginia. The South Branch of the Potomac River runs through it, on its way to Washington DC and eventually to Chesapeake Bay. Under a cloudless blue sky, I'd driven another motorhome-testing hairpin road, that took me out of George Washington National Forest, past countless Civil War sites to Monterey, Virginia, where I turned north and headed into West Virginia. This road traverses a wide valley lined by dilapidated trailers, mildewed manufactured homes and abandoned, pioneer, log buildings constructed of squared, interlocking logs—ten logs between the floor and the ceiling—topped by vertically planked second-floor attics and external stone chimneys. I didn't see a single one that had been restored. Logs and fridges, trash cans and dog food bowls sat on verandahs built in front of trailers mounted on breeze blocks. Wherever I stopped, dogs howled.

It can be easy to drive through here and miss the beauty—the cracked timbers of the old homes, tobacco-curing barns on hillsides, spreading oaks, comforting horizons. The road I was on was once the Great Philadelphia Wagon Road, bringing Scottish-Irish settlers, the Ulstermen, into West Virginia. They brought with them the arts of whisky-making and the temperament of independent spirit that still stews the troubles in Northern Ireland today.

Whisky-making was profitable. Whisky was a drink, a disinfectant, an anaesthetic, a sedative, a solvent, a unit of currency. It was worth a whole lot

31

more than the corn it was made from. Arthur told me about the Whiskey Rebellion and the whisky tax, dropped soon after the rebellion but reimposed by Abraham Lincoln in 1862 to raise money for the Civil War. Franklin County, where I was driving through, was the heart of moonshine country. Judging from the number of stills that are discovered each year, around one each week, Franklin County hooch-makers are still producing millions of quarts annually, mostly for inner-city shot-houses in the surrounding cities only a few hours away—Charlotte, where I'd come from, Raleigh, Richmond, Washington. It looked quiet in the surrounding hills but an entrepreneurial spirit was hard at work.

I didn't stop in the town of Franklin but Upper Tract was a treat. The white clapboard Post Office's sign was hand-painted black on a white background, 'POST OFFICE, UPPER TRACT W. VA'. A newer hand-painted sign over the grey entrance door gave more accurate information: 'United States Post Office, Upper Tract WV 26866'. Across the road, damage to a door of a building now used for storage was repaired with a 1961 West Virginia licence plate. Under an oak tree on the sloping front lawn of Upper Tract's pretty white clapboard Presbyterian church, Macy found a fallen branch, chewed, rolled and kicked the air with joy. I sat down with her and soaked up the mid-morning sun.

The AGS *West Virginia Guide* describes the inhabitants of Smoke Hole, descendants of Hessian soldiers who served in the Revolutionary War, as 'tall, muscular and bronzed'.

The Smoke Hole people are shy with strangers and resent 'city airs' but with patience and tact their reticence can be overcome. Barter is still the common practice at the local store. Their speech is quaint, containing many archaic forms handed down from the first settlers of the eighteenth century.

I was hoping to meet people who said 'clumb' for 'climbed' and 'holp' for 'helped', but Smoke Hole was deserted. Macy went fishing in the river but as the rain came I decided to head on.

*   *   *

Moorefield, West Virginia, is a quaint, red brick and grey-painted clapboard town where second-floor balconies overhang the sidewalks on Main Street. I stopped there for a bite to eat and wished I hadn't. A stench of cooked chicken lay over Main Street, emanating from a town centre processing plant. It lingered in the motorhome for the rest of the day. I think even Macy found it disgusting.

'How do you put up with the smell?' I asked my waitress, a quizzical, blue-eyed, pimply chinned, shaven-headed girl in her late teens, who for some inexplicable reason reminded me of Homer Simpson.

'Pilgrim's Pride? They own us.'

'What do you mean?' I asked.

'They don't just cook chicken. They got hatcheries, feed mills, processing plants. If you don't work for 'em you still depend on 'em. So who's gonna complain 'bout the smell. Besides, the

33

PRESBYTERIAN CHURCH, UPPER TRACT, WEST
VIRGINIA

smell ain't the problem. What they do to the environment sucks.'

'What do you mean?' I asked once more, like an old broken record, for those who remember broken records.

'You know how much chicken shit a million chickens make a week? Where does it go? The whole South Branch of the Potomac is polluted. You can't even fish or swim in it. They got bacteria in their water right down in Washington from it and there's algae in Chesapeake Bay from it. Our gov'nor, Bob the Wise, he won't regulate what Pilgrim's Pride does with their chicken shit. He won't even sign any agreement like the other states have to stop polluting Chesapeake Bay 'cause of the votes he'd lose. You know they process over a million chickens a week here? You know how those chickens have to live? Get too near a broiler house on a hot day and the ammonia'll make you gag.'

Most of us try to avoid thinking about animal welfare. It certainly wasn't in my mind when I was planning this trip. But when it pokes you in the eye, when you're confronted by the quite horrible reality of some of the industrial methods used to grow, house and slaughter animals, you can't help but take notice and ponder.

I drove on, thinking about Macy fishing in and drinking from the polluted river at Smoke Hole, and of a conversation I once had with Bernard Rollin, a Brooklyn-born bear of a man, sort of a Harley-riding John Bunyan who's now Professor of Animal Sciences at Colorado State University's vet school. I'd met Rollin when both of us were interested in the social and psychological roles

35

dogs and cats play in Western society. He'd just written *Animal Rights and Human Morality* and I'd just finished *Interrelations between People and Pets*.

Rollin told me how, in the 1930s, around the time the AGS books I was travelling with were written, a hen laid about 70 eggs a year. Today, a four-pound hen in a hatchery here in West Virginia probably produces around 275 eggs a year. The increase is because of improved genetics and nutrition and disease-control, but in no small measure to intensive confinement, to cages. Stuff hens in cages and they lay more eggs. Stuff them in too tight and productivity drops. Rollin told me that producers know that putting fewer birds in each cage leads to increased egg production, but they didn't do this because productivity is calculated per cage, not per bird. Cages are more expensive than birds. You make more money by packing them in, by accepting lower productivity per bird but higher productivity per cage. Their welfare just isn't part of the equation. No matter that they can't flap their wings, or peck at objects or dust bathe, or scratch for food, or exercise, or even move with a natural gait. No matter that they're lame or weak or have brittle bones. The only objective is to keep costs as low as possible.

Have you ever bought a chicken and found that the drumstick or thighbone was broken when it was processed? Well, it probably didn't break during processing. More likely it broke while the chicken was still alive, from osteoporosis caused by being nutritionally forced to reach slaughter size in six weeks rather than the biologically more natural five to six months. Are we so poor that we can't afford to spend another one or two or even three per cent of our income on humanely raised food? Economists tell us we've never spent as small a proportion of our weekly income on food, as we do now. If consumers really understood—if they saw with their own eyes—how appalling the conditions are for so many animals, would we let this continue?

During her first week in America, Macy enjoyed meeting her canine cousins. One morning she pirouetted, chased, rolled, tumbled and body-bashed with a black and white what-not staying at the same campsite. On another evening she engaged in a mutual bum sniff—it was, in fact, her first American bum—then dropped into a play bow and launched into unalloyed, gleeful figure eights, leaped over the other dog, collided a few times, then as quickly as the encounter began, ended it. Later that evening, that dog, a lanky hound, returned and trotted off with her ceramic food bowl in his mouth. I loved watching Macy's antics. She's a dog-orientated dog and has excellent social manners. Because I've written dog behaviour books, I watch her with professional as well as proprietorial pride.

My mobile phone rang. 'Hello, this is CBS calling. You're the world's leading authority on dog behaviour.'

'Is that a question or a statement?' I asked.

'We'd like to interview you. Can you arrange to be in New York on Friday.'

'I'd love to help,' I lied, 'but I'm in the Blue Ridge Mountains, in a motorhome with my golden retriever Macy. Why not try Peter Borchelt at the Animal Medical Center or Nick Dodman at Tufts near Boston?'

'Can I call you back?' asked the CBS voice.

I wondered how they got my mobile phone number and concluded they must have phoned my veterinary clinic and were told I was in the States. I stopped for food at a Winn-Dixie, where their background music was interrupted by announcements that watermelons were reduced in price, there was a two for one offer on Sara Lee bread and that Winn-Dixie supports America's fighting men and women who are keeping the country free.

CBS called again while I was at checkout.

'We'd like to come to you,' the voice said. 'It'll make great television. We'll need you for a day and your dog is perfect for what we want.'

'I appreciate your willingness to send a news crew to spend the day with us and I'd love to help. I know that CBS would do a good job, but my dog's not too pleased with what's happening at the moment and I don't want to upset her any more. The next time I'm in the States, I promise I'll help in any way I can.'

As the till rang up the final item, the checkout man turned to me and asked, 'Can I have your autograph?'

'My autograph?' I questioned.

'If CBS wants to send a crew out to you, you must be somebody.' I autographed a traveller's cheque and departed. Stardom beckoned but Macy, like all dogs, is too wise to be fooled by celebrity.

I took an instant, visceral dislike of Pennsylvania. Maybe it was the fat guy by the Hagerbuss Taxidermy sign, smoking a fag, nonchalantly walking down from his house to the road where a road-kill deer lay. Perhaps it was because Pennsylvania doesn't allow camping with pets in its State Parks. Mind you, Shawnee State Park, a well-ordered place—more a city park than a country one, where the grass is kept perfectly cut and every picnic table is numbered—is part of a 'pets in campgrounds pilot programme'. According to this programme, 'A house pet is limited to any dog or cat commonly kept in household captivity'. Hell. Is Macy my captive?

'A pet is not a vicious or dangerous animal, like any animal attacking without provocation'. And what's happened to grammar in Pennsylvania?

Twelve more rules followed, ending with advice that the trial programme 'will be monitored very closely to determine the positives and negatives with allowing pets in State Park campgrounds'.

Most of all I disliked Pennsylvania because of the Penn Pike, one pig of a road. What temerity the State has to charge a toll to use it. The surface is crap. Ask Macy. She bounced all over the motorhome as I drove its corrugated surface and was topped and tailed by unending lines of 18-wheelers. The westward tunnel of the mile-long Tuscarora Mountain Tunnel was closed. The single file of trucks going east, with me embedded among them, didn't slow down as we entered the tunnel, a place that looks like the world's longest urinal. The unending flow of trucks heading west, bearing down on me from the opposite direction, pushed the motorhome towards the wall with each passing air stream.

I drove through Harrisburg, across the high floodwaters of the Susquehanna River, left the Pike and headed towards Lancaster, but near its airport, traffic ground to a halt. Sitting in a traffic jam put me off. No. That's not true. Seeing signs extolling me to visit 'The Amish Experience', enjoy 'Dutch Wonderland', take an 'Amish Buggy Ride' irritated me. My veterinary school services a part of Ontario peopled by hard-working, frugal, God-fearing, devil-hating, Old Order Mennonites—Anabaptists—originally from the German-speaking cantons of Switzerland. These fine, calm, unostentatious people still travel by horse and buggy, the women wear bonnets and the men wear beards. They plough their fields with two- or sometimes four-horse hitches, and the only outward indications of their presence in Ontario are the wide shoulders on the roads and the occasional Department of Highways pictographic sign warning of horses and buggies on the highways.

The Amish here in Pennsylvania are a branch of Mennonites (followers of Jacob Ammon), just as conservative as Ontario's Old Order Mennonites. Yes, yes, I'm turning into a grumpy old man, but it annoys me that their presence was being turned into a spectacle. 'Dutch Wonderland'? Good God, the only thing Dutch about these retiring people is that their Swiss forefathers probably embarked from Rotterdam on their voyages to America. 'Dutch' is Americanised *Deutsche*, German, what they once called themselves.

I headed north-east. Near Virginville I found a private campground on the banks of the Maiden River. While I settled in, Macy investigated the river then ambled across the field to one of the permanent old trailers, mounted on a concrete base, with a roofed, mildewed and unpainted wooden verandah added in front of it. 'Fuck off, dog,' growled its inhabitant, and he threw the remainder of his coffee towards Mace. Pennsylvania was really growing on me.

*   *   *

Isn't it amazing how the weather affects your state of mind? Overnight the temperature plunged into the fresh, comfortable, low fifties. Cool air streamed in through the motorhome's screened windows. Now, the sun in the morning was blindingly bright and the air clear. And, presto, I quite liked my down-at-heel campsite, Mace and I took our now usual long, morning walk, then I gave her her usual breakfast and fried up eggs and bacon I'd bought from a farm in Virginia. I can't tell you how magnificent my motorhome smelled after that. I sat outside on its step, wiping the plate with bread I'd flipped in the frying pan's bacon fat, drank jet-black coffee and decided that this was a life—independent, free, curiously innocent—that I could easily get accustomed to. A psychiatrist friend, Aaron Katcher, once described dogs as not quite human, but not quite as animal as other animals. Aaron says that in our minds, dogs are more like Peter Pan, caught somewhere between nature and culture. That's how I felt this morning.

The overnight drop in temperature produced a thick, almost white dew on the grass. Macy left her footprints as she raced figure eights, tucked her head down and somersaulted. I felt like doing the same, but us Brits don't do such things. Maintain your decorum, I reminded myself.

In Kutztown, where the AGS *Pennsylvania*

41

Guide says there was a 31 feet in circumference white oak tree, the grass police were everywhere. There wasn't a single lawn that hadn't been immaculately razor-cut. Peonies and gladioli bloomed in geometrical rows behind white picket fences. Kutztown is a Main Street, America kind of town. The Stars & Stripes hung from every house verandah and street lamp post. I could have stopped at the Kutztown Diner for breakfast, shopped at Dunkelbergers for jewellery or gifts, or visited the niche-market Cut and Thrust-Edged Weapons Museum. Kutztown University, a liberal arts college, is the charming centrepiece of town. Mind you, I don't know how happy I'd be to have a name like that on my CV.

Near Allentown, I drove north a few miles to Fogelsville. This was a pointless diversion but as I was so close I thought I should visit—just because. At the Fogelsville Post Office I asked the counter attendant how the place got its name. He didn't know, nor did anyone waiting at the counter. Across the road, at the quaint Fogelsville Hotel, I asked the same question and got the same reply. The AGS *Pennsylvania Guide* says that Fogelsville is 'a neat farming village at the edge of Pennsylvania German country'.

The Fogel who first settled here was probably a Swiss-German Vogel whose name got changed at American immigration. My name, Fogle, got changed even more. My dad's grandfather was an innkeeper in Kaunas, Lithuania, where the merchant class spoke German. (He moved to Glasgow, according to apocryphal Fogle family history, when the Customs man at the Prussian border, with whom he was in tobacco-smuggling cahoots, told him there was going to be a crackdown on smuggling. His son—my grandfather—left Glasgow for Ottawa, Ontario, because that's where his wife—my grandmother—wanted to move to. Her best girlfriend had recently moved there.)

While the word for 'bird' in German—is *vogel*, across the Baltic in Swedish, it's *fogel*. My family's name probably changed to its present spelling when my great-grandfather arrived in Scotland. Incidentally, if you think that the Scottish 'Bruce' and German 'Fogle' sound unique, think again. There are three more Bruce Fogles registered for frequent-flyer miles with United Airlines.

I was getting close to 'the beginning'. Newark Airport was ahead of me, and beyond it the New Jersey Turnpike. This time I headed north on it towards Long Island and Sag Harbor, where Steinbeck's travels began. The night before, looking at my maps, I decided the straightest route to Long Island was across Manhattan, past La Guardia to JFK, then north. On my way, at Jersey City, a sign to Liberty State Park caught my eye. I turned off and drove to this park I'd not heard of. A refreshing breeze wafted in from Upper Bay. Macy and I walked from the parking lot, past the tree-shaded picnic area, across an open lawn, to where Upper Bay meets the mouth of the Hudson River. Across from us was the Manhattan skyline and there, right there, only 600 yards away was the Statue of Liberty. I didn't know you could get so close and remain on dry land.

I hadn't expected this. A park five times larger than Hyde Park in London, a thousand acres of open parkland, grassy knolls planted with young

43

trees and shrubs, boardwalks undulating out over the reeds and rushes, bricked pathways rising on concrete stilts that connected the erratic shoreline and allowing Macy and me to walk up the Hudson River for almost a mile.

We passed Ellis Island and—I'd never thought of it before—I wondered whether this is where my mother's father, born near Kiev in the Ukraine, landed when he reached America in 1882. Over one-third of all Americans today can trace their ancestry in the United States to people—Italians, Poles, Ukranians, Russians, Lithuanians, Latvians—who were channelled through Ellis Island, scrutinised for disease or disability, registered and moved on. On an adjacent information board I read that Ellis Island opened in 1892, ten years after my grandfather's arrival. So much for gazing wistfully at my family's first landfall in America. Besides, my mother's mother's family had arrived in Canada years before that.

As I'd done everywhere, I let Macy wander off leash. I knew this was illegal but trusted my ability to call her and her ability to obey. We left the shoreline boardwalk and walked up a grassy knoll where Macy saw and was intrigued by a young, West Highland white terrier carrying a fluorescent orange tennis ball in his mouth, and I was equally taken by his owner—an attractive woman in her thirties wearing a black New York Yankees baseball cap, black sunglasses, shiny black shirt, pinstripe denim trousers and flat-toed cream suede shoes. She had a white sweater or windbreaker tied around her waist and an ivory-coloured cellphone hung on a strap around her neck. Her shiny, dark hair, blonde at the tips, was pulled back in a

44

ponytail. For the first time since I arrived in America I recognised someone I was familiar with—a city chick. It felt good.

Macy did a Bambi gambol over to the couple. I tried to do the same but somehow the action got lost in the translation. The Westie saw Macy coming, dropped his ball and ran to meet her. He reached the limit of his extending leash and the woman commanded, 'Socrates. Stay.' He didn't and she came tumbling after him.

In the meantime Macy stole his tennis ball and ran off. I commanded her to 'Come. Drop,' both of which she did and I returned the ball, with apologies, to Socrates's owner. I wanted to say, 'Hey, you're the first attractive woman I've seen in weeks,' but I didn't. Instead I said, 'Socrates? Your dog's name is Socrates?'

'Well, his dad's name is Studmuffin and I wanted to get as far away from there as possible.'

Socrates wore a bandana around his neck and a gleam in his eye. As far as he was concerned Christmas had come early. Macy was hot stuff. While his owner tried to calm his lust, I explained how surprised I was to find such a large park so close to Manhattan.

'This was just a dump. It was the New Jersey Railway terminal for people arriving from Ellis Island, but by the time I was a child it was just a wasteland. The first part of the park opened for the bicentennial in 1976. I love coming here. Socrates and I are here every day.' She looked across at the Manhattan skyline, the skyscrapers all standing at attention beneath a crisp blue sky. 'I saw the Twin Towers go down. I videoed it.'

A memory got released from a recess in my

mind, a plane journey I once took from Toronto to New York. We'd had a strong tail wind and arrived early. Our pilot explained, 'We are here early and with the flight controller's OK we'll now take you down the Hudson River. Those of you on the left can see Manhattan.' And we did and it was one of the most glorious sights I had ever seen, the entire panorama of Manhattan, ships docked beside it, the island tipped by the Twin Towers, Ellis Island and the Statue of Liberty isolated in the Hudson River. We banked just beyond the Statue of Liberty then headed up the East River to land at La Guardia.

Two years on and this woman wanted to talk about the Twin Towers attack. I wondered whether this horrific and defining event was still so overwhelmingly dominant in people's minds that they needed to talk about it. A visual response to that traumatic attack was everywhere I had travelled. Stars & Stripes on car windows. Stars & Stripes on mailboxes. Stars & Stripes on buildings, lamp posts, bridges. Patriotic messages in supermarkets. 'Together we stand', proclaim signs. 'Proud to be American', state others.

Americans have always been flag-wavers and good for them. This is a country peopled by immigrants—people like my grandparents who moved to North America and reinvented themselves. They're proud of what they've achieved, proud to express their love of country by flying their American and Canadian flags. This is a country that changed 'God save our gracious queen! Long live our noble queen!' to 'My country, 'tis of thee, Sweet land of liberty.' Good for them. But something troubles me about the intensity of this patriotic surge. Propaganda thrives on flags. I get the feeling that patriotism is being manipulated.

*   *   *

I headed towards Manhattan to the massive sign HOLLAND TUNNEL, above the two black holes that penetrate under the Hudson River to reach New York City, the end of Steinbeck's travels and a symbolic beginning of mine. I don't know why, but my hands were sweaty as I approached the toll booth.

'Got any propane.'

'No, I don't.'

'Drive ahead and see that man there.' That man was a cop.

'Good morning, sir. It's a beautiful day today. This is some rig. Restore it yourself?'

I had a tail of traffic behind me and this pleasant round-faced young man, in a short-sleeved black shirt, wanted to shoot the breeze.

'No. I bought it fully restored.'

'Where are you planning to go today, sir?'

'I'm heading for Long Island.'

'That's nice. Tell you what to do. See that man over there? Drive over and he'll open that gate and let you through. Go round that circuit and that'll take you back in the direction you came in. Go south to Exit 13. Take that exit. That takes you over Staten Island to the Verrazano Bridge. That takes you to Brooklyn. As soon as you're off the bridge, take the Shore Parkway and just follow it. Have a nice day.'

I crossed Staten Island and in Brooklyn

descended to the Shore Parkway, and worried when I saw a sign warning that a pedestrian archway over the road gave a clearance of only ten feet two inches. I realised I didn't know how high the GMC was. Or how much higher it was with its roof storage pod and twin air conditioners. Traffic was dense but moving at the speed limit as I drove past Coney Island and Brighton Beach. The next sign warned of a nine-foot eight-inch clearance. As we neared the overpass I edged the GMC into the middle of the road and straddled the white line, driving under the highest part of the archway. The driver to my left was not amused.

Another warning sign. This time, clearance was eight feet eight inches. I did the same manoeuvre to similar annoyance from other drivers. As we passed under this archway almost immediately there was another sign warning of a seven-foot eight-inch clearance. There were no exits from the Parkway, just sign after sign of ever-reducing road clearances. What do you do? You can't turn around. All you can do is drive on.

Shit! Now a clearance sign warned of a seven-foot two-inch clearance. That's the height of a tall SUV. I visualised the storage pod and air conditioners lying in a row on the asphalt and the next archway opening the motorhome like a sardine can. Why did the cop send me this way? But now I felt comfortable driving the GMC. I felt at ease manoeuvring in traffic. It felt like home.

*   *   *

Cedar Point Park was already filling up with families when I arrived. 'When the sun comes out

48

so do the New Yorkers,' the woman at reception told me. I settled in and walked Macy, through the baseball diamond, where she dumped on third base and I cleaned up with fallen maple leaves, to the beach. We walked the north side of the 200-yard-long sandbar to the lighthouse, isolated on an island until a hurricane on 21 September 1938 created the sandbar. Macy found a large, dry, green crab shell to carry cockily in her mouth. The lighthouse itself was unlike any I had ever seen, shaped like a square, Vermont granite, Boston mansion, resting on a massive concrete plinth. The windows and doors were sealed shut. We returned on the shallow southern side of the sandbar, Macy torpedoing through the sparkling water. Back at the GMC, kids crowded round to stroke Macy. 'Where does she live?' six-year-old Jesse, with his security blanket, asked.

'London, England.' I explained. 'She flew over to Newark.'

'Awesome!' Jesse replied.

By dusk every single campsite was filled. Families unloaded barbecues, firewood, tents, chairs, tables, lanterns and bicycles. There's an urge—I think it's a biological imperative—to return to the land. We may love the thrill of urban life, but cooking a meal over a campfire, resting under the trees, sleeping under the stars, these are primitive, soul-satisfying activities. I was surrounded by contented people as I made myself a pasta salad, topped with bits of Homeland-brand salami, still in a shopping bag proclaiming it was 'proudly made in America'.

Later, feeling an attack of the nibbles, I went to the camp store to see what was available and drooled at the thought of hot dogs. I'd forgotten how easy Americans find it to tell total strangers about almost any aspect of their lives. Is it the weather? Sunshine? Latitude? Why are Swedes dour and Italians outgoing, British reserved and Spanish voluble? I don't know. While the store operator entertained me with stories of his diving golden retriever and his wife told me about her macular degeneration, I watched the hot dogs roll. Once they were cooked I went outside, released Macy from where I'd tied her to the wooden rail and walked down to the beach, where we sat, ate our hot dogs and water-gazed. The taste of salt water was familiar to Macy. The view, the food, the surroundings and the people here were familiar to me. I hadn't realised how much of this was still part of me.

*   *   *

Back at our campsite, I sat at the picnic table and Macy lay at my feet. The sight of dozens of flickering fires among the trees reminded me of a gypsy campsite I drove past one evening in Slovenia, in 1964. That summer a buddy and I spent four months criss-crossing Europe in a fire-engine-red Sunbeam Alpine convertible. We'd planned to hitchhike but my older brother worried about my safety, bought a British car, arranged for me to pick it up from the Rootes showroom on Piccadilly in London, tour Europe then bring it back to Toronto. Looking for a place to camp one night in northern Yugoslavia, we saw the flickering flames and slowed down to join them, only to accelerate away when dishevelled men scrambled towards our car. In an aspirational sort of way there was probably a bit of gypsy in the thoughts of my fellow campsite dwellers who chose to spend the weekend here rather than in their homes in the city.

As we sat there, first Macy then I became aware of a presence in pyjamas. Jesse, complete with security blanket, had wandered over from his tent. 'Can I hug Macy?'

Not all kids love dogs. Some are frightened by them, but Jesse wanted another warm touch from Macy. A cultural anthropologist friend from Boston, Connie Perin, once told me she thought that dogs and cats were 'transitional objects'. Kids—or us adults for that matter—graduate from the warmth and security of mommy's breast, to the satin-edged blanket, to the soft, squidgy teddy bear to the sensuous fur of a cat or dog. It's certainly true that when you stroke your own dog, your skin temperature drops, your heart-rate slows and your senses are soothed. I bet Jesse didn't know that was what he was after. Preston, Jesse's dad, quickly arrived and apologised, but Jesse performed a Broadway-quality strop and I offered to let Macy walk him back to his tent.

At Preston's campsite I was offered a cup of coffee from an enamel pot warming over their open fire. Preston was a Wall Street lawyer. We talked kids. We talked camping. Then we talked politics. Preston was a Democrat, financially conservative but socially liberal.

'You'd expect me to be a Bush fan, but I can't take to a man with no integrity. He's the type of general who'd lead you into battle from behind. Your Mr Blair, he had a good relationship with

President Clinton. You tell me, how'd he get suckered by Bush? Do you think he can talk any sense into him? Not that he'd listen.'

Preston was pretty vehement. I agreed I was surprised that these two men from opposite ends of the political spectrum seemed to tune in to each other's wave length. 'Don't get me wrong,' Preston continued. 'I'm a fiscal conservative. I like Bush's tax plans. What I can't abide are his social policies. Give him slack and women will have to go to Canada for an abortion, even if they've been raped.'

'What about Iraq?' I asked.

'Hm. We all got suckered on that one. Bin Laden hates Saddam. Saddam's a shit but he's a secular shit. Women don't wear veils. We've just done his dirty work for him. He must be chuckling in his cave. Get this one wrong and Iraq goes the way of Iran. Then what?'

Jesse was back in his tent and I planned to be out of the park before anyone was up next morning, so I thanked Preston for the coffee and conversation and returned to the GMC. Tomorrow, I'd visit Sag Harbor and try to find the exact street where Steinbeck started his travels.

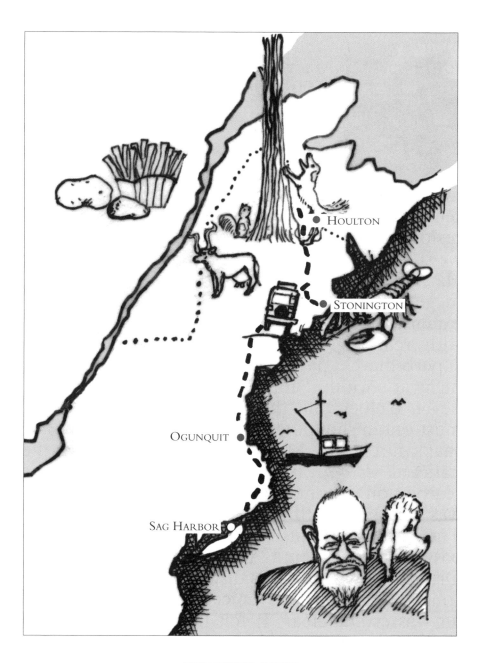

HOULTON

STONINGTON

OGUNQUIT

SAG HARBOR

CHAPTER TWO

NORTH THROUGH
NEW ENGLAND

 Macy and I had now journeyed over 1500 miles together. We'd settled into our trip, into our routines, but only now had I reached the geographical start of Steinbeck's travels. I wanted to find where he lived, but first I was curious to visit Sag Harbor, to see the town he chose to settle in after a lifetime of residing in and writing about California.

At 7.00 a.m., the road from the campsite to Sag Harbor was already crowded with lean, sweaty joggers and countless bicyclists wearing seriously expensive bike clothing and aerodynamic helmets with rearview mirrors. All were travelling the superb bicycle paths that made up a third of the highway's width. People were mowing their lawns. Seven o'clock and they were cutting grass! This must outdo shopping as the national pastime. No, that's not right. Mowing your own lawn is the national *dream*. It's aspirational. Here in Sag Harbor, on this cheerful, warm Saturday morning I was seeing the fulfilment of that national dream. The homes are just wonderful: picture-perfect, cosy clapboard and wood shingle structures. Driving slowly towards town, I could hear the songs of chickadees, titmice and nuthatches. The air was crystal-clear. It felt blissful. As I drove I thought, I could live this dream.

I stopped at the Bagel Buoy Bakery for still-warm bagels, then walked Main Street, stopping at a coffee shop for a great caffe latte. It was in-your-face obvious that town planners had not given planning permission to restaurant or store chains.

Not a Starbucks or a Gap in sight. Sag Harbor's charm was preserved. Steinbeck probably would have liked that. At 8.00 a.m. the only store open was the hardware store, where I bought a screwdriver and self-tapping screws to carry out a minor repair to the interior of the GMC. We walked down to the harbour where there's a small sandy beach. Macy danced in the water, then trotted over to Denise, Angela, Karalyn and Kali, four big Jersey girls here for the weekend, eating enormous breakfasts on a picnic table by the shore. Everyone was smiling. Was it for me? For Macy? Because of the sunshine? Or was Arthur right—people on vacation are just happy people.

Denise told me about Mimi, her corpulent Beagle. 'She's fat because she doesn't get enough exercise.' Angela told me about Maxine, her Maltese, who's on medication for separation anxiety and staying with Angela's parents while Angela visited Sag Harbor.

I went back to Java Nation for another coffee and, in the warm, morning sunshine, Macy sat at my feet as I read the *New York Post*. A feature article, written by Carol Vinzant, included 'Five ways to get Fido into the co-op'.

1. Supply letters of reference.
They're especially strong if you can get someone on the co-op board who knows the dog.
2. Train for an interview.
Many boards require you to bring the dog to your co-op interview. Run through some practice sessions to make sure he'll be quiet and well-behaved.

3. Get a doctor's note.

No kidding. You can have your therapist declare that your canine companion is necessary for your 'emotional support'.

4. Band together.

If other dog-owners in the building like you, they'll give you an in.

5. Invoke the 'three-month rule'.

Here's one of the stranger laws on New York City's books. If a dog has been living with you openly for three months—even if you brought him without permission to a 'no dogs building'—he is legally allowed to stay. In other words, sneak your dog in when you move and hope nobody notices for three months. The risk is that someone will sniff him out and then it's heave-ho for Fido.

As I read, an elderly woman, of whom there are very many in Sag Harbor, came up the stairs to the coffee shop. 'Oy!' she proclaimed, as she pushed to lift herself up the first step. Macy sat up and her ears perked forward. 'Oy!' repeated the woman, accompanied by a man who may have been her grandson, as she mounted the next step. Macy leaned forward. 'Oy!' she said again, and Macy started to wag her tail. She was perplexed. In London, Mace understands that 'Oy' is Cockney for 'Hey!' It alerts her that someone wants someone's attention. I explained to her that Britain and America are separated by a common language, that here 'oy' is usually followed by 'vey', that she wasn't wanted and should settle back down.

As I walked over to visit the Presbyterian

church, everyone we passed either smiled or stopped to talk to Macy. The AGS *New York Guide* said the church's steeple, shaped like a sailor's spy glass, dominated the village and beaconed homebound mariners out in Gardiners Bay, but a hurricane in 1938, the one that threw up the sandbar that attached the island Cedar Point lighthouse once had been stranded on, to Long Island itself, had hurled the steeple into the churchyard. At the church a lumberjack of a man, vacuuming the entrance carpet, told me his father was picking up his mother from the house to the right of the church, what was then the telephone exchange, when the steeple fell onto what was now the car-filled front drive.

I asked him why there were so many cars there so early on a Saturday morning and he explained, 'It's for Hebrew School. Part of the local Jewish community needed a synagogue, so we let them use the chapel. Services don't start for another half-hour but moms are dropping off their kids for Hebrew School.'

A mother explained to me that this was the Conservative Synagogue of the Hamptons. 'There's been a Reform Temple here for ever but we wanted something more traditional. Isn't it wonderful we have such a beautiful and historic church for our *shul* and our *cheder*?' I thought it wonderful too.

Back on Main Street, in an antique shop, the owner commented on Macy's excellent figure and explained, 'My Jack Russell, she looks like a small gas tank. My wife feeds her twenny times a day.' As we walked, guys as well as women said hello to my dog, most frequently by saying, 'Hello, puppy.' It's perfectly obvious to anyone that Macy is no pup. Just as Mace was confused with the meaning of 'oy', it now dawned on me that Americans now use the word 'puppy' as a term of endearment, not as a description of the chronological age of a dog.

We went into the Paradise Bookstore close to the harbour.

'Hello, baby,' the woman at the till said—and I just knew she wasn't talking to me. She reached behind her, to a shelf filled with reserved books, got down a box of Milkbone dog biscuits and gave one to Macy. This was obviously a very doggy town, somewhere that Charley would have been welcome. Another dog, a Clumber spaniel, and his owner came in. I'd never been in a bookshop where there were an equal number of dogs and customers. Neither women knew where John Steinbeck lived, nor did the store have a copy of *Travels with Charley*, although I was pleased to see they had multiple copies of my recent books, which I subtly rearranged. It was the same story in the other local bookshop so I returned to the harbour, to the Chamber of Commerce hut, to ask where Steinbeck lived.

'We can't tell you that,' the neat, sprightly, smiling, grandmotherly woman on duty replied. 'Would you like to buy a Sag Harbor T-shirt? Hello, puppy.' A couple buying T-shirts asked why I was interested in where he lived and I explained, pointing to ever-present Macy who was sniffing the leather shoes on the bare feet of the man's extraordinarily hairy, stumpy legs. Do these guys really think there's anything remotely attractive about Bermudas, gorilla legs and slip-on, shiny leather shoes?

Grandma listened to our conversation and after she completed her sale, produced a *Sag Harbor Chamber of Commerce Directory*, opened it at the map in the middle and with an unsteady hand drew a line from the wooden windmill where we were, up Main Street, turning into Bayview Avenue. 'No, that's not right,' she said, more to herself than to me. She drew the line into Glover and repeated, 'That's not right either.' Then she extended the line up to Otter Pond and on to John and she smiled and said, 'He lived somewhere around here but his place is best approached by boat. Now you can't say I told you exactly where he lived,' and she radiated a warm, helpful and slightly conspiratorial grin.

In increasingly warm, fresh sunshine we walked up Main Street, past the Old Customs House, past a closed used bookstore to Otter Pond, and turned right onto leafy John. The street was lined with mature maples and oaks on the lawns of comfortably aged, perfectly kept New England-style clapboard, shingle and red brick homes. A small SUV with the New York licence tag LUVPEACE passed us, parked further ahead and the driver started to unload. Out first came Riley, a large, dark golden retriever who stretched, then trotted towards us to greet Macy, who enjoyed his attention. Riley's owner was returning home now that her summer renter had gone. We talked and eventually I walked on, with precise knowledge of exactly where Steinbeck's journey began. The serendipity for me was that the point he lived on had the same name as the point on Lake Chemong in Ontario where I spent my first twenty summers. Dogs barked from their backyards as we walked by, but my city-raised dog didn't even break stride. We arrived at the Steinbeck home and Macy dived into the reeds on the shoreline, where Charley probably frolicked. We'd reached the geographical start of the journey.

We were at the exact spot where Steinbeck's wife kissed her dog goodbye as her husband and dog departed on their three-month travels. I took pictures of Macy, then we both walked briskly back to Main Street. Canio's new and used bookstore had opened and the vendor had a paperback copy of *Travels with Charley* which I bought, the same edition the man in Cornelius, North Carolina, had, with Steinbeck and Charley standing by an oak tree I now recognised was still growing only a few hundred yards away.

'Do you know we're trying to create a John Steinbeck Learning Center at the library?' explained the proprietor. 'A sculpture of Steinbeck has already been commissioned. Kimberly Monson, the sculptor, who's from Queens, spent a lot of time here this summer getting to know where he lived and worked, and people who knew him.'

I went back to Java Nation for another cup of coffee. I was wasting time. I didn't want to leave. I liked it here, but knew I had a deadline to be in Ontario, to help my father close down the summer cottage, so I picked up the GMC, drove back to John and down to Steinbeck's home, turned around and set off on his route out of Sag Harbor and onto the south and north Shelter Island ferries. Macy was happy for a chance to lie down. She'd been streetwalking for almost six hours, most of the time on her leash.

At Orient Point I bought my ticket for the ferry

that crossed Long Island Sound to Connecticut.

'Keep up the good work,' the clerk replied as she handed me back my credit card and ticket.

That was a thoughtful touch. The credit card says 'Hearing Dogs for Deaf People' and shows a scruffy Jack Russell terrier-type dog wearing its Hearing Dog coat. No one in Britain ever comments on the card. With time to spare, we sat on the beach and I had lunch, a garden-fresh, sliced beefsteak tomato, salt and pepper, on a soft Sag Harbor bagel. Perfection.

Macy was good on the ferry. She came with me as I checked out what was available and was happy I ordered some French fries from the canteen. The girl serving me meticulously put every single French fry in the paper container. Later, she came over to where Macy and I were eating them and, with a look in her eyes that reminded me of Jesse, said, 'Please?' looking at Macy.

'Sure', I replied, and she gave Macy a deep, deep, heartfelt hug. Macy is not averse to affection from strangers. She leaned into this woman, who responded by laying her head on top of Macy's neck and stroking her body. Almost immediately two other girls—blue-eyed, dark-haired women in their early twenties—joined her and they too stroked and petted and hugged Macy, who looked up at me and shrugged her shoulders.

'Guess you've lucked out,' she said.

I asked the trio where they were from and with a bashful smile the first girl answered, 'Russia.'

When I asked where in Russia, she explained she and her friends were from the Caucasus although she didn't specify exactly where. 'I miss my home,' she said, giving Macy long, slow caresses. 'I have German *ovtcharka*. Very goot. Very reliable. Very intelligent.' She was describing a German shepherd.

I asked her about Caucasian dogs.

'Caucasus *ovtcharka* is big. Not always goot. Asian *ovtcharka* is not goot dog. Bad with people.'

The United States may be misunderstood throughout the world. It may be laughed at by some, demonised by others, but it's still the world's most powerful magnet. These girls had found their summer jobs on the ferry via the Internet. Soon they'd be returning to the turbulence of their homeland. With a strong breeze coming off the Sound, I used the opportunity to give Macy a full body rubdown. Acres of moulting hair wafted over the gunwales back towards Long Island. We walked upstairs to the sun deck where I leaned against the railing and soaked in the heat. Macy sat beside me but it was soon obvious she was uncomfortable. She got fidgety, unable to settle. At work, I sometimes wonder how dumb dog owners can be, to allow their dogs to suffer needless injuries. Here I was on a metal deck in the heat of the sun and I hadn't realised that Macy was standing on a hot frying pan.

We moved to the stern, shaded by the bridge, but as we got there the ship's horn right beside us blasted and Macy tried to dive overboard. As I calmed her, an officer came down from the bridge, stroked Mace and, as I was now getting used to in the States, launched into conversation.

'Ya know, there's a seasonal couple we take back and forth. They got a brown Newfoundland and the dog won't go up or down those stairs.' He nodded to the open metal stairs down to the next deck. 'When he was a pup, he was carried. Now they made it into an art. One picks up the front and one picks up the back and the dog goes rigid like a piece of statuary . . .

'Ya know, I bought my house for 185 grand in '88 at the top of the market. Negative equity for years. Just refinanced. Ya know how much the bank wants to loan me? Three hundred grand. Ya know what? My neighbour just sold his home, just like mine, for 350 grand. I live in a blue-collar town but the way things are going I'm gonna have to sell my old station wagon and get an SUV. . .

'Ya know how damp and humid it's been this summer? I wanted my house painted, but each time the painter came with his moisture meter the wood was too damp to paint. He tells me as long as it's over 35 degrees his epoxy paint still works. I sure hope I can paint my house before winter . . .'

At New London, Connecticut, I phoned Julia who sounded fraught with worry about our son's dog Inca and her six pups, all of whom she was looking after while Ben was on a promotional tour for a book of his that had just been published.

'Inca's so uncomfortable,' she said. 'What can I do?'

I explained that what Inca was 'suffering' from, suckling pups with sharp teeth and claws, was simply normal. The very reason pups have such pin-sharp teeth is to induce mothers to end the period of breast feeding. It was only natural for her to be irritated by their constant demands for milk.

I also spoke to Emily, our eldest, at home—for the first time in years—recuperating from some needed and unavoidable surgery for an ovarian cyst. Then I phoned my mother in Toronto. 'I've felt so alone, not being able to talk to you,' she said in a maternal sort of way that was bound to induce guilt in me. And here I was, traipsing through New England. What was I doing?

*   *   *

Steinbeck had driven west in Connecticut, to visit his son in boarding school, but I decided to aim north for Maine and rejoin his route near Bangor. I love Maine and headed to a favourite place— Ogunquit—a sleepy village by the sea, with a wonderful bakery, rocking chairs on the porch outside, that bakes the best and biggest raisin bran muffins I've ever tasted. Over a mile from the village, traffic snarled to a standstill. I'd never been there on a warm weekend, only out of season, and the ambience was disheartening. It was dark but the stores were still open and the sidewalks clogged with designer-dressed bejewelled shoppers.

It wasn't what I expected but I couldn't pass up a meal at the Ogunquit Lobster Pound, 'established in 1944'—the same year I was. You line up and choose a lobster that suits your appetite or your wallet. We were asked if we wanted hard or soft shell, male or female.

A diner asked, 'What's the difference between a male lobster and a female lobster?' Before the pound keeper could answer, another diner interjected, 'The female lobster talks a lot more.' The pound keeper then explained that the male has bigger claws and a smaller tail, while the female has smaller claws and a bigger tail. 'Funny,' said another voice from the line. 'My wife has a neat little tail and just massive claws.' This was good. It felt like home. Everyone's a comedian. You're on your verbal toes.

The helpful and friendly server at my table was Valentin, from Bulgaria, who, like the Russian girls, had found his job via the Internet. 'This is my fourth year in a row,' he explained with a proud smile. 'I go back home to Sofia in three weeks.' Valentin prepared a doggy bag of bread and butter for Macy.

Back at the campsite I was bugged by mosquitoes for the third night running. For there to be so many so late in the year, it must have been a very wet summer. Then the night went toe-curlingly cold, so cold I called Macy over for warmth—a call she more than willingly responded to. I still hadn't bought a blanket. I wished Julia were with me.

There was once a curious experiment, carried out by psychologists at the University of Toronto. Students listened to tapes of interviews of people applying for a skilled job and were asked to choose whom they'd employ. The job applicants were all actors and they made sure they presented the same business and experience credentials. Who did the students unanimously choose to hire? The guy who, during the interview, said 'Whoops, I'm sorry. I just spilled coffee on me.'

We prefer a little imperfection with our perfection. I certainly do when it comes to cities. Some folks find Venice smelly and decrepit. I think it's the most soul-satisfying city in Europe.

Ogunquit has been fashionable for decades. The AGS *Maine Guide*, published in 1938, explained that even then, there were sixteen hotels in town

65

and a thriving Ogunquit Playhouse. On this viewing, however, the quaintness seemed gone, replaced by a perfect, manufactured tweeness. In Sussex, England, where I live, there's an old church in a nearby field. Inside there were faded Saxon wall paintings. With no electricity, on Christmas Eve, tealight candles were lit in green, plastic, washing-machine detergent balls nailed to the ends of each pew. The place was alive with ancient history. Then English Heritage got wind of the church. The wall paintings were restored, the ceiling beams painted brown, the pews sanded and polished, the graveyard cleared and planted. Now it feels like a museum, preserved in aspic. Ogunquit somehow reminded me of the horrors of over-restoration.

Maine reminds me of where I grew up in Ontario. I've travelled through here many times before: through rustic Wells, picturesque Kennebunk with its scroll-saw Wedding Cake House, built by a sea captain for his bride who had been deprived of her wedding cake when he was ordered hastily to sea, and antique market-dominated Arundel, named after my local town on the River Arun in England. I decided to scoot up I-95 until just past Portland, then return to US 1. It wasn't just that I was familiar with the coastal road I was bypassing; the question now in my mind was whether I should take the old highways, as I had planned, and spend more time in the motorhome, or drive the interstates more often, spending less time on the road and more at stops and destinations. 'Take the interstates,' Macy advised.

'Good morning,' I said to the toll collector as I entered the Maine Turnpike.

'Dollar fifteen,' he replied, not raising his scrawny, weather-beaten head.

This was a peaceful road, scant traffic, no concealed, unmarked police cars as there were further south on I-95 in Maryland and Virginia, only pine, spruce, birch and maple forest. The road signs gave miles and kilometres in equal sized numbers. That meant I was close to Canada.

Back onto US 1, I passed through uninspiring terrain. Road signs said, 'Caution—watch for moose on the highway', and I did, but to no avail. I hoped that Macy would help out but she didn't. Some dogs are lookers and some are dozers. My son's black Labrador Inca is a looker. She hangs her head out of car windows, her eyes following anything or anybody interesting. Macy was proving to be an Olympian dozer, a real bore. I wanted her to take advantage of seeing sights she'd never see again. I can't tell you how many chipmunks playing chicken-across-the road I'd seen and she'd missed. Their gazelle-like leaps would have had Inca in a reverie of delight. Occasionally Macy did arise from her torpid state, look out the window, look at me and mutter, 'God! More fast-moving trees,' circle, lie down and return to her dog-dreams. There may have been moose among those trees, but I didn't see any. Incidentally, do you know that in Sweden, in a typical year, more people are killed by moose than by handguns?

I stopped to shop in Freeport. This pleasant, tree-shaded town was named after Sir Andrew Freeport, a character in Joseph Addison's *The Spectator*, who represented the London merchant class. How apt—although Freeport's merchants are no longer shipbuilders, shoemakers and crabmeat packing plant owners. When Steinbeck travelled through Maine (coincidently with Addison's *The Spectator* as part of his reading material), he passed factory-outlet stores selling locally manufactured shoes and clothing. Now, every major world-fashion brand seems to have an outlet in Freeport. Downtown's historic buildings have been transformed into an upmarket Main Street, America, mall. I headed for L.L. Bean's massive Mecca for outdoor activities and it was still as wonderful as ever. I bought a camping chair and stool, a locally made wool carpet for the motorhome's living room, a blanket and bedspread, waterproof L.L. Bean walking boots (made in China), mugs, plates and a cutting board.

*   *   *

North of Freeport—Down East as it's called here—is a different land. Southern Maine oozes success. Every home is freshly painted, every garden perfectly manicured, every business, even every car lube station, announces its presence with a hand-carved, gilded wooden sign. There's a moneyed mien to southern Maine. Heading Down East, the further I drove the poorer it looked. There was nothing but used trucks for sale and yard sales. Cheer was provided by pastures filled with goldenrod and occasional fields of tangerine-coloured pumpkins, and green or russet squashes and gourds. I stopped at one roadside stand and bought a gallon of freshly pressed cider and a basket of Northern Spy apples, a long-forgotten variety. The juicy, tart sweetness of the apples zapped my taste buds with memories of a flavour that once was but somehow, in the international homogenisation of apple varieties, is no more. We stopped at a county walking trail, which led through the hilly woods. As always, tail held high, Macy led the way, darting through the birch and maple, then the pine and reddening blueberry scrub bush, over lime-green deer moss, leaping with delight from spongy, green ground onto smooth grey granite. Unexpectedly, the summit of the hill was a burnt-out wasteland. A pungent, almost acrid, smoky smell hung in the air. All around was blackened, soot-covered desolation, the trees naked but for the tallest that still had browned needles at their tops. There must have been a lightning strike and forest fire here only a day earlier, with the fire probably extinguished by the following intense rain. In a startling way the scene was mutely beautiful.

At Damariscotta, I saw a group of men with long wooden sticks tapping the beach exposed by low tide. I guessed they were clammers and wondered how clean these clams were, but drove on, through attractive red-bricked Camden where a GMC driver heading south flashed his lights, honked his horn and waved as he passed. Hey. I'm part of a fraternity!

By now it was 80 degrees and brilliantly sunny. Traffic was heavy heading south, but scant as I continued north-east past York, Scarborough, Cumberland, Falmouth, Yarmouth, Gloucester, Durham, Richmond, Chelsea, Bath, Bristol, Newcastle and Woolwich. The names were all familiar, not only from England but also from south-western Ontario where I was born. Now US 1 paralleled the coast. We stopped at Camden Hills

State Park. Macy did her usual Bambi-in-the-woods routine, arriving at the cliffs overlooking the ocean where two men, one wearing diving goggles, were standing hand in hand contemplating the ocean vista.

'Hello, puppy', the goggled man said to Macy, and he gave her a rub and a clenching hug.

Macy muttered something like 'Bugger off' and scampered down the steep, rocky incline to the Atlantic waters gently swelling against the smooth granite shoreline.

As she nosed through rock pools, goggle-man explained, 'Forgot my glasses. These are the only prescription lenses I have with me.'

I followed Mace down to the shoreline and, looking north, saw that the ocean's landfall was gentler, with forests abutting the sea. In the warm air was the sweet smell of salt and seaweed. It was good.

Back on the road, helmetless, sleeveless, bandanaed, moustachioed herds of bikers were heading south. I could say, 'And that was just the women,' but that wouldn't be fair as it was difficult for me actually to tell the guys from the gals. All rode Harleys, all dressed in leather and all were quite past their prime. The Hell's Angels of my youth are now getting old-age pensions. I assumed these OAPs enjoyed biking in Maine because they didn't have to wear protective helmets. A few other states give bikers the same freedom but with strings attached. In Florida you need to show a medical insurance policy. In Texas you have to complete a safety course. In Pennsylvania you have to be over twenty-one, but here in Maine anyone over fourteen can ride helmetless.

At a roadside antique market by an abandoned, snow-sagged Victorian house, I stopped to buy wild blueberries and for a bite to eat. According to the AGS *U.S. One Guide*, in Maine I could expect 'Eggs Canadian: eggs scrambled with maple syrup' for breakfast; 'Soused Clams: freshly shucked clams stewed in vinegar' for lunch; and 'Roast Venison: leg or saddle of venison thoroughly larded with pork, basted with claret while baking, served with gravy made from pan drippings, garnished with currant, barberry or wild plum jelly', for dinner. I went into a restaurant down the road and asked for succotash—corn stewed with green beans. 'We don't have none,' the waitress replied, 'but my grandma makes it so I know what you're talking about.'

I settled for a grilled cheese sandwich, kept half for Macy, then walked the antique market learning that a good set of moose antlers 'on the bone' costs $500–$700 and 'sheds'—antlers that have naturally dropped—are $10 a pound. 'Who wants them?' I asked. 'It'll cost you five times as much in New York City,' I was told, which answered both who and where.

*   *   *

Steinbeck stayed with a friend in Stonington, Maine, a fishing harbour at the tip of Deer Isle. At Bucksport I was back on his track as I turned off US 1, south onto State 175, towards Stonington, This twisting, turning, roller-coaster of a road passes through land that looked as it if had once been cleared for agriculture but had long since reverted to nature. Old farm buildings, scrub bush and thin trees straddled the road. When Steinbeck travelled this road in Rocinante, he was met by thundering trucks filled with timber. I passed only pick-up trucks with local licence plates and a 1968 red Chevy Corvette from New York. Macy hated this road. She rolled from side to side. Her stomach met her brain as I crested interminable hills, but it was 40 miles to our destination and there was no alternative route.

The bridge from the mainland to Deer Isle was unexpected—an elegant, faded green, arching, stringbean of a suspension bridge, so narrow that I wondered what would happen if I met a large truck coming from the island which, naturally, I did. I slowed to snail speed. He thundered north. Leaving the bridge the road continued on an elongated, stone-built, S-shaped causeway across vast mudflats. It reminded me of Chichester Harbour at low tide.

Stonington, at the southerly tip of Deer Isle, lying as it does off the mainland, seemed physically and mentally separated from the land I'd been travelling through. Deer Isle reminded Steinbeck of Dartmoor in south-west England and Stonington, he thought, resembled Lyme Regis on the Dorset coast, though I don't see why. Perhaps it was because this region was settled by people from the West Country and because speech in Maine retains the double vowel sounds of West Country English. This wondrous, melancholic village is to me more reminiscent of a Newfoundland outport, clinging to its granite, forested shoreline, speaking to the sea, oblivious to the land behind. I doubt Stonington has changed at all since Steinbeck visited a friend here over

STONINGTON, MAINE

40 years ago. The 'Island Fishing Gear' store where he bought a kerosene lamp is still there, still with the same sign outside. Macy and I clambered over clean pink and grey granite, then spongy, seaweed-smothered smooth rock to the cockle- and mussel-littered shore and the dark waters of the harbour. Macy beachcombed, successfully finding a piece of neoprene to carry with her. We walked past the sheds, landed boats and warehouses on the south-western side of town, all nestled in dense greenery polka-dotted with the crimson heads of wild rosehips. It was idyllic, compromised only by the signs from the Commissioner of Marine Resources on the utility poles, warning, 'This area closed to all digging of clams, mussels, quahogs, oysters, carnivorous whelks or oysters because of pollution or paralytic shellfish poison'.

The streets were so empty on an early autumn Sunday afternoon that I let Macy wander off her leash, commanding a 'Sit' when I heard or saw the occasional pick-up truck, filled with black metal lobster traps, cruise slowly by. There were piles of lobster traps beside most homes, and orphan piles sitting in yards between buildings. Somewhere, probably in the warehouses on the north-eastern side of town, were lobster pounds teeming with green-black lobsters.

Walking past the lone hotel, a converted family home, a tall, elegant, crop-haired woman in her mid-seventies beamed a broad grin. Nodding towards Macy who was sniffing the sidewalk, she commented, 'I have one of those. Her name's Mollygoddamit, but now that she's grown up I just call her Molly.'

I drove back up the island to a fork in the road leading to a private campsite I'd located in my camping directory. It was closed for the season. I contemplated staying put for the night but remembered passing a veterinary clinic further up towards the rainbow suspension bridge and drove to it, parking on the Deer Isle Veterinary Clinic's gravel and earth forecourt. The sign on the door told me it was open on Tuesdays and Thursdays and for urgent problems to contact the Eastern Maine Emergency Veterinary Clinic in Brewer, a virtual suburb of Bangor at least an hour away. My mobile phone wasn't working here, nor had it in most parts of Maine so I couldn't call for permission to stay, but a pick-up truck, filled with transparent bags bulging with used soda cans, pulled into the drive of the home across the road where I was met by a woofing, three-legged, black Labrador.

'What happened to him?' I asked.

'Oh, he was crossing the road to check out what was happening at the vet's, when he was hit by a car. They took him right in but couldn't save his leg, so it got amputated.'

With their approval we camped at the vet's overnight. I returned to the GMC, made my bed with the L.L. Bean blanket and bedspread, fed Macy—who picked at her dog food but gobbled the remaining bagel from Sag Harbor—then made myself a southern Maine dinner of blueberries, mixed green salad leaves, olive oil and balsamic vinegar, finishing off with some home-made soft oatmeal, raisin and walnut cookies I'd bought in Sag Harbor. The night cooled. I brewed a cup of coffee and settled into my new camping chair, propped my new walking boots onto my new campstool and watched Macy like a hawk. No way was she going near that road to visit the Labrador on the other side.

*   *   *

Like most dogs, Macy has a few simple ways of waking me up each morning. Catlike in her love of dawn, she gets up while it's still dark, stretches then shakes. Hers is a vigorous morning shake, so much so that the GMC rolls a little. Her shake also rings her bell, the brass nametag on her collar. I'm a dawn riser too, so I'm pretty much aware of her morning ritual, but usually I stay in bed waiting for Part Two. This begins with her walking like a ballerina on points over to my bed, where she stands and stares. Ask any dog owner and they'll tell you that we all know when our dogs are silently staring at us. I lie there pretending not to notice and after a few minutes Mace utters short, plaintive, high-pitched squeaks, so high some of them, I swear, are in the ultrasound range. I respond by reaching out to touch her and she replies by dancing as if her feet were on the sun-heated deck of the Long Island Sound ferry. I pull on the clothes I dropped by the bed the night before, open the GMC's door and she bounds out, followed by me. This morning when I let her out, she bounded straight for where I'd dumped the remainder of her unfinished meal last night, where a large feral cat was munching on her Eukanuba.

In *Travels with Charley*, Steinbeck wrote about 'the coon cats, huge tail-less cats with grey coats barred with black . . . they live in the woods and are very fierce'. He may have been commenting on the breed now called the Maine Coon, although these cats have luxurious tails. I've lived with one, our silver tabby Millie. The breed descends from cats transported from England to Maine where, in the survival of the fittest, those with the most insulating coats and those large enough to catch winter rabbits were the ones that survived. The cat eating Macy's leftovers was a big tabby that hightailed it into the woods behind the veterinary clinic, with Macy in hot pursuit. Mace returned a few minutes later and I decided to forego early morning exercise and instead made breakfast for both of us.

Tidying up afterwards, I looked out the motorhome front window and saw she'd wandered across the highway. I jumped out and with urgency in my voice commanded, 'Stay.' On that firm and explicit command she cantered towards the highway and me. Hearing no traffic, I shouted the command, 'Come.' Obedient Dumbo came to an abrupt halt in the middle of the road. I ran towards her, but now I heard a truck coming. The driver saw her and slowed down. Regardless of how many times I shouted 'Come,' all Macy did was stand and cower. 'Like a deer in headlights,' the driver smilingly shouted as she accelerated away. I dragged Macy back to the motorhome, tossed her in and headed back towards the mainland.

*   *   *

It's easy to get lost on the byways heading back towards Bangor, and I did. Roads twist back and forth on themselves. Some routes divide in two, the same route number going in different directions, one to a dead end, the other out of the maze and towards US 1. Passing roadworks, I was surprised to see the road crews were driving trucks with Quebec and New Brunswick licence plates. I asked the driver of a cement truck from the firm Ciment Quebec what he was doing and he shrugged a Gallic shrug and said nothing. Either he didn't speak English or was giving his impression of the taciturn Yankee.

Just beyond Sedgwick I drove past three wild turkeys in a clearing. As I slowed down, they lofted into flight. Wild turkeys are now commonplace, even pestilential in some regions, but I was excited by the sight. This once numerous bird had been a long-extinct species in New England and adjacent Canada. Over-hunting and deforestation by logging were probably the causes. I remember unsuccessful attempts in the 1960s to release game farm-reared turkeys. They were too far removed from their ancestors to survive harsh New England winters. It wasn't until around 1970 that prescient game biologists in Georgia and South Carolina realised that turkeys trapped in the wild and then moved to other suitable habitats would survive and multiply. The turkeys I just saw were descendants of around thirty wild turkeys released in New England about the time I graduated as a vet. In the following 35 years they've multiplied to around 50,000 individuals although all the descendants I can so far account for is three. Curiously, while most of us at Christmas eat white turkeys, birds with their origins in Spain, my commander-in-chief always buys a 'domestic bronze', a descendant of these North American wild turkeys.

At North Sedgwick I stopped for gas, where the burly, tattooed attendant offered Macy a Milkbone.

'I could make a million bucks writing a book describing the different reactions dogs give me when I give them a bone.' Ogling the GMC, he asked, 'Restore it yourself?' But before I could lie, he continued, 'It's amazing that folks can drive those converted buses with a Class C licence. If you could see what I see here in the summer you'd never go back on the road.'

I asked the best way to Bangor and he suggested an alternative route that would save me fifteen miles. 'Once you're past the blueberry plant, just follow your nose.'

Blueberry plant. That was intriguing. We undulated along, Macy and me. People waved in the friendly way I was once used to in rural Ontario. I felt completely at ease, at home. I motored on, past white clapboard homes almost all in need of a couple of coats of paint. The wood shingle barns were either natural wood or had long ago been painted red. 'Proud to be an American', stated the flags attached to mailboxes, neighbour reminding neighbour of their patriotism.

I stopped at the G.M. Allen & Son Blueberry Factory, hoping to buy fresh blueberries, but was three days too late. 'We froze last week's final harvest on Friday,' the short, blonde-haired, blue-eyed assistant in the Blueberry Patch retail store told me, 'but we have frozen blueberries, blueberry syrup and lots of blueberry jams. Want to try some?' She offered me samples from a variety of jam pots, one of which actually tasted like fresh blueberries so I bought that and ten pounds of frozen berries.

Here's what I learned from a US Department of Agriculture brochure I picked up at the Blueberry Patch. Blueberries have more antioxidants—phytochemicals that scavenge cell-damaging chemicals called free radicals—than any other fruits or vegetables. Good stuff. I also learned a few more surprising facts. 'Wild Blueberries' is a trademark and this factory had just finished processing two million pounds of Wild Blueberries. Maine's crop of Wild Blueberries is around 70 million pounds. Another hundred thousand pounds of wild blueberries are also harvested but these blueberries don't have capital letters. These are grown organically while Wild Blueberries are grown using fertiliser, herbicides and pesticides. Now that hand-raking on the blueberry barrens had finished for the year, the fruiting plants would be cut back to the ground and left next year to grow in size but not be used for harvest. Harvesting takes place in the second year after pruning. Once pruning was finished the locals, including the shop assistant's parents, were off to Florida for the winter.

I visit Sweden several times a year with the chief, who deals in old, painted, Swedish furniture, and, as far as I know, in Sweden a 'wild blueberry' is just that. Each August thousands of pickers arrive from Poland and the Baltic States and work their way through Sweden's woods, picking blueberries and lingonberries, delivering them to locals who set up weighing and buying operations in their car garages. It isn't as efficient as here in Maine. The Wild Blueberry Commission of Maine states in one of their brochures that yields have

NORTH SEDGWICK, MAINE

increased enormously since 'integrated pest management' and 'integrated crop management' methods have been devised and used. I remain a blueberry Luddite. I want to go for a walk in the woods and know that the blueberry I've just picked was fertilised by moose poo and pruned by grazing white tail deer.

*   *   *

Beyond Bucksport, heading towards the Canadian border, laden logging trucks thundered back towards the Bucksport paper mill, while empty ones, mostly with New Brunswick licence plates, roared past me as I cruised at my regular 55 mph. I stopped near Bangor to get some new food for Macy and phoned Emily who was leaving hospital that day and sounded perky as always, but explained that her grannie, my wife's mother, had had a mild stroke. I called Julia but she wasn't answering her mobile. Soon after, she phoned back, sounding brittle, tense and worried. I drove on, working out what to do and the best way to get back to London.

The landscape north of Bangor was probably attractive but I wasn't concentrating on it. Should I be here, selfishly enjoying myself while Julia had so many responsibilities back at home? I know that majestic white pines now appeared, towering above the surrounding forest, because you just can't miss them. Beyond Island Falls, individual trees shone in vivid autumn colours. A Hyundai Accent passed me, with a large yellow Labrador lying on the lap of the front-seat passenger. Macy muttered, from under my legs where she was resting, that she wished she had Julia as a front-seat passenger, to lay her head on.

At a lookout vista facing Mount Katahdin in distant Baxter State Park, a couple with a 27-foot Airstream trailer came over to have a good look at my GMC. 'Restore it yourself?' I asked before they could get a word in. They had, and, just to prove it, showed me photos of the trailer's step-by-step restoration.

'How long did it take to restore yours?' the husband asked.

'Bit by bit, I guess around five years,' I replied nonchalantly, fingers crossed behind my back. I took pictures of them and they did of Macy and me, and I returned to I-95.

On an overpass I tried, successfully, to avoid running over a concentration of five, plump, dead racoons, one slightly larger than the others. This was probably a mother and her now almost fully grown spring litter, all wiped out together: a mother leading her young to their deaths. The sight was painfully sad.

$$*\qquad*\qquad*$$

Steinbeck intentionally headed for Aroostook County in north-east Maine, to visit the potato capital of America. He wrote at length about spending an evening with a French-Canadian potato harvesting family. I stopped at the Houlton Visitors' Center to ask about the potato harvest.

'The local farmers don't grow potatoes the way they used to, but we do a good broccoli,' explained the bureau's attendant. She gave me the name and telephone number of the local potato professor, who also runs the Old Iron Inn Bed and Breakfast, but, what with Julia's mother and the dead racoon family, I wasn't much in the mood for dry-calling Mr Potato and asking how Maine had lost out to other markets.

Just beyond the Visitors' Center, across the road from a massive Irving gas station truck stop, was a Tim Hortons. I hadn't realised this Canadian coffee, donuts and bagels chain had moved across the border into the States, but I knew that a couple of pecan butter tarts would give me the sugar-surge I needed. Tim Hortons in many ways typifies the Canadian personality. Practical, unpretentious, classless, it has quietly innovated and oozed into every nook and cranny in the confederation until today you can't visit a Canadian airport, hospital, gas station, tyre store or, it now seems, border town without being offered a Tim Hortons coffee, bagel and cream cheese, or donut. Horton was a calm, cool defenceman for the Toronto Maple Leafs hockey team, a heads-up player with a powerful slap shot. He opened a donut and coffee shop in the early 1960s, near where I went to veterinary college, and soon had a dedicated following, including me, for his apple-fritters and Dutchies—square, glazed, raisin-filled leviathans. The chain garnered another generation, my kids, in the late 1970s, when they introduced small round 'donut hole' donuts called Timbits. In Canada there are thousands of Tim Hortons, even in the sleepy rural hamlet of Bridgenorth, Ontario, where I spent my summers and where once only dew worms were for sale.

Canadians eat to live rather than live to eat. Their gastronomic highlights are *poutine*—French fries smothered in melted cheese and brown gravy; and *pemmican*—wind-dried buffalo meat. But there are two other Canadian foods, found nowhere else in the world, that really are tasty if you've a sweet tooth—the Chelsea bun and the butter tart. The Canadian Chelsea bun is based on the bland, dry, English version. The English variety is a small, baked wrap of dough wound around seven raisins and a dash of cinnamon, and topped with sugar crystals. Even freshly baked, it tastes like it's two days old. The Canadian Chelsea bun is a lighter but chewier, baked dough-wrap, wound around zillions of raisins drenched in brown sugar, butter and cinnamon, topped with a dark brown sugar glaze. In the United States it's been rebranded as the cinnibun.

The butter tart is a pie-dough tart filled with a mix of brown sugar, butter and raisins—or pecans—then baked. Every Canadian supermarket sells butter tarts in packets of six or mini butter tarts in packs of twelve. It makes my chest expand to see that Tim Hortons is now quietly advancing Canadian cultural imperialism on unsuspecting American border towns by exposing their citizens to these icons, these epitomes of Canadiana. Leaving Macy in the motorhome, I went in, bought some butter tarts and a coffee, and asked the counter assistant if Canadians still came across the border to harvest potatoes. She giggled. 'You kidding? It's died a death here. It's a lot better on the other side. School "potato break" starts next week.'

By 'the other side', she meant in New Brunswick where she lived. I asked why it was better on the other side. 'You know, the Maritimes are owned by the Irvings and the McCains, eh? Except for Prince Edward Island. That's owned by McDonald's. They're changing the name of Nova Scotia to Nova Cain.' I don't know if she knew how funny that was. She was smiling, but she was serious.

'Do you know anything about the potato harvest?' I asked. 'Why are so many of the potato fields I've driven past brown and lifeless?'

'The plants are killed a few weeks before harvesting. That gives the potato skins time to thicken and it also means they're protected if there's an early frost.'

'How do you know that?' I asked.

'My dad grows potatoes. This year he planted Shepody. They got harvested last month and they're for French fries; and Ontario, they're for potato salad; and he's trying Yukon Gold. They're yellow, not white, but he says the gourmet market wants them.'

'But what about harvesting? Are potatoes still hand-picked from the ground?'

By now my font of knowledge was surrounded by three other Tim Hortons employees, all smiling and nodding as she explained potato culture to me.

'Harvesters do everything. They dig the plants out and lift the potatoes onto the conveyor. You need someone there to pick out the rocks and stuff but the conveyor drops them right in the dump truck. If you want to see it, why don't you cross into New Brunswick? It's really dead here.'

I'd planned to continue north on US 1, as Steinbeck had, paralleling the Canadian border, through Madawaska to Fort Kent, then, rather than swing back south through Maine, as Steinbeck had, divert off his route into Quebec, returning to it in New Hampshire. On my potato expert's advice I decided instead to cross the border here and travel north on the New Brunswick side. I followed the signs through Houlton to 'Canada'.

Just before the border, two black unmarked Chevy Blazers, with flashing blue strobe lights on their roofs, were parked at angles on each side of the road, reducing the normal two lanes to one. Four men wearing wrap-around sunglasses stood between the cars. It was cloudy. They looked ridiculous. In their twenties and early thirties, they wore dark blue combat trousers tucked into black jackboots, guns in black leather holsters, dark blue shirts and dark blue baseball caps, with US Customs embroidered in gold thread on them. There hadn't been enough time, I assumed, to rebrand their caps US Customs & Border Protection, as they now were. Under their baseball caps, their heads were obviously shaven. I finally arrived at the front of the line of cars.

'Turn off your engine.' I did.

'Where you goin'?' OK. I'm at the border but it's no time to get facetious.

'Canada.'

'What have you got in your RV?'

'Myself and my dog.'

'Where do you live?'

'England.'

'Let's see your passport.' I gave him my UK and Canadian passports.

'You're Canadian! What else you got inside?'

His raised voice and exclamation 'You're Canadian!' brought his fellow goons over.

'Some food and utensils,' I answered.

All four wandered to the back of the motorhome, stared, frowned, then trooped back to my window.

'You got a North Carolina tag. You gonna sell this in Canada?'

'I'm not going to but what is it to you? That's something for the Canadians to worry about. It's not your problem.'

As I spat out those words, I realised I shouldn't have. They conferred, then my interviewer hefted himself back to my window and said, 'Lemme see your dog.' I raised Macy from her sleep and cupped her head up towards the window.

'Proceed.'

A minute later I was in Canada.

CHAPTER THREE

EASTERN CANADA AND
VERMONT

Canada is where I'm from. It's a country where six-packs of beer are designed for you to carry while wearing your winter mitts. It's where Halloween costumes are made to fit over snowsuits, where car engines have their own plug-in electric heaters, where there's nine months of winter and three months of poor skiing, where newspapers devote eight pages to news and twelve to hockey. Canadians define themselves as 'not Americans'. Canadians don't think Cuba's a 'problem'; it's a cheap place to go for your holidays. We're metric, not Imperial measure. We drink 'pop', not 'soda'. We eat 'chocolate bars', not 'candy bars'. A Canadian understands the following: 'Please pass me a serviette. I just dropped some *poutine* on the chesterfield.' Mind you, for variety, French-Canadians define themselves as 'not French'. Canada, French-Canadians say, has the largest French population in the world that never surrendered to Germany. In essence, it's almost impossible to tell a Canadian from an American, unless, that is, you make that very comment to a Canadian.

Across the American border, at Canadian Customs, I entered the Atlantic Time Zone, an hour behind Eastern Time and two decades behind the rest of North America. At the New Brunswick Visitors' Centre I stopped for Mace to have a little exercise and for me to pick up a provincial map. As we walked in, a uniformed woman of medium height and sallow complexion came forward. 'We can't allow her inside. There are health reasons. Allergy.' And as she spoke, she put a black comb to her upper lip, clicked her heels together and shot her right arm into a straight-armed salute.

Pompous officials really get up my nostrils but I wasn't going to challenge her, so I put Mace in a 'Sit' and went inside asking why New Brunswick is called New Brunswick.

'New York, New Jersey, New Hampshire, New England, Newfoundland. My ever-diminishing grey cells even understand Nova Scotia, but where's Brunswick?' I asked.

My little Maritime Nazi didn't know but another young official came over.

'Nice dog. A lot more obedient than the last one who came in.' He'd given the game away. Macy was barred because of annoying behaviour by one of her brethren. He handed me a photocopied paragraph of information that said:

New Brunswick was given its name from the House of Brunswick, which ruled England at the time this province was established in June 1784, as a result of the great influx of United Empire Loyalists leaving the newly independent United States.

Odd, I thought. Wasn't it the House of Hanover that ruled England at that time?

I drove north, through Bristol and Bath, past United Empire Loyalist hillside cemeteries and on to Perth-Andover. This region was the site of the Aroostook War between Canada and the United States. The 1783 peace treaty between Britain and the United States was vague about the exact

91

boundary between New Brunswick and what was then greater Massachusetts but would become, in 1820, the State of Maine. When Maine began granting land in this region, the King of the Netherlands was asked to arbitrate and although the British accepted his arbitration the US Senate rejected it and authorised a force of 50,000 militia to meet the emergency. Daniel Webster, of *Webster's Dictionary*, using a map he said was marked with a red line drawn by Benjamin Franklin himself in Paris in 1782, persuaded Maine to accept a compromise in which Britain paid both Massachusetts and Maine sums of cash and the US government reimbursed Maine for expenses incurred in mobilisation.

Local towns here are now dominated by McCains potato processing plants. Do you know or are you even remotely interested in the fact that one out of every three French fries eaten on this planet comes from a processing plant owned by a business headquartered in this backwater?

Now, the Saint John River marked the border between the US and Canada. The names of towns changed. Bellefleur, Saint Leonard, Sainte Anne de Madawaska, Riviere-Verte. As well as the provincial flag and Canadian national flag, I passed a home flying a French tricolour embellished with what appeared to be the Star of Bethlehem.

Just past Saint Jacques, I pulled into Les Jardins de la République Provincial Park, bought firewood and settled in for my first night in Canada. As evening drew in, the air cooled. I put on a scarf and coat and took Macy for a walk along the Madawaska River. That name was familiar. My

Aunty Nettie had once given me a tie woven by the Madawaska Weavers. Now I knew where they wove. By the river we met a dark golden retriever, fat like most other dogs we'd encountered so far on our travels, being walked on her leash by a couple—he, taciturn, in a red wool hunting jacket with orange reflective lining, toothpick in mouth; she, accommodating, warm and outgoing. Seeing Macy, she let her dog, Chanel, off her leash. Both dogs play-bowed to each other and took off, running, body-bashing as their paths crossed. While we talked, Chanel broke off her dog play and rolled in the grass.

'Any-ting dis-gus-ting, she roll in,' he muttered through his toothpick, in French-Canadian inflected English.

'Chanel Numero Sept,' responded his wife.

They were a local couple, from nearby Edmundston, enjoying a final week of camping before winter set in. I asked about the flag I'd seen.

'Dat's d'Acadian flag,' Toothpick explained.

'My husband is Acadian. I am Quebecoise,' his wife continued, in accentless English. 'His family has been here for hundreds of years.'

Toothpick remained silent.

'Where did the family come from?' I ventured.

'They were from Nova Scotia but were exiled to the Saint John River, near Fredericton. In the American Revolution his family fought on the British side, but afterwards the British told them to leave their homes to make way for Loyalists. You know—Catholic ethnic cleansing. They moved up the river to Madawaska.'

Back at our campsite, a chipmunk in a branch above the motorhome screamed obscenities, swore at us, and intentionally threw bits of bark and pine needle as I built a fire. We ate our dinners and when the Acadian couple walked by I offered them the remainder of the large bag of dog food I was abandoning, as Macy simply didn't like it. 'She roll in any-ting and eat any-ting. If it's dis-gust-ing, she roll in it then eat it,' Toothpick responded, in controlled thanks for the food.

*   *   *

The temperature dropped to near freezing overnight. I'd tried to light the furnace in the motorhome but it wouldn't start. Now, the foggy morning's frosty air rasped my nose and lungs with an invigorating freshness. Autumn colour had touched the crowns of trees, producing a bedlam of warmth in the still predominantly verdant landscape. There's a delicious smell in the air, as summer gives way to autumn. It prepares you for the cycle of life about to be enacted: death, followed by stillness, followed by reawakening. Seeing the first signs of autumn, smelling the cleansing air, on a crisp, clear and bright morning, still takes my breath away. Pictures of North American autumnal colour only tell part of the tale. Believe me. You must be in it, enveloped by it, to experience its truly inspiring splendour. I love autumn here.

I turned on the motorhome stove's gas rings to take the chill out of the air, donned hat and scarf, wished I had gloves, and took Mace for a 45-minute walk through the park. She barked at a camping bicyclist who went past. With his parka up tight around his face he probably didn't notice, but

I did. *Bad dog*. This trip was bringing out the dog in Macy and I wasn't particularly pleased.

While I fried up bacon and eggs and brewed coffee, Macy wandered towards the nearest campers around 50 metres away, just emerging from their tent.

'Come on in,' I heard the woman say, and Mace disappeared through the tent flap. I went over to apologise and retrieve her, noticing the Ontario licence on their pick-up.

'Vacation?' I asked.

'We come back each year,' Alice replied. 'My husband's from Nova Scotia. We'd live here if there was work.'

Alice and Jack live in Mississauga, Ontario, the most godawful of Toronto's dormitory exurbs.

We talked dogs. We talked Maritimes. And I mentioned the Acadian couple I'd met the previous evening.

'Hey. It could have been my family, eh, that moved them off their land? They were Loyalists from Pennsylvania who settled in Nova Scotia after the American Revolution. The Americans don't know they created two countries, not just one. If it hadn't been for them, eh, Ontario and the Maritimes would never have been settled. It would've all been French.'

'So there's lots to be thankful for in America,' I commented.

'Yeah, like thank God we're not part of them, eh? A pea-brain for a president, eh? I hate Chretien, but thank God he stood up to that blackmail and we didn't go to war in Iraq.'

Jack rubbed his hands together and smiled as he spoke but his anti-American feelings were harsher than the envious form I was more used to hearing from Canadians. Did he hold a grudge because his side lost the war and emigrated to Canada?

I turned to Alice. 'What do you think of Maine?' I asked, shifting the subject.

'Beautiful. Beautiful. They didn't vote for Bush. They're more like Canadians than Americans, you know. Maine's nice.'

The sky turned Caribbean-blue as we drove up Route 185 in Quebec, heading for Rivière-du-Loup on the St Lawrence River. A sign to the town of St-Louis-du-Ha! Ha! caught my attention and I turned off the highway and into the village, dominated by its towering, red-doored, orange brick, silver-spired church. In front of the church was a memorial, Christ with arms outstretched, to soldiers killed in World War I. In front of the nearby post office I saw three elderly men chatting, so I stopped and got out.

Unlike most English-speaking Canadians, who expect all other Canadians always to speak English, and Parisians who are so up their backsides they think Canadian French is too plebeian, I love Canadian French. Rather than that excitable, emphatic, pretentious, posturing accent you hear in Paris, here in Quebec the language is more sibilant, more amusing. Think of a laconic Midwestern American drawl, Fargo in French, add a little mirth and there you have it, Canadian French. You could also say that Canadian French is in many ways purer than European French: the European *le weekend* is *la fin de la semaine* here; the Parisienne's *le shopping* is the Canadienne's *la magasinage*. Mind you, a car is *un char*. I enjoy hearing Canadian French. The trouble is, I don't understand it. Used to once. Not any more.

'*Bonjour, messieurs,*' I pronounced in French not spoken for 40 years. '*J'ai honte mais je parle seulement un petit peu de français. Parlez-vous anglais?*'

They shrugged in a manner that only elderly men can shrug, looked at each other then one said, '*Tu comprends anglais. Tu vois la télévision anglaise.*'

'*Mais seulement pour les jeunes filles,*' he responded.

More incredulous shrugs followed.

'*Le nom, St-Louis-du-Ha! Ha!, c'est curieux. Connaissez-vous pourquoi?*'

I didn't know where in my brain my fractured French was coming from, but it was enough to get an answer.

The tallest of the trio explained that when the first white settler arrived, he looked at the mountain and exclaimed, 'Ha! Ha!' Then he looked at the lake and exclaimed once more, 'Ha! Ha!' At each 'Ha! Ha!' all three men raised their arms high and wide. This was indeed worrying for these old men were probably my age and I wondered how my arm gestures were evolving. I thanked them for their gesticulations and departed towards Rivière-du-Loup. Suddenly, before me was the St Lawrence River—mighty, imperious, overwhelming—almost black in colour, its distant shore only visible because of the hills on the north shore. This isn't just a river. At this point on its journey to the Atlantic, it's an irresistible force of nature, a behemoth, frightening even on a cloudless, warm day in its awesome, forbidding darkness. Here at Rivière-du-Loup it must be

97

twenty miles across.

This could be the most northerly point on our journey, just under 46 degrees of latitude. I turned south-west onto the old south shore river road, now called the *route des navigateurs*. The road was empty of traffic, easy to drive, and I made a steady 55 mph. Narrow strip fields of potatoes and corn, both awaiting harvest, as well as fields of stubble from already harvested wheat, occupied the sliver of land between the river and the cliffs to the south. Roadside shrines of Christ on the cross every few miles reminded me to drive carefully.

Just past a Poulet Frit du Kentucky, I slowed down to buy fresh smoked salmon from a roadside stand and the break pedal stuck. My first mechanical glitch. Better the brake, I thought, than the accelerator. Continuing along I noticed that some houses had provincial fleurs-de-lys flying in front. Others had fleurs-de-lys and national red maple leaf flags, but only post offices flew the national flag alone. The Quebec flag, by the by, is the ancient flag of the French navy. The provincial motto, *Je me souviens*, 'I remember' or to some 'I know who I am', seems equally historic but was created almost as an afterthought by the architect of Quebec's Legislative Assembly Building and added below the province's coat of arms only in 1939.

We stopped at a federal government migratory bird sanctuary on the river, and while Macy gambolled, I phoned Julia to find out about her mother. Her voice was plaintive. 'It never rains but it pours . . . I miss you more than I can say . . . Certainly not. I can take care of everything . . . I love you . . . ' Then her voice broke and she could say no more. I spoke but there was no response. I said I'd phone back, and still no response. I said goodbye. No answer. This was supposed to be a carefree adventure but it was as clear as a fish's eye I should be in London right now, not enjoying myself in Quebec's autumn sunshine. I had no stomach for lunch and continued towards Quebec City, planning where to leave Macy so I could return to my family; with a veterinary friend in Montreal or, if time allowed, with my brother in Toronto. I felt glum and heavy-hearted as I drove over the bridge above the St Lawrence, through leafy, suburban Sillery to the Plains of Abraham, just west of Quebec City's ramparts, where, in spite of my anxiety, both our spirits were uplifted. Macy rolled in the grass and I just gazed as rollerbladers, girls in Lycra halter tops and shorts, guys in check shirts and chino trousers glided by. All that was missing was a bunch of hockey sticks. Even on a warm sunny day, with Macy kicking her legs up in delight, watching the rollerbladers skate effortlessly, twist around and do laps skating backwards then rotate forward and accelerate, what I thought of was the Canadian poet Gilles Vigneault's, *'Mon pays, ce n'est pas un pays, c'est l'hiver.'* (My country, it's not a country, it's winter.) This super sight made me know I'd truly arrived home.

The province of Quebec is unique and Quebec City is one of the great towns from the European colonial era in North America. French explorers landed here in 1534. 70 years later, while Shakespeare was writing his plays, Samuel de Champlain founded the city, and for the next century and a half this was the political and economic centre of New France. Then, in 1759, as every schoolchild in Canada learns, on the heights of the Plains of Abraham, General Wolfe's British forces defeated those of the Marquis de Montcalm, concluding the Seven Years War and altering the future history of the heartlands of America. Unlike their later actions in Nova Scotia, the victorious British did not undertake a wholesale removal of the French-speaking population. In the most surprisingly tolerant way, the right to speak French remained, the Catholic clergy were left alone, French law was retained. Indeed, when the Napoleonic Code was enacted in France 50 years later, it was adopted as civil law in Quebec and remains to this day the basis of civil law in the province.

We walked, Macy and I, through Quebec City's lower town, then to upper town, and in the late afternoon sun along the Dufferin Terraces boardwalk in front of the Château Frontenac, a hotel part Scottish baronial, part Loire River valley château. Other dogs trotted by. A black cocker spaniel played retrieve with a ball her owners were throwing ahead of her, and when the ball bounced over the escarpment of the cliffs of Cap Diamant, plunging down to lower town, I was pretty sure the spaniel, being a spaniel, would follow suit. It didn't.

Macy didn't know what to make of the flute players, puppeteers and accordionists she met on our walk, but with the day drawing in we left to find an overnight campsite.

At Lac Megantic I checked into the Baie des Sables Municipal Campground where a lean, young woman, yet another Celine Dion lookalike,

QUEBEC CITY

checked me in. Celine asked if she could practise her English on me. I hoped this was an excellent chat-up line but it was, in fact, her earnest attempt to try her almost non-existent English on what I took to be a rare English-speaking camper. We had a problem. Celine couldn't find much more than a word of English and as the sun dropped to the horizon so did my French. Unlike most other campsites I'd stayed in, where an open bottle of booze was grounds for expulsion, here the camp store was 90 per cent wine, 10 per cent other supplies. I bought a large screwtop bottle of New York State red, phoned Buddy, who told me where to look for the breaker button to get the furnace working, then went for a walk with Macy.

'Viens ici,' a camper beckoned as Macy trotted past, and my multilingual canine responded and walked over to her. She gushed to me, but I couldn't understand a word she said. How, I wondered, did I understand the guys in St Louis-du-Ha! Ha! yet not understand *un mot* here? I explained that neither my dog nor I understood what she or her friends were saying. They laughed, but didn't understand a word of what I was saying. It was disheartening. Here were people in their thirties and forties, living on a cultural island, cut off from anything good, bad or indifferent in the culture surrounding them. You can say this is an improvement from the time French speakers had to learn English to take over their own destinies, but to turn your back on the language of the people that live around you is surely introspective parochialism in its most denying form.

Back at the motorhome, with the furnace fired up I made a meal—flakes of hot smoked salmon on a blueberry-sprinkled green salad—had a shower and while Macy chased cats in the woods, I lit a fire, drank my wine and planned the next week. I contentedly fell asleep to the soothing, sonorous sounds of freight train horns, moaning plaintively, distantly through the trees.

*   *   *

Ben phoned at 7.00 a.m. while Macy and I were out walking, and we talked about his Grandma Jean. Julia had been telling him she'd take care of everything and Ben, knowing how protective his mother can be, thought he might get a clearer picture of what was happening from me. I told him what I knew and what I was planning to do, to fly home if Jean didn't improve. I wanted to see her and knew that she'd feel better seeing her son-in-law. Ben advised me not to come home; that his mother and grandmother would feel guilty if I interrupted my trip and that he'd take care of what needed to be attended to.

My dog and I walked along, criss-crossing snowmobile trails through dense autumn woodland, crossing streams, turning bends, climbing hills, then descending towards more streams. Mace stopped at each one, sampling the cool, sparkling, running water. Soon we emerged onto a dirt road that led down to the Baie des Sables public beach. The lake was mirror-smooth, with a low morning mist hanging over it. Above the mist I could see the trees on the far shore and above the trees an electric blue sky with a clarity that only autumn brings. Around me the ground was covered in a profusion of wild flowers, yellow buttercups and silverweed, white anemones, purple milkweed and pink bindweed. Yellow pond lilies and white water lilies, some with a faint pink glow, floated in a still pool separated from the lake by a curve to the shoreline. Blue and green dragonflies hovered over the beach in the reflected warmth of the morning sun. Smaller red dragonflies soon joined them. Macy missed all of this. She entertained herself by running circuits in the shallow waters, leaping, arching like a salmon swimming upstream through rapids, snow-ploughing the still water with her nose, acting the fool. We walked and played for another hour and then it was time for breakfast. I called Mace to 'Come' and she did, racing past me, up the dirt road, and then between the two trees we had emerged through, returning to the wooded trail. She raced ahead and at each trail intersection she stopped, checked I was there, then turned left, right, or trotted straight ahead. The land was anonymous and I'd lost track of which trail was which, so I just followed her. Imperious and grand, and confident as the St Lawrence itself, with her tail held high and trotting with such ease that her feet didn't seem to touch the ground, she led me for a quarter of an hour until we reached a clearing above which the campgrounds were.

L'Ami du Passant, the Wayfarer's Friend truckers' stop, just outside Lac Megantic, was exactly the type of diner I'd planned to have breakfasts in, but by now I'd got into the habit of making myself breakfast when I fed Macy, so we passed it by and drove through town where the best view over the lake is from the cemetery. Lac Megantic holds an annual *Festival du Crevette*, a crayfish festival. I spent my childhood summers lifting flat rocks in the shallows of our lake, catching crayfish to fish with. The idea of anything other than a fish wanting to eat one never entered my mind until I started visiting Sweden and attended a *Kraftfest*, the crayfish-eating gastronomic highlight of late summer. The Swedes now get their delicacies from crayfish farms in the southern United States. I guessed that in Lac Megantic the crayfish were still local.

I stopped for another walk in the woods, where yet another little bugger of a chipmunk swore at us and bombarded Macy with bits of tree. Living in Europe for so long I'd forgotten how extrovert chipmunks are. They're the Jack Russells of the woods—small, opinionated, feisty packets of mayhem. Surrounding us, the mixed forest here in the Eastern Townships produced a brilliant palette of autumn colours—the scarlet of red maple, orange-red or sugar maple, the glowing yellow of black maple, golden yellow of birch, light tan of beech and russet of oak—all backed by the verdant landscape of evergreen spruce and pine. To my eye, this is nature at its most wonderful, an explosive burst of vitality before winter, an exuberant, final reaffirmation of life. As was now routine, Mace missed it.

On I drove, past professionally painted signs proclaiming 'VERS À VENDRE' (Worms For Sale). Dew worms, the currency of the local economy, have been taken over, it seems, by big business. Just before La Patrie the road was being rebuilt and a detour took us bouncing into the woods. The logging trucks and the GMC struggled to maintain five miles per hour on this track, but on the far side

105

of La Patrie we returned to the highway and entered rolling farmland. This was the heart of the Eastern Townships, a unique part of Quebec. Elsewhere in the province, the feudal seigneurial form of land management prevailed. The *seigneurs*, granted land by the King of France, in turn granted rights to work the land to their vassals, their *habitants*. The *seigneurs'* mill ground the *habitants'* flour and taxes to the *seigneur* took the form of farm produce.

The land we were in was never part of the seigneurial system. It was settled in the late 1700s by Highland Scots, mostly from the Isle of Lewis in the Outer Hebrides, people removed by their landlords from their land in the Clearances, to make way for more profitable sheep-grazing. By the early 1800s the Eastern Townships held the third largest, Scottish Gaelic-speaking population in the world, after the Highlands and Cape Breton in Nova Scotia. These immigrants named their towns after the places they left behind: Stornoway, East Angus, Tolsta, Gisla, Lingwick, Ballalan, Keith. And because this region was then unexploited territory, farms were set up according to the planning model used elsewhere in Canada. The result is that the shapes of the fields and the positioning of homes and farm buildings resemble Ontario and New England rather than the rest of Quebec.

Vestiges of Scottish influence remain. Just past West Ditton I saw an excellent herd of Ayrshire cattle. The ancestors of these animals, with their white and pale brown and red-toned coats, originated in the mountainous regions of Ayr, on the south-west coast of Scotland, where the harsh environment had already adapted them to the difficult climate of a Quebec winter. I'm told that Ayrshires remain the second most numerous breed in Quebec. Withstanding the pressures of the last 40 years, there is still an Anglo presence here. Some farms flew the red maple leaf flag. It reminded me of my high-school history classes, of the defiance of the local Scottish population in the early 1900s when the French-speaking population increased in the area to a near majority and the locals formed the Protestant Defence Alliance hoping to import more British immigrants.

I stopped near Eaton to drive through a covered bridge, built in 1886 over the Eaton River. If this bridge were in New England or Ontario, it would be a major tourist attraction. Here, in the depths of the Eastern Townships, I was able to park in the middle of it, get out with Macy, take pictures and return, knowing it was unlikely there would be any traffic on the road from either direction. Just beyond, I braked hard as a kamikaze deer leapt towards me and then across the road. At East Clinton I tanked up with gas. On paying, the gas station attendant said, *'C'est bon.* 'Ave a nize day.' It was the first spontaneous English I'd heard in Quebec.

The drive was taking longer than I'd calculated. I'd forgotten how large Quebec is—seven times larger than Britain, twice as big as Texas—and I'd been travelling through a tiny fraction of its south-western corner. South of East Clinton, the road veered through what must be one of the prettiest villages in Quebec: St Malo. This is a relatively new parish. The signs indicated it was founded in 1863 and the tall, friendly, white clapboard church was built by loggers in 1900. The village itself is on high ground: the sign said 585 metres (1920 feet). I climbed an observation tower, staring down at Macy who was wondering what I was doing, and, on this clear day, looked back to Mount Megantic in the east, Mount Orford to the west, and across rolling farmland and forest blazing in all the reds, oranges, yellows and browns of the spectrum.

The church was unlocked and, with Macy on her leash, we went in. Vestments hung from garment racks, green for Masses and Sundays, white for Saints' Days, gold for Easter and Christmas, purple for Lent and Advent, red for the Feast of Martyrs. On tables were silver chalices, patens and cruets. I'd stepped into yesteryear, a land where church property was left unlocked and unguarded because the local people still felt no one would possibly think of stealing from a church. I'd forgotten there were places like this.

*   *   *

Steinbeck backtracked through Maine and I planned to hook up with his route in New Hampshire and Vermont where he sped through, spending a single night at an unlocked but empty motel. The American immigration inspector didn't know what to make of a Canadian driving a motorhome with a North Carolina licence plate so she called over a Customs inspector.

'Got any meat? We don't like Canadian meat.'
'Only meat I've got's my dog.'
'Can I see her?'
I raised Macy's sleeping head.
'Pretty puppy!'

I passed a 'Welcome to New Hampshire' sign, followed shortly by another announcing 'The 45th Parallel, equidistant from the Equator and the North Pole'. American flags flew once more from every utility pole in every town. Eventually I turned west, into Vermont, and past a still smouldering burnt-out shack. I stopped five miles further along the road where a Vermont State Trooper car was parked beside a house by a grass landing-strip, and while I reported the burnt shack, Macy worked the landing-strip, raising at least twenty wild turkeys.

This route we were on, paralleling but just north of where Steinbeck travelled, is not part of tourist Vermont. It's Linda's Discount Grocery Store run from her ramshackle home, trellis tables by the roadside supporting 40-year-old soda bottles labelled 'antiques'. It's overgrown fields where, if you cut the grass you find abandoned cars. It's trailer homes with peeling paint. There's poverty here, similar to what I saw in West Virginia but harsher, more desperate, more forbidding, because of the fierce winter climate.

It's always a surprise to see the vast areas of economic hardship in America. It shouldn't be. On a continent where countries have been created by people, mostly Europeans like my forebears, who often changed their names, changed their languages, truly reinvented themselves, poverty is looked on by many as a stepping stone, a stage you have the opportunity to evolve from. That's the American dream. You may be poor, but in America you have the potential and the right to leave that behind. There's an in-built optimism within North American cultures. The future can be good. You make things happen. In Europe we're inclined to view America's 'can-do' spirit as naive, provincial, parochial. Certainly in Britain the prevailing attitude, it seems to me, is to keep your head down and hope nothing bad happens tomorrow.

Just past Island Pond, my mind was taken off these thoughts by the biggest bumble bee in New England. Its bulging pollen sacks made it look like it was carrying two, huge, yellow, Lulu Guinness handbags. After a fast buzz around my eyes, it landed on my lap. The GMC is fitted with vertically hinged glass vents just outside the driver's and passenger's windows. Turn them one way and they bring fresh air in. Turn them the other and they suck the air out. I turned the glass vent to suck mode, nudged the fashion-conscious bee up and to the left and, whoosh, out it rocketed.

Near Derby, I passed three white and green Chevy Blazers marked 'Border Patrol'. I've seen vehicles like these by the Mexican border but never before by the Canadian border, only minutes away, where Beebe Plain, Vermont, and Stanstead, Quebec, form a single town straddling the border. In this twin town, one side of Canusa Street is in one country, the other side in an other. If you want to cross the street, you report to your appropriate Customs office at the bottom of the road. Haskell Opera House's entrance and audience are in the United States, while its stage is in Stanstead, Canada. The opera house is now also a library and, fittingly I thought, the books reside on the Canadian side. The border patrol vehicles made me wonder how the 'war on terror' was coping with this quirkily admirable international situation.

110

Throughout Vermont the names of businesses, like Poulin, Gendreau, Prudhomme and Desrochers, reminded me that French Canadians have oozed over this border for centuries, giving the state its distinctive ambience today. Newport, at the bottom of Lake Memphramagog, dominated by the Catholic church on top of its tallest hill, looked like a place in the process of evolving from lumber town to tourist town.

At Lake Champlain I arrived at a private campground on Grand Isle and parked in the most distant site, alone in the woods, just feet from the shoreline. After dinner I set up my camp stool on the shore and watched Mace trudge through the water, plunging her head to the bottom to investigate what tickled her feet. I looked across the lake to the Vermont shore. Here I was in one of the smallest states in the union yet its size was almost overwhelming. And I thought more about how American and European cultures had diverged. Growing up in North America, and there's not much difference which side of the border you grow up in, you take the freedom to be yourself, to do your own thing, to get away from crowds, to get away from everyone, to be alone, you take these freedoms for granted.

It's the size. North America's magnitude is incomprehensible to Europeans who haven't experienced it. Grow up here and, from Atlantic to Pacific, from Arctic to Gulf of Mexico, there are worlds of sights to see and places to go, and the liberty to move at will. There are virtually no borders, no language barriers, no regional conflicts, no restrictions where to travel or where to live. People have all they need in their vast landscape—forests, farmlands, flatlands, badlands, lakes, mountains, deserts, oceans, monuments, vistas, towns, cities—to satisfy almost any of life's desires. You need to experience North America, to understand how, as well as its 'can-do' spirit, a more worrying isolationist frame of mind also evolved here.

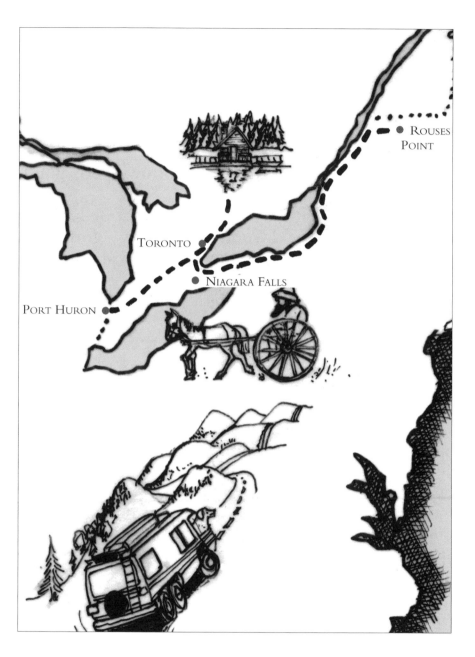

CHAPTER FOUR

NEW YORK AND ONTARIO

 In upstate New York State at Rouses Point, on the rural road traversed by Steinbeck, I stopped at the Blue Note Restaurant in North Clinton for breakfast: $1.61 at the counter.

'Here to hunt?' asked the hollow-eyed, gaunt man sitting beside me.

I pegged him either as a local farmer or Ichabod Crane's ghost. He'd seen Macy, my 'gun dog', looking out the front window of the GMC and my Bean's waterproof boots. I was wearing a green T-shirt and trousers. To his eyes I was a visiting rifle.

'What's good up here?' I countered.

'That extra month shoot'n' time for squirrels gives good target practice for white tails. Nutt'n' but pests, squirrels, but they're tasty pests.'

I can't say I've ever tasted squirrel but it's been part of the American frontier diet since the year dot. I'm told it's like rabbit only the meat's sweeter, richer and darker. Millions of these tree rats are eaten by Americans each year, but around ten years ago there was a real scare. We all know about mad cow disease. Scrapie, a sheep brain disease, got transmitted to cattle when cattle were fed dead sheep. The infectious agent modified in cattle and became highly infectious for cats, mildly infectious for people and not infectious for dogs. This got scientists thinking about other similar animal diseases that might spread through food.

A classmate of mine looked back at brain specimens from Alberta deer with chronic wasting

114

disease and saw that the brain lesions were similar to mad cow disease. Scientists checked out deer and elk eaters and found no relationship between eating either species and developing new variant CJD, the human equivalent of chronic wasting disease in deer or mad cow disease in bovines. Other scientists worked backwards. They looked at the eating habits of people who developed new variant CJD to see if there were any common denominators and, in August 1997, a couple of neurologists from Kentucky reported in the British medical journal, *The Lancet*, a cluster of five cases of CJD in squirrel eaters, or to be more specific, squirrel-brain eaters.

Now you and I might think twice about cracking open a squirrel's cranium to feast on its contents. You may be saying to yourself right now that people who eat road-kill rodents deserve to die, but the nugget of this story was the dilemma of cause and coincidence. As with venison eaters, when squirrel eaters as a population were studied, and there's a whole lot of squirrel eaters in America, the statistical relevance of the five cases vanished. It is safe, it seems, to gnaw on squirrel.

'I've never tasted squirrel. What's it like?' I asked.

'Squirrel,' he responded, plainly and logically, and we both continued our breakfasts—white toast smothered in salty butter, with mugs of black coffee. 'Scoped semi-auto 22. Look for acorns or beech nuts. That's where squirrels are. Easy to bag six a day. Bear hunt'n' starts day aftah tamarrah. You can use last year's licence 'til the end of the month. Never been bear hunt'n'. Turkey shoot starts October 1st but this year it's only for

115

seventeen days. I like spring turkey hunt'n'. I sound like the sexiest hen you ever met. Toms fly in from Canada when I call.'

'How do you call turkeys at this time of year?' I asked.

'It's sort of a kee-kee. That's what lost young 'uns call.'

'So, I guess you're looking forward to next month,' I commented.

'Yep. Saturday, October 18th. Been scout'n' a monster white tail buck. First saw the spread of his antlers in the snow where he'd been feed'n' last spring. Monster. I figger he's up to 250 pounds. Already interested in my doe bleat. Sunrise, October 18th, he's mine.'

Here's a personal inconsistency I haven't yet reconciled. I don't mind this guy killing and eating squirrels, but I do mind him wanting to kill this buck simply because the buck's regal and elegant and has trophy antlers. Isn't that the exact animal to leave alone, to let breed and multiply? When Steinbeck travelled through the north-east, each day he wrapped Charley's tail in red Kleenex, fastened with rubber bands, so that hunters wouldn't mistake his standard poodle for a white tail deer. Macy and I were travelling through a few weeks earlier than Steinbeck did, just before the hunting season began, so I didn't have to take similar precautions, but the matter-of-factness of my breakfast companion's conversation was corroding.

I spend my working life trying to relieve pain or discomfort in animals. Even when working with livestock, the objective is the same. The last time I worked with pigs, sheep and cattle, as a temporary

116

veterinary inspector during the foot-and-mouth disease outbreak in 2000, the farmers I met— people who raised livestock for meat, people used to cyclical slaughter—were universally distressed at the suffering caused to their stock by movement bans. Stock had been restricted to where they were—in muddy fields, in cramped pens. It was impossible to get feed to some, impossible to allow movement for others. I processed numerous humane killings of livestock because farmers preferred their animals dead rather than see them live in appalling conditions. 'This isn't what farming's supposed to be about,' I'd be told over tepid tea in farmhouse kitchens, as we filled in paperwork.

Good farmers raise livestock, knowing their animals will meet an inevitable death. It's their business, often the family business for generations. On good farms, and I've been on many, the livestock are healthy and content, and death, when it comes, is humane. But I've got a problem with hunters killing only for pleasure. In England, the people I know who hunt do so because it's a social custom. Shoots are for the upwardly mobile or those already there. In North America it's more testicular. You could argue that here, too, hunting is a social custom, a vestigial social memory of the time when it was necessary to capture and kill wildlife simply to survive. I've talked with people who tell me this is why they hunt, but the more they explain, the more their body language emphasises how they engage in their 'sport', the more evident it is that hunting and killing are deeply tied into their feelings of masculinity. It's a basic, biological impulse.

117

*   *   *

I don't think I've ever before paid attention to road surfaces, not until this trip when I saw their effect on Macy. US 11 was freshly paved, a pleasure to drive on. It was littered with road-kill, all skunks and racoons, no squirrels. Were they all shot in target practice? The land looked tired, wan, listless. Even the signs, 'Sale—Pine trees—U dig', suggested a terse harshness to life in this north-eastern corner of the state. There are numerous Veterans of Foreign Wars Posts on US 11 and directional signs to State of New York Department of Correctional Services facilities—first one, then another, then another. The VFW and American Legion Posts flew both American and Canadian flags, all at half-mast. I turned on the radio and learned it was September 11. That sobered the drive.

The AGS *New York Guide* says that 60 per cent of the population of Malone speaks French. There's a St Vincent de Paul 'nearly new' shop sponsored by Notre Dame church just down from the gas station where I tanked up the GMC, but when I asked the station attendant whether anyone still spoke French, he chuckled, 'Not in my lifetime.' I asked him about the 'correctional services' I'd passed.

'That's the only growth industry between here and Rochester. More new prisons than anything else. State does fuck-all for farmers and ships its criminals upstate. Expects farmers to move into law enforcement.'

At Malone, following Steinbeck's trail, I turned

118

onto State 37, through truly uninspiring countryside, Only concrete silos remained where once there had been bustling farmhouses and barns. The U-Haul trailer rental sites were emptied of their rentals. I bet none ever come back. Here were more abandoned farm buildings, farmhouses and homes than I'd seen anywhere else. A handwritten sign on the front lawn of a 1960s manufactured home said 'Typing—by chance'. No wonder Steinbeck wrote nothing until he arrived at the Niagara Falls border crossing to Canada. Just past the Akwesasne Mohawk Casino and the Hookers and Hunters Store, I stopped for Macy to gambol on the edge of the St Lawrence.

'Stop! Spit that out!' I shouted at her, as she slaked her thirst with river water. 'That water's been through Cleveland!' I admonished her.

I must say that the roads in New York State were the best of any I had travelled on. The 1940 AGS *New York Guide* describes a new form of road marking, just introduced in New York State:

> White lines painted down the middle of the road, already copied in Canada and in all probability soon to be extended throughout the United States. The sign, 'Unlawful to cross solid line on your side', erected at intervals of five miles or more, might seem at first difficult to understand; but referred to the lines before you, it is clear and simple.

At the western end of Lake Ontario State Parkway, I pulled into Hamlin Beach State Park, showing my driver's licence and, as requested, Macy's rabies vaccination certificate. Apparently, last year,

119

racoons in the park had confirmed rabies. We settled into our evening routine: a good long walk, on this occasion along the Lake Ontario shore where fog was already moving in from the lake, then dinner for both of us, a log fire, branches to chew on and leaves to roll in for my dog, pictures to download and notes to transcribe for me. Mosquitoes were back, but I left the motorhome door open, lounged by the campfire and finished off my New York State plonk. I relaxed, but Mace was twitchy, jumping back into her home, then peering out each time something spooked her. Lots of forest noises did. Rabid racoons?

*   *   *

In mid-August, when goldenrod releases its pollen, the whole of eastern North America begins sneezing. Growing up across the lake in Ontario, I was taught that eye-catching goldenrod, the most prominent wild flower both in Ontario and here in upstate New York, was the major cause of hay fever. In fact, this wasn't true. Goldenrod pollen is too heavy to travel on the wind. The true causes of sneezing, itchy eyes and drippy nose are the ragweeds—inconspicuous plants without showy flowers—that grow near goldenrod, flowering at the same time. Some of the large goldenrod colonies I was now driving past were probably over a hundred years old. The colony spreads from its rootstock. Sometimes, in really dense colonies, the central plants die back, creating a yellow ring, but here the colonies were as dense as planted monoculture crops. Back in England I see this plentiful weed grown as a garden ornamental.

120

While driving through these fields of wild flowers, I passed unexpectedly a farm with dozens of what looked like rows of large shipping crates for dogs. It was a vealer calf operation. Holstein calves, probably all males, were tethered in each plastic vealing crate. Some were standing, some were sitting. None could turn around. Each tan-coloured crate—there were probably about sixty of them—was around two feet wide and five feet long. That's a little narrower and only a little longer than the crate Macy travelled over the Atlantic in. Macy was in a crate in which she could stretch and turn around in, for almost fourteen hours. These calves would probably be tethered in these crates, unable to turn, for fourteen weeks. The thought was stomach-churning.

It's worth repeating. Most of us don't give much pause as to where our meat comes from. Price is paramount. But think about it. We spend less of our income on food than any previous generation or any other culture. We're the richest, most successful society ever. We've got so few worries about filling our stomachs, we worry instead about our leisure activities; where to go for holidays, what sports to participate in. Surely we have a moral obligation that every sentient animal under our control—farm animals, lab animals, zoo animals, pets—is allowed to experience life in an environment that its genetic heritage has predisposed it to.

This isn't a radical new idea. It was articulated perfectly well 40 years ago, in the British government's Brambell Report. That report said that farm animals should have food, water and fresh air according to their biological

121

requirements, safe housing with enough room to prevent injuries and to allow them physical exercise, a sufficiently stimulating environment that leads neither to boredom nor to fear, daily supervision to monitor for and provide help for injuries or illness, and sensible handling throughout all the stages of life, to avoid unnecessary suffering.

The calves I saw here were probably bought at around a week of age from local dairy farmers. If they were the norm, they were separated from their mothers within a day of birth and probably pail-fed their mothers' milk to provide them with colostrum, the first milk that provides temporary protection from some diseases. After a week, they were most likely sold at local barn auctions as vealer calves.

There are simple alternatives to veal crates. We use the alternatives in the UK. Loose housing these calves in groups of six to eight allows these poor creatures to exercise and interact with each other. Don't forget, cattle are, like us, socially gregarious. They enjoy social contact with their own kind. There are, no doubt, risks for the farmer with loose housing. Common bedding, drinking water and feeding makes it easier for disease to spread. And there's the crux. If a farmer uses loose housing, he has to ensure higher quality standards. Let me give you an example. For decades, antibiotics were called 'growth-promoters' and added to livestock feed. (In many countries they still are.) Animals on antibiotics grew to market weight faster than those not given antibiotics in feed. Then one country—Sweden—banned prophylactic antibiotics in animal feed. They were concerned about both increasing antibiotic resistance among infectious bacteria and about antibiotic residues in our food.

Immediately after the ban was implemented, Swedish vets were faced with an explosion, literally and figuratively, of diarrhoea—'scours'—in livestock. But within two years this problem had completely abated and, unexpectedly, livestock were reaching market weight earlier than when they were fed antibiotics as growth-promoters. The use of antibiotics had simply masked poor husbandry. In the absence of prophylactic antibiotics, farmers either improved their animal-rearing techniques or went out of business. Tethering vealer calves is a cop-out for lazy farmers unwilling to invest either their brains or their wallets in better husbandry methods. It's shocking, but because veal units like this one are out of sight and out of mind, we do little to ban them.

*   *   *

Steinbeck had planned to cross into Canada at Niagara Falls and travel through south-western Ontario to Michigan. I was crossing here too, to visit my parents, then take the route he'd abandoned because he didn't have a rabies vaccination certificate for Charley. 'Please understand,' he was told. 'It's your own government, not ours. We are simply advising you.' Steinbeck turned around and took the longer route under Lake Erie.

At the border crossing, high roadside barriers were under construction, creating a protected concrete funnel. Unlike the backroad border crossings I'd been through in Maine and New Hampshire, this was a major Customs crossing. Canadian Customs officers wore Kevlar bulletproof vests. Car and motorhome traffic formed eight lines. Several more were dedicated to 18-wheelers. The Customs officer at the head of my line had chosen today to be his country's chief inquisitor. We sat there for what seemed hours. One vehicle in our row moved forward for every seven or eight in adjacent lines. In my rearview mirror I saw chaos. Cars behind me were pulling out of our line whenever it was possible. Like a malevolent football referee my Customs man was rigorously asking questions, looking in car trunks, then handing out yellow cards and instructing drivers to drive to the left and park for fuller inspections. The flashy SUV in front of me, with Ontario plates and a large Chinese family, proved a particularly juicy treat. The inquisitor pulled a Polo Ralph Lauren shopping bag from the trunk of the car, held it high and issued a yellow card. Forget about guns. Forget about drugs. Forget about international terrorists. He's caught a Canadian who'd been shopping at an American discount mall!

Now it was my turn.

'Birth certificate or passport, please.'

I gave him my Canadian passport.

'Where do you live, sir?'

I told him England.

'How long?'

I said 33 years.

'How long do you stay in Canada?'

I said five days.

'Are you importing anything?'

I said only my golden retriever.

'Now, did you bring your golden retriever all the way from England?'

I answered in the affirmative.

'Have you done this before? I'm under the impression your golden retriever will be quarantined for up to ten weeks when you return home. I'm worried about your dog getting back to the UK.'

Like Steinbeck, I had a Customs officer whose prime concern seemed to be my dog.

I explained there were new rules and that her papers were in order.

'Take care,' he said, and I was back in Canada.

At Niagara Falls we walked the length of the riverside park, from the boiling rapids to the Canadian Horseshoe Falls, then further east until we were opposite the American Falls, and then back. Returning to our home we walked past a new Hilton where the doorman—grey hair, military moustache, peaked black military hat, wearing a blue suit with sky-blue collar and cuffs—came down the steps.

'Hi. May I say hello to your dog?'

Macy was by now listless from what had been for her a long, boring walk and showed no emotion as Ron hunched down and gave her an experienced scruff-tickle.

'I like all dogs, but goldens sure are something special,' Ron explained, and now Macy was responding with a head-press.

'Their greatest pleasure is to please. Isn't it something? They can be so selfless?'

Ron was right. It is fascinating that through

THE 'MAID OF THE MIST' APPROACHING NIAGARA
FALLS

selective breeding you can choose for traits such as selflessness. And if in dogs, why not in us too?

We talked for some time. Ron told me of his four-year-old golden who had died a few months previously from lymphoma, a tumour of the lymphatic system. I explained that was an extraordinarily rare event in my experience. As a vet I never see lymphomas in dogs so young but he said this was common in Ontario. He also told me of his other golden.

'I live on the Welland River. My dog saw a chipmunk go down a hole and has spent the rest of his life staring at that hole.' He had another golden that retrieved stones from the bottom of the river. 'And if you don't throw one in, he'll stand looking through the clear water until he sees the stone he wants, then swim down to it, six feet down, and retrieve it.'

Ron's story wasn't unique. It was surprisingly similar to one I was told by my hot dog provider at Cedar Point, Long Island.

Rather than take the QEW, the Queen Elizabeth Way, a freeway to Toronto, I opted for rural Highway 20, once the main route. Road signs to it were atrocious but, following my nose, I eventually found myself heading in the right direction, through flat, bland, anonymous, monotonous, suburban lands. The roads still have their original names: Regional Road D, County Road 9, Concession Road 17, Service Road 26. There's a dour Presbyterian logic to this sensible system. I thought it soulless when I lived here and even more so now.

I stopped for apples and more apple cider, and spoke with Julia who once more was tense and terse. Ben phoned around the same time and gave me his opinion on what was happening in London. 'Don't come back,' he reiterated. Forty-eight kilometres out of Toronto, traffic ground to a halt. It took another two hours to get there, fighting the worst mannered, poorest disciplined, most discourteous drivers I'd come across. I fantasised about transforming into white van man. After all, I was 10 feet tall and 27 feet long, but my motorhome was too precious to damage so I told my hormones to relax. By early evening, blood boiling, I reached my parents' condominium in Toronto.

'Good evening,' I said to the security man at the gate, a man whom I've met frequently on previous visits.

'You can't bring that in here,' he said eyeing the GMC, and directed me to park outside the complex and walk in. I parked, fed Macy, let her attend to her needs, then put her on her leash and walked her in.

'You can't bring dogs in here,' said the security man, running over to cut us off on the sidewalk.

'We've both come from England to see my parents, the Fogles.'

'I'm sorry but no dogs are allowed,' he replied, now with hands on his hips.

'I'm sorry too, but piss off.'

'Do you want me to lose my job?' he countered.

Well, of course I did. He could move to New Brunswick and work in the Visitors' Centre, but I didn't say anything, just went in, up to the seventeenth floor where I was greeted with chicken and broccoli soup, and Macy with cuddles and tickles from my parents.

128

We had been on the road for less than a month, but I was now attached at the waist to my new home. It was comfortable and comforting. My brother had arranged for Macy and me to sleep in his guest room in the coming days, but we both declined, preferring to live on his driveway. Each morning Macy and I arose just before dawn and walked the suburban streets to the local Tim Hortons where I had a butter tart, toasted bagel with cream cheese and coffee, while Mace survived on handouts from other early morning customers. On these walks, she worked the banks of grassy lawns. She was the squirrel police, instructing these fluffy-tailed vermin to return to their trees. My brother had warned me to be careful on these walks. 'Don't go near the Catholic school. The neighbours call the police if they see a dog there.'

I hadn't realised how dog-friendly Europe is until now. In Britain, I can walk my dog freely on virtually any public footpath. Parks are open to dogs unless signs state otherwise. Signs may say a dog must be 'under your control', rather than 'on a lead'. In continental Europe, especially in Belgium, France and Italy, visiting a restaurant with your dog is an absolute pleasure. As often as not, a water bowl is provided for your dog before a drink is offered to you. In North America, I was experiencing the opposite. In every federal, state, provincial and municipal park I had visited, dogs were either banned or restricted to leashes no longer than six feet. Here in Toronto, police seemed to have nothing better to do than to enforce dog laws. Rob explained there was a park, a half-hour drive away, that allowed dogs, but that he and local dog walkers, communicating by cellphone, found local green areas where they illegally let their dogs off their leashes. He took me to an illegal dog walk.

This was excellent fun. Suburban families arrived at the appointed time, 9.00 a.m., equipped with collapsible water bowls, litre-bottles of water, poo bags and assorted 'chase' toys. As we arrived at the grounds, a grassy and wooded couple of acres at the far corner of a school playground, two Jack Russells were running in unison like demented wasps. A golden retriever bounded up to me, dropped a ball at my feet and impelled me with his eyes to throw it for him. All the time I was there, this dumb dog kept mistaking me for his owner. Another retriever worked more efficiently, but rather than bringing its ball back to her businessman owner, it brought it back and dropped it in her water bowl. A truly obese man in seriously unattractive, soft cotton gym shorts, wearing a large bum bag lost in the surplus fat of his waist, cruised the playground like the Pied Piper, followed by a trail of dogs that knew he was there to dispense dog treats. Looking at him I could only think, Please, don't bend over. In all, there were around thirty dog owners and twenty dogs. Seemingly relaxed on this warm summer-like day, they were, in fact, alert to any car that slowed down on either of the two roads visible from the playing field, ready to flee if the police arrived.

Regrettably, my brother introduced me as a vet. While Macy gambolled and stole toys, I was asked, 'Why does my dog's hind leg quiver?' 'Do you think my dog's fat?' 'See those eyes. They look grey. Is that a problem?' 'Is this lump something I should worry about?' 'I've treated my dog for fleas, but she's still scratching. Can you have a look?' 'What should I feed my dog?' 'Do you mind looking at a little cut on my dog's paw?' 'How can I get my dog to lose weight?' 'What's the life expectancy of standard poodles? I just lost my other one to lymphoma. She was only six years old.' That question pulled me up short. Ron, the Hilton doorman in Niagara Falls had told me his four-year-old had died of lymphoma. I never see deaths as early as this at my clinic in London. I'd check this out with a teacher-classmate.

The common dog-walk subject was diet, and rightly so. Some pooches were obese, but now I could see why there is such an epidemic of fatness in North America. Macy is lean and muscular because her diet is sensible, but also because she thrives on physical off-leash exercise. At home she runs for at least an hour each day, usually much more. Here in North America, she was getting much more exercise but it was all illegal. I'd been admonished several times already for allowing her off her leash. Urban dogs here, and they make up the majority of dogs in North America, simply don't have the opportunity to burn calories. Sure, the market responds. In Toronto there are 'dog spas' offering 'thousands of square feet of indoor and outdoor exercise area, sleepovers and personal trainers'. Vets offer weekly, corpulent canines' anonymous meetings where dogs attend weekly weigh-ins and owners of fat dogs discuss the problems they have fighting canine flab. It makes me glad I've spent my time practising clinical

131

veterinary medicine. You don't need vets to run these meetings, or puppy socialisation parties, or manage separation anxiety problems. Veterinary businessmen look on all of these ventures as new 'revenue steams'. I guess that's true. But does it really take six to eight years of higher education to qualify to conduct these events?

For that matter I've got a problem with other aspects of what's happened to veterinary medicine in North America. I had dinner with old friends who told me their interpretation of their veterinary experiences. 'Your dog's still breathing?' the vet asks. 'I'll remove her cataracts. She won't see any better but we should do it.'

'What can you do?' asked my friend. 'You love your dog so you tell the vet to go ahead. I've paid for all his children's weddings.'

The American veterinary profession promotes the humanising of our relationship with our pets, our 'bond' with them. I guess I'm partly to blame. I was one of the eleven individuals in Dundee, Scotland, in 1979, who created the term, 'The Human-Companion Animal Bond' and I chaired the following year's international meeting of that name. I edited the first text on the subject, *Interrelations between People and Pets*, and wrote the first popular book, *Pets and their People*. I did so because I was fascinated by this powerful relationship. I hoped it would be taken more seriously. It sure has—by business. Vested interests now play on our emotions. 'Their teeth are as important to them as yours are to you,' says an American veterinary leaflet. That's crap. Oral hygiene is as important, but that's a whole lot different. We're being manipulated, in the name of 'the bond'.

*   *   *

I'd promised my father I'd go with him to the summer cottage, around 100 miles away, to close it down for the winter. My mother, the spokesperson in their marriage, sat in the front passenger seat while my dad sat in the black leather armchair in the living room section of our home.

'Morris, you'd like this. We could use it to drive to Florida.' He nodded and smiled.

Like many couples who have lived together for so long, my folks have a classic love-hate relationship. They squabble like four-year-olds then miss each other deeply when separated for a day. My mother gave my father an achievement medal which he wears proudly: 'For living with me for 65 years'. That doesn't diminish their need to needle.

At the cottage, I backed down the hill and around the point to our summer home on the lake, built over 55 years ago by my dad and still standing. Once down, there would be no room to turn around. My brother, his wife and dog drove out in their car. Macy squirrelled up and down the point, played with our neighbour's woolly, white shepherd, dug in the thick seaweed that had accumulated on the beach and waded in and out of the lake. She ran across the lake's rocky bottom, emerging to say hello to visiting neighbours then returning to the waters to play with the dogs that joined her. It was, to me, a surreal experience, seeing my English dog frolicking where I as a child and my kids as children had played.

My mother told me that beginning a few summers back the birds had all disappeared from the cottage, and it seemed true. There was no birdsong in the air and few visible birds in the trees or on the utility wires. At my brother's home in Toronto, I'd seen a brilliant-red, male northern cardinal and a debonair cedar waxwing. While we sat in yet more warm sunshine, Macy marched into the lake towards a flotilla of trumpeting yellow-billed herring gulls, just offshore. Further up the lake I could see two velvety black loons, the most primitive, and to me the most arresting, of all waterbirds, floating in the still water. Either these were immature birds, born this spring, or adults that, in preparation for winter, had lost their black and white chequerboard-patterned topsides and their Art Deco striped, black and white neck bands. I'd have to wait until nightfall to hear their wild, laughing call, the best sound in Ontario lake country.

This warm, shallow lake always attracted waterbirds. I've seen double-crested cormorants, cackling coots, stocky, pied-billed grebes, spotted sandpipers and, of course, countless mallards, all floating on its waters. I once saw a whole flock of green-winged teals land on the lake for a day. A silent great blue heron—in Scotland it's called a flamingo dressed by Presbyterians—nested each summer in a dead elm tree, at a bend in the small bay where our summer cottage is located. It or its descendant was still there. Sparrow hawks used to work the pastureland behind the cottage. Mourning doves whoo-hoo-hooed in the first soft light of dawn. Hundreds of chattering, starlings lined the telephone wires. Raucous crows imperiously roosted in the trees, descending on planted fields. Black and yellow goldfinches were common, especially in mid-summer when thistle and goldenrod were abundant. We called them wild canaries. Orange-breasted Baltimore orioles were less common, but still an annual summer presence. Robins swooped down wherever I turned over rocks looking for earthworms to fish with, singing their rising and falling chirilly, chirilly, chir-up, chir-up refrain. Purple martins lived in roosts in the eaves of unoccupied neighbours' cottages. Noisy blue jays flew out of the oak and pine woods, seemingly scolding the adjoining pasture land. Plump little energetic nuthatches, with their tinny voices, hopped from tree to tree. Red-headed woodpeckers knocked themselves silly hammering on the cedar trees on our front lawn and ruby-throated hummingbirds knocked themselves senseless, flying into the cottage's slanted picture-window facing the lake. Kingfishers nested in the sandy cliff at the top of the point. Sparrows were in abundance everywhere. Today the skies were blue and still but virtually empty of birds and I didn't know why.

Rob reminded me to check Macy's feet. Zebra mussels had moved into the lake around ten years ago and their razor-sharp shells, clogging water pipes out of the lake to neighbours' cottages, were a hazard to dog paws.

Taking a break from work, Macy and I took a walk up the hill, across the paved county road, to the dusty gravel and dirt concession road beyond, that led to deep woods filled with fields of trilliums in the spring and, around a bend, to a hilly vista of rocky pastureland and crops of mature silage corn. The red-brick farmhouses and weathered cedarwood barns here were all built in the mid to late 1800s, when Scottish and Irish immigrants thought this land might be fertile enough for successful farming. It wasn't.

Of all the places I've ever been, this is the most idyllic sight. The dusty sides of the road were dense in late summer wild flowers. And it was only now, with the experience of living in Britain for so long, that I realised how many of these colourful plants were immigrants from Europe. In this part of Ontario, the most common tall wild flower at this time of year is blue-flowered chicory. Among the roadside borders of chicory were tall stocks of curly dock, groups of thin-stemmed plantain and miniature forests of stout, ramrod-erect, yellow-flowered great mullein, some as tall as I am. Butter-and-eggs, looking like miniature yellow and golden snapdragons, grew at the edge of the road, mixed in the bird vetch and bladder campion, bound together by pink, flowering bindweed. There was red clover, pink sweet peas, violet-blue alfalfa, lavender teasel, purplish burdock and bull thistle, pinker knapweed and yellow sow-thistle, dandelions and buttercups, banks of tall, slender, oxeye daisies and shorter chamomile. Tall loosestrife added a red-purple background. And everywhere there was Queen Anne's lace, the wild offspring of carrots brought to this region by early settlers, that had escaped from their gardens and reverted back to their ancestral form, and in doing so provided my father, a florist, with the most exquisite of lacy, creamy-white blooms for June to September weddings. All of these wild flowers were imports, perhaps all from Britain, where I

136

knew them well. And in return? Britain got goldenrod and me.

Further down the road were banks of orange day lilies—another import, this one from China. And among all these incomers were natural wild flowers, milkweed, black-eyed Susans, goldenrod, mauve-white fleabane, purplish fringed asters, white cow parsnip, pinkish fireweed and a few stems of evening primrose. I don't think I've ever seen such a vivid array of late summer wild flowers before. I had my camera with me and took countless photos of Macy among them.

Back at the cottage, we finished battening it down for winter. I visited the hardware store, a few miles away in Bridgenorth, for antifreeze for the pipes, and watched as my father, now 96 years old, once more showed his sons exactly how to drain the pipes he'd fitted when he built the cottage, cedar board by cedar board, in the mid-1940s. This was now the old bear's den, the place he returned to each summer. For the last few years, his knees have bothered him. Aspirin helped but, a practical, can-do man, he looked in his tool box and decided WD-40 might be the answer. He's been spraying his knees ever since. When he started doing so, to be safe I checked out what WD-40 contained and found it was formulated in the early 1950s at the San Diego Rocket Chemical Company. Its name came from a project to find a 'water displacement' compound, an enterprise that proved successful with the fortieth formulation. The Corvair Company bought the stuff in bulk to protect Atlas missile parts, and when workers began smuggling it out to use at home, the makers knew they were on to a winner, although they didn't count on my father using it to treat his arthritis. The stuff gets its distinctive smell from a fragrance that is added to the brew.

I've come over each spring to help him open up the cottage after its winter hibernation, to tidy away the debris left by animals that moved in over the winter, to make sure water flowed up from the well, to help repair frost-cracked pipes, to tidy up and stock up, knowing that he'd settle into a daily routine, driving into Bridgenorth for an occasional newspaper and weekly food supplies. Everything was now much as it had been when I visited five months previously. We finished our work, settled comfortably back into my mobile home, and while my mother entertained me with stream-of-thought comments and stories, my exhausted father fell into a deep sleep in his armchair. Macy lay beside him for the drive back to Toronto. She'd loved her visit to Lake Chemong and so did I. Faded as it was, the cottage and the landscape it resides in have been part of my life all my life, a constant in an ever-changing world. I don't want to live there but still feel it's home.

*   *   *

Not yet 6.00 a.m. and Highway 401, the east–west freeway across northern Toronto, was already sixteen lanes of stop/start, bumper to bumper tail lights. There's something mutely attractive about the vigour and vitality of such dawn activity, but as I churned my way through 40 kilometres of transport trucks and seemingly displaced New York City taxi drivers, all weaving from lane to lane, all bent on gaining a car length's advantage

138

on other commuters, I just wanted to get out of this metropolitan mayhem. Did you know that when the restaurant chain TGI Friday decided to open in Toronto, they changed their name to TGI Monday to appeal to the local work ethic? That's not true.

Leaving behind urban congestion and driving another 40 kilometres further along Highway 401 I turned off onto a familiar road that would take me to Rockwood, a conservation area a few miles from Guelph, the university town where I'd spent eight super years. Along the road, what was once productive farmland was still farmland, but it had changed. Farmhouses, farm buildings, farmland, all were now impeccable. Ancient split-cedar fences were lovingly restored. Hanging baskets of flowers garlanded entrances to farms. Young maple trees, looking like gawky, skinny teenagers, lined driveways to repointed, repainted, red and yellow brick farmhouses. Rocking chairs sat on verandahs. Even on an overcast day like today, the freshly whitewashed stone foundations of cedar plank barns reflected a simple purity. Luxury pick-ups and SUVs rested beside red-painted farm outbuildings. Sleek horses nuzzled each other as they grazed.

This was now commuter belt, transformed by affluent Torontonians into their idealised vision of what the countryside should be like. Don't get me wrong. It looks wonderful, but I wondered where farming had moved on to, now that this land, the most fertile in Ontario, was out of production. Driving on, I passed a Lincoln Navigator, parked on the shoulder of the road, its hazard lights flashing. A sturdy woman stood in anticipation by the roadside, waiting for a break in the traffic to rescue a turtle hunkered down on the central yellow line, as transport trucks and my old motorhome thundered past on both sides.

At Rockwood, in the woods on the banks of the Grand River, there are hundreds of perfectly circular potholes seemingly drilled into the hard, rocky ground. Some are small, less than a metre across and a metre deep. Others are enormous, six or seven times larger and deeper. Mature trees grow out of some, while others, especially those near the river, are water-filled, pungent stews of decomposing vegetation, fallen branches and autumn leaves. These potholes were formed by glacial waterfalls, moulins, that poured down through crevasses, eroding and drilling deep round holes in the dolomite rock below. I used to come here at least once a week when the weather was good, just to wander and ponder. I parked in the conservation area, to give Macy an opportunity for some early morning exercise and me the chance to meander in solitude through a familiar landscape. The river was still, the wooded, far shore reflected in full perfection on its mirror-like surface.

Macy was not still. There was wildlife in abundance and she did hurtling leaps over fallen trees and small sink holes, systematically working the ground with an utter and absent delight. A black squirrel, with gazelle-like bounds, sprinted away from her to the edge of a large stagnant pool, where it continued its escape, leaping miraculously from fallen tree trunk to fallen tree trunk until it reached the far side of the six-metre-wide soupy pothole where it scaled the imposing five-metre-high distant wall, disappearing into the far woods.

Macy followed. The bog looked solid green. But it wasn't. Her propulsion took all of her to the first fallen tree, but only her front legs to the next. Her hind quarters crashed into the green mire. She clambered up and over that tree and found herself in deep, thick goo. She disappeared under the gunk.

Macy doesn't swim. She's had the inclination but never the fortitude or courage to try. When playing in the English Channel with Inca, the Labrador, she waits for Inca to retrieve from deep water and swim into the shallows, then steals the item from Inca's mouth. Now she was submerged, out of sight, in thick, malodorous gloop. Her head surfaced, then her forelegs, pawing vigorously at the sky. Her momentum took her to the bog's far rock wall, but there was no place on its smooth surface that she could gain a foothold with her forepaws. She fell back under the slime, submerged, then reappeared desperately trying to save herself. She fell back into the muck and sank again, emerging barely recognisable as a dog, her head garlanded in slimy green vegetation. Her powerful thigh muscles pumped like pistons, all four legs trying to climb the vertical surface, fighting desperately to escape. I shouted her name, I screamed her name, but in her splashing and in her concentration she was oblivious to me. And there was no way I could reach her. The bare, spindly branches of the fallen fir trees in the bog made it impossible for me to wade, walk or swim to her. To my right was a four to five-metre sheer rock face to climb to get to the far side of the bog. To my left was an impenetrable mass of black decomposing vegetation. Even if I could get to the

141

other side, I couldn't get down the vertical wall to grab her.

I continued to shout, 'Macy! Macy!' Finally she heard her name and turned towards me, swimming powerfully through the thick debris, over a fallen tree, through more mire, then over another trunk, more putrid gunk, then the spindly branches of a third tree and finally to me. She emerged, dripping green from head to tail, smelling of one hundred years of decomposing frogs, shook on me, eyed another squirrel and shot after it into the woods behind. Dogs, lucky buggers, they don't suffer from post-traumatic stress disorder.

Reunited, I marched her to the conservation area's campground, sat her under a water tap at an RV site and washed her down. There was black sediment through to the depths of her coat. She smelled like she'd been swimming in a septic tank and, no matter how much I rinsed, I couldn't flush away either the debris or the smell.

Her stench helped me arrive at a decision I already wanted to make. Rather than visit the veterinary school as planned, I decided to take a short diversion north to Elmira, to the heart of Old Order Mennonite country. I drove north ten miles and exactly as it was, 40 years ago, the presence of these unassuming farming people is apparent only by the wider shoulders on the roads and the signs to watch for horse-drawn vehicles. In Elmira's municipal car park, spaces are reserved for buggies. There is no commercialisation and I was glad I'd skipped Lancaster, Pennsylvania.

On the county road I continued on, many farms had hand-painted signs, 'Maple Syrup For Sale. Not Sunday'. I stopped at one and, surrounded by

MACY EMERGED FROM THE BOG DRIPPING GREEN
FROM HEAD TO TAIL

myriads of fluttering monarch butterflies, still to embark on their 4000-kilometre migration to Mexico's Sierra Madre mountains, I bought from a Mennonite family a half-litre of Canada No. 1 Light maple syrup, six turkey eggs, a kilo of cheddar cheese curd and 500 grams of farm butter. Dinner that night was perfection—buttermilk pancakes, smothered in fresh churned butter and maple syrup, and a melt-in-your-mouth cheese omelette. Sublime.

*   *   *

Pinery Provincial Park is on the shore of Lake Huron. Macy frolicked on the lakeshore while a forbidding dark storm raced across the lake and a rainbow arced back towards our campsite. Park information says, 'When you take your dog for a swim, remember that dogs must be on a leash no longer than six feet at all times.' Am I just getting pedantic or do these state and provincial park regulators really need a lesson in clear English?

My firewood had been examined by park rangers when I checked into the park. Asian emerald ash borer beetles, green flying aliens, resident in Detroit for some years, had migrated into Windsor, Ontario, in 2002. This park, with 1000 campsites among coastal freshwater dunes and rare oak savannah, has the largest remaining forest in south-western Ontario, home to four different species of ash. Ash log firewood is *verboten*.

The storm coming off the lake arrived just as I lit my campfire. It bucketed down and I stood with my folding chair above the flames, keeping the fire

144

dry. An hour later, other campers were amazed we had such mature, roaring flames. Two couples joined me, hunkering down on their haunches beside my smoky chair, fire-gazing. They talked, almost absently, about the local Goodrich Celtic Music Festival, about nearby Chemical Valley, about the weather. They stared into the roaring flames.

'Any suggestions on where I should go in Michigan?' I asked.

'Why not head across Canada?' Jeff asked.

I explained I was following, sort of, Steinbeck's route.

'We're vacationing at home this year,' he countered. 'A symbolic rebellion against Big Brother.'

'The States?' I asked.

'They've always taken us for granted, eh? Nothing we could do about it because we needed them. That nuclear war was going to happen over the DEW [Distant Early Warning] line, but at least that protected us down here. Now that Russia's gone, they're just as arrogant. Except we don't need them now. They need us. But all they still manage to do is try to humiliate us. Don't get me wrong, eh. Most Americans are good people, but this government they got right now thinks it can tell everyone what to do and everyone follows because they say so.'

Jeff pulled an old folded piece of paper from the back pocket of his jeans, an email off the Internet.

To: Anne; Bob; Colin; Gwen; Cliff; Jeff; Michelle

145

This is an actual radio conversation between a United States Navy aircraft carrier (USS *Abraham Lincoln*) and Canadian authorities off the Newfoundland coast in October 1995. This radio conversation was released by the Chief of Naval Operations on 10 October, 1995 as authorised by the Freedom of Information Act.

CANADIANS: Please divert your course 15 degrees South to avoid a collision.

AMERICANS: Recommend you divert your course 15 degrees to the North to avoid a collision.

CANADIANS: Negative. You will have to divert your course 15 degrees South to avoid a collision.

AMERICANS: This is the captain of a US Navy ship. I say again divert your course.

CANADIANS: No, I say again, you divert your course.

AMERICANS: This is the aircraft carrier USS *Abraham Lincoln*, the second largest ship in the United States Atlantic Fleet. We are accompanied by three destroyers, three cruisers and numerous support vessels. I demand that YOU change YOUR course 15 degrees North. I say again, that's one-five degrees North or counter measures will be undertaken to ensure the safety of this ship.

CANADIANS: We are a lighthouse. Your call.

He grinned as I read it. It was probably another Internet myth, but perception is more powerful than truth. The email reinforced his attitude and

146

I wondered whether Americans realised how dramatically attitudes of one-time friends such as Jeff had changed from respect and admiration to suspicion and doubt. Next morning, after a crispy night, the first since Quebec, we walked the banks of the Ausable River. Macy eyed a chipmunk, but it stood its ground and shrieked expletives at her. She stood, quizzical, tipping her questioning head from side to side. I'd planned on driving down County Road 21, through Petrolia, Oil City and Oil Springs. This once swampy land was where North America's first oil was discovered. Not a lot of people know that. The region eventually produced over 10 billion barrels of oil. By 1860 it was the site of the world's first integrated, exploring, drilling and refining oil company. Chemical Valley is its legacy, a maze of refineries and chemical plants strung along the Ontario side of the St Clair River. Pipelines from Alberta on the Canadian prairies, thousands of miles away, now feed oil for refining into Chemical Valley.

I didn't take that route. I headed for Michigan, through fields of silage corn, yellowing on the stock, and green fields of potatoes not yet killed for harvesting. In Forest, parked semis lined the road outside the Tim Hortons. At 7.30 a.m. over a hundred cars were already parked at the Forest Golf Club. Department of Transport tractors were grading the wide soft shoulders of the highway. All was normal and as it should be in rural Ontario.

I hooked onto Highway 402. Starting eight kilometres from the Bluewater Bridge connecting Sarnia, Ontario, and Port Huron, Michigan, were signs, 'Trucks use right lane only. Do not block ramps'. This was obviously a busy border crossing but today it was a breeze.

'Who else are you travelling with?'

'Just my dog.'

'Where's your dog?' Pause. Smile. 'Pretty puppy!'

I was back in the States.

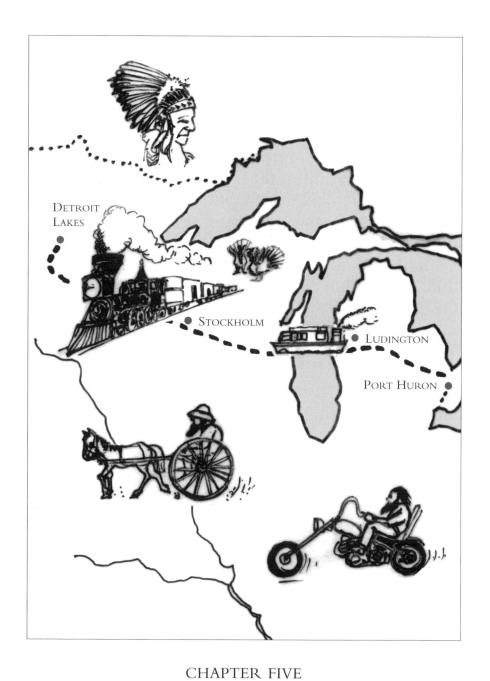

CHAPTER FIVE

The Midwest

Another lesson. Stick to the old roads and you miss the state or provincial welcome centres. These great places for browsing brochures are all located on main routes, on the Trans-Canada Highway or on the American interstate system. My American Guide Series maps were wonderful, but up-to-date state maps pinpoint state parks and, more specifically, which ones permit overnight camping.

I had planned to follow Steinbeck's path under Lake Michigan to Chicago, then head north towards Wisconsin, visiting Oak Park and River Forest on the way, to search out Frank Lloyd Wright buildings. From the AGS *Illinois Guide* I'd learned of the Illinois Pet Cemetery, opened in 1926. Old pet cemeteries fascinate me. Visiting one is like having a local social history lesson— pets' names, types, ages, memorials. The AGS guide says:

> Funerals follow a fixed routine. Birds and other small animals are buried in white plush boxes, larger animals in grey and silver-pine caskets. The hearse is a seven-passenger car, with a compartment for the dead pet. The tract of six acres, in charge of a caretaker, contains numerous granite monuments, appropriately engraved. Some have inlaid photographs of the pet. A cross marks the grave of a dog that saved its master's life.

I was going to stop there too, for a gander.

At the Michigan Welcome Center I discovered there was a seasonal car ferry across Lake Michigan to mid-Wisconsin, and it was still operating. I instantly dumped Steinbeck and opted for this vintage boat route. I asked the attendant what was worth stopping for between Port Huron and Luddington, on Lake Michigan, where the ferry departed to Wisconsin from. 'Nutt'n', he answered. It sounded like it would be a tedious drive.

Just outside Port Huron I saw a road sign to Pontiac, Michigan. For a moment I went all nostalgic and seriously thought about visiting my motorhome's birthplace. Steinbeck had taken a dogleg trip up through Pontiac and Flint, into Michigan lake country, before heading back down to continue to Chicago, so I'd be back on his trail.

Trucks have been built in Pontiac for over 100 years, since Max Grabowsky's Rapid Motor Vehicle Company opened there. That business eventually became part of General Motors, evolving by 1912 into GMC Trucks. Between 1973 and 1978, at GMC Trucks' Pontiac factory, 13,000 GMC motorhomes were built, the most advanced motorhomes of their day. At least 10,000 of them, like mine, are still on the road.

In 1960 when Steinbeck travelled, surprisingly there were no RVs, only trailers. Steinbeck had Rocinante built for him, a cabin on the back of a 3/4-ton pick-up truck. Forty years later I can choose from literally thousands of different styles, lengths and layouts. While visiting Florida early in the year I looked at Winnebagos, Isatas, BT Cruisers and Lexingtons. I drooled at the seamless shell of the luxurious Coach House Platinum, built

151

locally in Nokomis. Motorised sofabeds, outside hot and cold shower, back-up video camera, leather seats, DVD player, flat-screen TV, automatic satellite dish—this was pure luxury. But nothing met the panache, the sophistication, the sheer presence of a vintage GMC motorhome that I chanced upon at a local RV dealer's.

You could tell, just by its unique shape that this was a vehicle decades before its time. Uniquely it had front-wheel drive—no drive shaft—better brakes, better suspension, better gas mileage—a whole eight miles to the gallon—than its competitors. It drove more like a car than a truck or a box on wheels. There was even an integrated vacuum-cleaning system inside. Just plug in the hose and it sucks.

Through the Internet I visited the specialist sites: gmcclassics.com, gmcmotorhome.com, gmcmi.com and, in Florida, gmcss.com. I phoned members of GMC Motorhome Clubs, the GMC Elegant Cruisers in southern California, Sunshine Statesmen in Florida and Dixielanders in Dixie. I spoke to commercial dealers: Alex Sirum at gmcmh.com, Buddy Bethune at bethunesales.com, Cliff Golby at golbymotorcorp.com. I soon had the feeling that, with a vehicle that generally cost from $6000 to $60,000, a middle-of-the-road model would have the reliability to take me where I wanted to go. Buddy Bethune had the right vehicle at the right time. That's how I ended up starting our journey in North Carolina. Decoding the VIN, the vehicle information number, I knew mine was one of the last produced: number 12,359 in that production run of less than 13,000.

Rather than detour to Pontiac I stopped at an

outlet mall for more supplies. In a store I caught sight of myself in a mirror and saw I'd lost weight. So had Macy. Was this a consequence of increased exercise or an insufficient diet? Either way my commander-in-chief would not be pleased. She liked us the way we were. As I paid for some cushions a shopper asked how things were in England.

'How do you know I'm from England?' I asked, surprised, even startled at such accurate recognition of what I assume remains a broad Canadian accent.

'We're from Norfolk, visiting our son who lives here. I couldn't help but hear you when you spoke and recognised your voice from the *Jimmy Young Programme*.'

We talked about Jimmy Young, just retired after 40 years of presenting his BBC daily radio show, and another couple came over.

'We just love *Animal Planet*. Hello, puppy. You should visit Frankenmuth while you're here. Just like Germany.'

'What part of Germany is it like?' I asked a bit cynically. I'd seen the signs beckoning me to Frankenmuth for a Bavarian chicken dinner.

'Dunno. Never been there.'

On we drove, through a spatula-flat landscape and while Macy dozed I listened to NPR, National Public Radio. This network transmits a variety of BBC Radio 4 programmes after midnight each night. Now, there was a public service message on behalf of the Michigan Association of Broadcasters and the Michigan Veterinary Association, giving tips on how to make your pet's senior years as comfortable and pleasant as

153

possible. If only there was a similar service for owners of elderly parents.

*   *   *

The empty heart of Michigan is a land of yard sales, trailer homes and detritus from the past. I stopped just beyond Idlewild, where every shanty, house, store and trailer by the road was vacant and abandoned. This is scratch the earth, dirt-poor territory, bypassed by the interstate system. Gas stations, car repair businesses, motels, farms, all were deserted. I knew that industry had abandoned Michigan, that it was part of the rust belt, but here in mid-Michigan there was never any industry to go rusty. Lumber and the railway, the only enterprises ever offering work, were gone. Nothing was left.

Ambling back to the road I, saw another car parked nearby and a woman—African-American, full-bodied, with her grey hair swept back in a bun—was walking her white toy poodle on a leash. Macy trotted over and I followed. Zora, from Cleveland, had stopped when she saw my parked motorhome.

'Hi, all. Thought you might be here for Idlewild.'

I asked what was happening at Idlewild and she told me about what it once was—a thriving summer resort for middle-class African-American families.

'My grandparents came here each summer. My parents came here each summer. I came here each summer. And I'm back. Duke Ellington came here. Count Basie came here. Louis Armstrong came

154

here. Marcus Garvey came here. Dr Daniel Hale Williams came here. Even the Four Tops came here.'

'I didn't know there were black resorts in Michigan,' I said. Truth is, I never thought about it.

'Folks came here, thousands of them, to sing and dance, to fish in the lake. We had a cottage right on the lake, but it's no more. We came from all over, from Detroit and Chicago and Milwaukee, even from New York City. After the Civil Rights Act, there was no more need for Idlewild. We could go where we pleased. We could go to Miami Beach. Folks are trying to restore Idlewild. I came to see what they're doin'. There are new businesses and new plans. I thought you might be here too.'

I was certainly there, but not walking through history as Zora was, only walking my dog.

*   *   *

Ludington. Large Victorian gingerbread homes, near the waterfront, testified to former wealth and grandeur. The lumber industry once made this a major Great Lakes shipping port. Lumber for construction in Milwaukee and Chicago was transported across Lake Michigan to Manitowac, Wisconsin, where I was heading by boat. James Ludington, after whom the town was named, came from Milwaukee. When the lumber ran out, the boat service turned from freight trains to cars. When I was a young boy at Lake Chemong, and Idlewild was jiving to Ellington and Basie, this faded town was, amazingly, the world's largest car ferry port.

155

Here's a bit of trivia, a Radio 2 factoid. The term 'stateroom', for a private room on a ship, was coined here. You could cross Lake Michigan in the state of your choice—Alabama, Delaware, Idaho—your preference if you booked early enough. Now all that remained was the SS *Badger*, over 50 years old, still with staterooms, and my short cut to Wisconsin. Tickets were available for the next morning and, after buying passage for me and my home, I read the regulations. 'PETS: Animals may be transported in the owner's vehicle or kept in a well-ventilated portable kennel on the car deck. Kennels must be provided by the owner and are strongly recommended during warm weather, as are windshield sun screens'. Highlighted in red letters it said, 'No pets of any kind are allowed in any passenger areas, and pets are not accessible during the cruise.'

I didn't like the thought of leaving her alone during the crossing, but Mace was now very comfortable in the motorhome. I'd make sure the four large windows were slid open to screens only and that she couldn't lie down by the front window where the sun might pour in.

'Neat rig. Restore it yourself?' a checked-shirted, barrel-bellied guy commented.

'Yup. Kept it in a garage in North Carolina ever since I bought it,' I said, straight-faced.

'Winters here in Michigan eat rigs like yours,' he replied.

I headed up the coast, through shifting, rolling sand dunes to Ludington State Park. The park and adjoining Manistee National Forest, to the north, occupy extensive sand dunes by the shore of Lake Michigan and deeply forested old sand dunes

156

behind these. Campgrounds nest in the dells created by the forested dunes. Unlike other state and provincial campgrounds I'd stayed in, this one was busy. Almost all sites were occupied. This was fortunate because within half an hour of arriving I'd lost Macy.

It was almost 5.00 p.m. when I checked in, three hours before sunset at this western edge of the Eastern Time Zone. Mace had been a good traveller, lying stoically by my side as we hammered on, travelling 300 miles from last night's campgrounds on Lake Huron. Before even plugging the motorhome into the campground electrics, we both charged deep into the woods for a refreshing walk.

These dense, sound-absorbing, pine woods have grown thickly upon ancient dunes of steep climbs and almost vertical drops. The land, and covering forest, roller-coasters for miles. Macy, as always, squirrelled. She bog-walked, painting her lower half a dark chocolate hue. After a twenty-minute walk from Cedar Campground where we had parked, we emerged in Beechwood Campground, walked through it and on to Lost Lake, a branch of Hamlin Lake, where I sluiced Macy clean. We retraced our steps and on a mossy, crested ridge between the two campgrounds, Mace caught sight of movement in the distance, raced down into the deep hollow, up the far ridge and over. Minutes later she returned to the ridge, but now something else caught her eye.

With elegant, greyhound grace she torpedoed along the crest of the ridge, then out of sight once more. I sat and waited. Nothing. I called but she didn't return. After five minutes I quick-marched down into the hollow and up the other side, shouting her name. I walked the ridge she had raced along, then, from a great distance, I heard it. Shrieks of pain: sharp, plaintive sounds. They were high-pitched, incessant, getting shorter and farther away. I took off at full speed in the direction they'd come from. 'Macy! Macy! Mace!'

Have you ever lost your dog, been personally responsible for losing your dog? I know the guilt and anguish people feel because, as a vet, I've been the dispassionate shoulder to lean on. Now, here I was in their situation. I tried to think sensibly but all I could hear in my mind were her piteous, painful shrieks. What had happened to her?

As best I could, I followed her visible tracks through the fallen leaves and damp humus. I came across what I thought were fresh ones heading back towards where I'd parked. Macy had impressed me in Quebec, knowing her way back to our campsite, and I followed these back to our home, ten minutes away. But she wasn't there. I told my neighbours I had lost her and returned to the woods, calling, calling, calling, but with no response.

It was now 40 minutes since I had last seen her. I went to the camp store, asked the staff to phone the park rangers and report Macy missing, and returned once more to the woods. I descended into each bog, looking to see if she had found herself trapped in mire. My AGS *Michigan Guide* says that bears inhabit this area. I knew that coyote and lynx had moved in since the guide was written. Is that why she yelped in such distress? Had she been carried away by a brown bear? My T-shirt clung to me, soaked with sweat. I climbed ridges,

158

descended hollows, circled back to where I'd last seen her, constantly, and now hoarsely, yelling, 'Macy!'

Eight o'clock. She'd been missing for two and a half hours. My mind reeled. Was she alive? How could I look for her once it was dark? What do I do with her body when I find it? Should I cremate it and take the ashes home? What if I find only part of her? How can I travel across North America with my dog if I don't have my dog? Do I still have a marriage? The sun was setting over Lake Michigan, a mile away. I'd planned to be on the beach with Macy for it. I walked back to our campsite, to check with my neighbours again, get a torch and return to the woods. I had decided to spend the night on the ridge where I'd last seen her alive. As I approached our campsite I saw a park ranger's pick-up truck with its driver standing beside our home. 'Just leaving a message for ya. Yer dog's at site 305. Wasn't on her leash, huh?'

This was one of life's truly happy moments. The tidal wave of heart-accelerating emotions crashed, followed by a still, quiet, calm. I'd be able to speak with Julia. I'd be able to tell her that Macy was getting more exercise and encountering more experiences than either of us had ever imagined.

I stripped off my wet T-shirt, put on another, gulped down a bottle of water, returned to the woods and clambered up and down and up and down and up and down, eventually reaching Beechwood Campground. I'd previously spoken to campers in its two loops, not knowing there was a northerly third loop. At its top, by the woods, I saw a forlorn dog on a makeshift rope leash, attended by four people. Macy saw me and her ears went

159

alert but her tail didn't wag. As I got within voice-distance, I said, 'Thank you for finding my dog . . . and saving my marriage.' Mace managed a feeble wag of her dirt-encrusted tail. She had appeared half an hour previously, emerging from the woods to the north, panting intensely—exhausted—then lay down under a tree while her whole body shook with panting. Sally had gone over, given Macy water and slices of bologna, while David bicycled to the park office a mile away to report a found dog. She'd been running in the woods on her own for over two hours.

I wanted to hug her to death but I'm a guy and people were around, so I told Sally and David, her saviours, how they could dine out on the story of how they saved the vet's dog and let one man and his dog continue their journey.

After profuse thanks—and I mean really profuse, embarrassingly profuse thanks—I put Mace on her leash which I'd brought with me. We walked down to Lost Lake. I guided her in and commanded 'Sit,' and with exhaustion she did, looking lost, tired and deeply unhappy. I rubbed her body in clear water that blackened with organic bog matter. After several moves to clearer water and lots of rubbing she was relatively clean. We left the lake but she was so exhausted she didn't even shake herself, walking by my side as we returned to our campsite where she lay down flat on her side and fell into a deep sleep. After an hour I woke her and offered her food—cheddar cheese curd, white bread and butter. She'd have none of it. She looked strained, stressed. I opened the motorhome door and, with an effort, she pulled herself up and climbed in, onto her own bed and into another

160

deep sleep from which she didn't emerge until the following morning.

Mace is usually sparky at dawn but now she looked edgy and worried. I brushed her thoroughly, pressing against her for reassurance as I did. I was reassuring myself she was alive and with me, as much as giving her contact comfort I thought she needed. 'Why did you abandon me?' she mourned plaintively with her eyes. It was already 6.30 a.m., but still an hour before dawn. The air was warm and dry. I took her to the shower house with me where I showered and shaved, and she stood gloomily, not showing interest even in the ferocious *Blazing Saddles* noises coming from toilet cubicles occupied by other early morning risers.

I packed and departed and as I drove back to the Lake Michigan shoreline, through the bare dunes, the sky turned pink, the advent of sunrise. I parked and we walked through the still, cool dunes to the wide sandy beach. Macy cheered up a bit when she discovered hidden in the dunes two massive Chinook salmon, each around 30–40 pounds, both almost as long as she is. Damage around their tail fins revealed white flesh. I could only guess why such delicious meals had been abandoned. Either they were caught illegally or the angler knew that University of Wisconsin scientists had found high levels of flame-retardant chemical in Lake Michigan salmon and recommended removing the skin and fatty tissue before cooking. I wondered whether there was an inverse relationship between the level of flame-retardant chemical and barbecuing time.

We continued to the ferry. I'd already decided

that if I couldn't remain with Mace on the lake crossing I'd cancel the booking and drive further north, over the top of Lake Michigan. I'd got out my stethoscope and had my story ready when I arrived at the dock.

'I know your regulations are explicit, but I'm a vet, my dog's not well and she shouldn't be left alone on the journey. Can we stay together?'

'I don't think that's a problem,' the woman on sentry duty replied, as she returned my ticket through the window and fingered the red stethoscope I'd left there. 'I'll speak to the second mate.' She spoke into her two-way radio. 'I've got a veterinarian here with a sick dog. Any way they can travel together?' Crackling back, I heard, 'No problem.' She turned to me. 'Introduce yourself to Al over there and good luck with your doggy.'

Blake, a young monosyllabic ferry company employee, backed the motorhome onto the ferry and, as he did so, Macy climbed up beside him and made him an offering of one of the stuffed toys she'd been given in Toronto. 'Will you take me home and care for me and protect me? That asshole in the back didn't.'

During the time Blake was in the driver's seat I read Ludington State Park's *Guide for Visitors with Pets*.

We are sure that the very fact that you have your pet with you is evidence that you sincerely care about the welfare of your pet . . . Please remember that the park is a strange environment for your pet. It may react much differently here than at home . . . Don't allow your pet to run loose at any time . . . Always keep your pet on a leash which must not exceed six feet in length . . .

Four hours after departure, we were in Wisconsin and in our third time zone. I was going to visit the Frank Lloyd Wright buildings in Stockbridge, Wisconsin, as an alternative to those in Oak Park and River Forest, Illinois. Every 1950s subdivision in Canada seemed to have been derivatives of that architect's designs and I wanted to see the originals from a half-century before. Macy looked so forlorn that I chose to head instead through rich dairy and arable farming land, past fields of barley interspersed with acres of ripe orange pumpkins, to the nearest state park. Mid-afternoon, surrounded by a chain of clear, spring-fed lakes, we settled into a shady campsite at Hartman Creek State Park.

Macy investigated the nearby territory. 'Stay! Sit! Come!' I commanded. It was time to start retraining both of us. I didn't want to put myself or her ever again through the emotional torment of the last few days' events. I made both of us a light meal of scrambled eggs, mine with a little maple syrup and cheddar cheese. The park was almost empty but for two other vehicles—a massive Pace Arrow RV with lights strung through the surrounding trees and green carpeting on the ground, and a GMC pick-up truck pulling a trailer. We walked around the lake, to Hellestad House, a restored log cabin, once the home of Ole and Anne Hellestad, a couple who emigrated from Norway to Wisconsin in the mid-1800s.

On our walk back we met the trailer owners, a dairy farmer and his wife, just retired two months past, now living in Sheboygan. I didn't get their names, but I'll call them Sam and Elsie. Bow-legged Sam wore a beaten-up International Harvester cap, brown shirt and jeans. He had a full head of snow-white hair, a creased, leathery but gentle face, and used a stiff branch as a walking stick. Elsie was broad, very, very broad, with surprisingly spindly blue-veined legs emerging from wide, baggy shorts. She wore small, thin, oval-framed, gunmetal-grey glasses. I thought Sam and Elsie were old, but they turned out to be younger than I am.

They complimented me on not visiting Wisconsin Dells.

'Yes, nothing but tourists there. Noah's Ark. America's largest waterpark. Millions go there. Nothing but tourists.'

I asked Sam what happened to his herd when he retired.

'Yes, no future in dairy. My son's an optician in Seattle. Interned on an Indian Reserve in Montana. We visited him there. Auctioned my cows.'

I asked him the size of his herd.

'Yes, 46. Enough to raise a family. My father raised his family with thirteen cows. You can't do that now. I computerised. High-energy fodder. BGH. All it did was make my cows sore. Gave 'em mastitis. Laminitis. They burned out young. I've been a dairyman too long to do that to my cows.'

I mentioned I was a vet, and was curious about BGH—that's Bovine Growth Hormone, also called Bovine Somatotropin or BST. Its use is normal in the US, but it's banned in Canada and the EU.

'Yes, they told me it'd increase my milk

production by 10 per cent. Showed me figures. I guess it works in big units with robot milking and dairy-go-rounds, but all I got was more mastitis and lameness. I was told to feed high-energy fodder, not to let my cows graze, but how can you do that after they've been confined all winter? I thought about going organic. That's big business now, you know. Milk gets not much more than $9 a hundred pounds, but organic gets over $18. Yes, they told me what I'd have to do to go organic and it'd take years. We're too old. So we sold out.'

I asked, and Sam explained that robot milking was increasing in Wisconsin. He said it was the future; cows liked it. The system involved computerised, automatic feeding, milking and monitoring. Cows, and farmers, first have to be weaned off the concept of routine twice-daily milking. Instead, the cows are trained to voluntarily visit comfortable robot stalls for free access to food, water and milking. A young dairyman, who switched, told Sam that at first cows visited the robot stalls at the same times of day they were previously milked. The dairyman also had problems with equipment breakdowns and backlogs of cows waiting to be milked.

'The idea's good,' Sam concluded. 'Cows early in lactation come to be milked three or four times a day. Later on, they visit the parlour twice a day. Everything's measured—fodder, milk, clots, activity. Yes, if I'd had the money and one of those technicians around I might have stayed on.'

All the while Elsie said not a word, then, out of the blue, unexpectedly, 'Your Mr Blair. He's a good man. A religious man.'

That's probably a fair description of the Prime

165

Minister: a good man, a religious man. I still feel he genuinely believes in what he's doing, that it's up to Britain and the United States—the old Anglo-Saxon coalition—to save Western civilisation, and this means confronting terror. I said I couldn't agree with his reasons for going to war in Iraq, but agreed with her that the British Prime Minister was a man of conviction.

'Our President is a religious man,' she added.

Sam nodded in agreement, then he continued, 'Mrs Thatcher. She kept Mr Reagan under control. I wonder what Mr Blair can do?'

'What would you like him to do?' I asked.

'Mr Bush is a good man, a religious man. But he has so many advisors. It would be better if Mr Bush and Mr Blair made the decisions themselves.'

'What do you mean?'

'They're honourable men but—and don't get me wrong—I'll do what my President tells me to do, but our President, he's surrounded by people who maybe aren't as honourable. God wants us to fight this war because it's the right thing to do. You're not supposed to profit from war.'

Sam spoke with what seemed a mixture of embarrassment and sorrow. Elsie's head nodded affirmatively as he spoke and, by my side, Macy chucked up her meal. This may well have been her way of rendering an opinion on my prime minister and their president but it sure was a conversation-stopper. I returned to our home and built a campfire—no, a bonfire—and spent the evening swatting mosquitoes. My left leg itched and was covered in a rash, either poison ivy or poison sumac, probably contracted the evening before in my frantic search for Macy. I cleaned the rash with alcohol swabs I'd brought along in Macy's first-aid kit, throwing countless swabs on the fire where each produced a blue-flamed fireball. Good way, I thought, to scare away any predatory bears.

*   *   *

I thought the names of Ontario's roads were the continent's most insipid, but Wisconsin's system is even more banal. All county roads are lettered A, B, C, D, then AA, BB, CC, DD. I detoured onto County Road HH, through Whiting where the Baptist church signpost had two cut-out cowgirls leaning against each edge of the placard which read: 'PRAYER MUST MEAN SOMETHING TO US IF IT IS TO MEAN ANYTHING TO GOD'. Road signs here were as detailed. 'GIVE YOURSELF A HUG. BUCKLE UP'. 'GIVE THEM A BRAKE. SLOW DOWN'. Back on arrow-straight US 10, I drove through unending fields of silage corn. Each barn had three or four silos. I passed a veterinary clinic, about as common a sighting as a GMC motorhome, and patriotic signs everywhere: 'Glad to be part of this great nation' covering the wall of one building; and 'Support our troops' on another.

The road quietly entered Amish country. I knew this because of the horse-drawn vehicle warning signs on the highway. Chance was on my side. At the Clark County Fairground, just outside, I came upon a twice-yearly Amish horse and implement auction, the largest horse auction in this or any of the surrounding states.

There can be few nobler or more dignified sights in North America than hundreds of Amish, converging on a sunny, early autumn day in horse-drawn buggies, sulkies, carts and surreys. The men and boys—all in straw hats with black bands, and denim, buttoned trousers with buttoned pockets, held up by black braces, and all wearing solid white, taupe, light blue, dark blue or dark green cotton shirts—wandering, chatting, testing the soundness of horses by hopping on and riding bareback, feeling the horse's gait through their own spines. And bonneted women and girls, far fewer in numbers—the girls giggling, walking in groups, chattering, smiling, watching. As in Ontario, Amish and Mennonite children in Wisconsin are exempt from compulsory school attendance after eighth grade—twelve to thirteen years of age.

The 12,000 Amish here in Wisconsin, those I bypassed in Lancaster County, Pennsylvania, and the Mennonites in Ontario are all interconnected. Products of sixteenth-century Europe's Protestant Reformation, at the heart of their faith is a belief in the authority of the Bible, adult baptism, the avoidance of ostentation and, above all, a commitment to peace and non-resistance. The Mennonites tell that Menno Simons, after whom they take their name, said, 'The regenerated do not go to war or engage in strife. They have beat their swords into ploughshares and their spears into pruning hooks and know no war.'

Amish and Mennonites first settled in Ohio and Pennsylvania where, combined, over 100,000 still live. In the early 1800s, Chief Joseph Brant, Chief of the Six Nations (Mississauga, Cayuga, Mohawk, Oneida, Onandaga and Seneca tribes) in Ontario, sold almost 100,000 acres of tribal reserve to a land speculator who travelled to Pennsylvania and convinced Mennonites there to purchase land from him and move to the area west of where I went to veterinary school, what would become Waterloo County. Today there are over 57,000 Mennonites in Ontario, thousands of whom are Old Order and live as their ancestors did hundreds of years ago.

So too do the people I was now among. I wandered through the fairground, to the sheds where the horses and their vehicles were parked, to the implement auction where milk churns, buggies, and ranges of iron 'things' were being auctioned. An antique dealer from Minneapolis had just purchased a hundred-year-old road grader and we got talking.

'I do my best business here,' he explained. 'Amish folk are leaving Pennsylvania and moving here. Pennsylvania's got too expensive and too commercial for them. They come here to preserve their way of life where their kids aren't exposed to as many temptations. Older farmers here like it because they get top value for their farms when they sell. I like it because the Amish sell off implements they find on those farms. Turnover's always good for me.

'Farm equipment salesmen and bartenders are never happy when Amish move in, but tell you what,' the antique dealer continued, 'go over there and try her pickled cantaloupe. That's something new the Pennsylvania Amish have brought with them. Delicious.'

Macy and I lazed about. We wandered through the commercial sales area where I could buy old leather saddles, subtle, supple masterpieces of hand-sewn, hand-tooled leather work, for a few hundred dollars, to the horse barns filled with

169

dapple-grey, black and, overwhelmingly, chestnut-coloured horses, all with auction numbers slapped on their haunches. I said hello to each child we met, but neither Macy nor I, outsiders, garnered any response.

Just down the road from the fairground, straw-hatted Amish men were emerging from the local Hardees with take-out burgers and fries. Across the highway from the fairground, even weirder, beside Chatty Belle, the 'World's Largest Talking Cow', was the Cheesemobile, a once refrigerated, glass-sided transport truck, now housing the 'World's Largest Replica Cheese'. At the time of the 1964 New York World's Fair, 16,000 Wisconsin cows contributed their combined output to produce a seventeen-ton cheddar, displayed in this vehicle at Wisconsin's world's fair pavilion. The cheese was allegedly eaten at the 1965 annual meeting of the Wisconsin Dairymen and Cheesemakers' Association. *Allegedly*. Seventeen tons of cheese eaten at an AGM? The pavilion, now sited beside Chatty Belle, is home to Neillsville's local radio station. It's also a cheese shop. A crumbled blue cheese from North Hendren Cheese Cooperative caught my eye and the saleswoman complimented me on my choice.

'That's an award-winning cheese from a dairy about two miles north of Willard. They only use milk from herds certified BGH-free and never add milk powder to up the butter-fat content.' I bought a pound and nibbled. Succulent as the most sublime Roquefort I'd ever tasted.

*   *   *

AMISH FARMERS AT A BARN SALE, NEILLSVILLE,
WISCONSIN

The year my GMC rolled off the production line in Pontiac, Michigan, the Norske Nook Bakery and Restaurant in Osseo, Wisconsin, was rated one of the nation's ten best roadside diners according to the book, *Roadfood*. Though I wasn't particularly hungry I dropped by for a meal, 'Smothered Denver Lefse Wrap'—scrambled egg, ham, hash browns, Colby cheese, peppers, onions, mushrooms, all wrapped inside Norwegian lefse bread, then smothered in hollandaise. Neither subtle nor Norwegian but very tasty.

Across the street in the window of an antique shop, I saw something I recognised, a carved Scandinavian mangle board. Mace and I went inside and among the expected old snowshoes and Currier & Ives prints were more Scandinavian objects: hackles, the teeth of which were used to separate coarse from fine fibres for spinning and weaving; a copper kettle on an iron stand of three spider-like legs; a wooden butter-mould; a large, painted pine wedding chest; a small, unpainted bentwood food box; ale bowls and, locked in a glass cabinet, two wooden tankards. Julia and I visit Sweden four to six times each year. I knew that what I was looking at were all Norwegian, between 150 and 225 years old—here, in the middle of nowhere, in Wisconsin. This would pay for my trip!

Nonchalantly, I asked to look at the better tankard: polychromatic-painted, carved from the burled growth of a birch tree, the lift for the lid fashioned in the form of a lion. It sat on three feet, in the form of resting lions. Its top was carved and painted with a lion rampant, the symbol of the Norwegian monarchy. I guessed it was 200 years

172

old, carved by an itinerant craftsman, probably in eastern Norway, near the Swedish border. In Norway a tankard such as this is part of the country's national patrimony. Export is forbidden. I looked at the price on the bottom. Damn! More than in Norway!

I asked the shop attendant, a lean, lanky, mousy-brown-haired man with a triangular face, and a slow, thoughtful pattern of speech about the tankard.

'Oh . . . Ya . . . It's Norwegian. 1790 to 1820. It was found at a farm auction in south-eastern Minnesota and sold to a Rochester, Minnesota, dealer, who sold it to a Rochester collector. My father purchased it from him.'

His 'ya' gave away his regional heritage.

Eric's father, Donald Gilbertson, was, I learned, more than an antique dealer. He'd bought this tankard while amassing information for his 1975 book, *A Treasury of Norwegian Folk Art in America*, one of the first books to illustrate what Norwegian immigrants brought with them to Wisconsin and Minnesota. Like many dealers, collecting is the genesis for dealing. Donald was now selling this wonderful tankard because he had even better ones. I bought it, 'Norwegian Tankard, c. 1780–1810, lion feet and thumblift. Old painted surface, as found with hairline crack up barrel'.

Eric realised I was genuinely interested in the trove of Scandinavian artefacts in his shop and showed and explained each in detail. I asked if treasures such as these were still out there waiting to be discovered.

'Ya . . . Just last month he picked up a 1672-dated powder container at a local farm.'

All the while, Macy hung around quietly. Eric asked about her and I mentioned we were on a trip together.

'Oh . . . Ya . . . Steinbeck . . . He travelled with his dog.' I sensed a hint of envy in Eric's voice. 'Ya . . . I'd like to do that.'

*   *   *

The Mississippi River is the physical barrier, the geographical divide between East and West, but it is only that; no more. The cultures of Nelson, Wisconsin, and Wabasha, Minnesota, across the river, are the same—openly, attractively, optimistically, typically libertarian Midwestern.

A sign told me that Wabasha, Minnesota, hosts an annual Grumpy Old Men Festival. If my dad's still around in February, I'll ask him if I can enter him. There's a unique bit of hydrology here on the Mississippi. While the upper Mississippi freezes solid and ice-fishing is a popular winter sport, a three-mile stretch of the river, south of Wabasha, remains ice-free. The river narrows just to the north—the southern end of a dilation in the river called Lake Pepin—and just to the south the Chippewa River flows in from Wisconsin. The combined current and water volume keep the river running, making it good winter hunting territory for bald eagles feeding off river chad.

Dried autumn leaves skittered across the Great River Road as I drove north towards Minneapolis St Paul, and from the heights, looking down on the Mississippi, white caps raging over its surface, black clouds racing in from the west, the wind buffeting me, it looked demonic and threatening.

It crossed my mind that when my parents were children, steamboats still pushed vast rafts of logs down river past Wabasha. The last raft departed in 1915.

We camped at Frontenac State Park where rain relentlessly pounded the roof and attacked the windows. I loved it. The sound was relaxing, my home comforting, soothing, embracing.

On our regular pre-breakfast walk I met a Munsterlander, a Doberman and two Luxembourgers, the latter the first citizens of the grand duchy I'd ever encountered. One was hairy and bulldoggish, with a neck as thick as the surrounding pine trees, the other was brown-eyed, slight and academic in his demeanour. They were on a fact-finding expedition, tracing the descendants of Luxembourgers who had emigrated to this part of America in the 1840s. The academic-looking Luxembourger was to write a book about their quest.

'Sometimes we were part of France, sometimes Germany. Many left for a safer life. In ten years we lost 80,000 people, one-third of our population,' he explained when I asked how they came to be camping on bluffs above the Mississippi.

'Some went to Pennsylvania and Ohio, but most came here to Iowa, Minnesota and Wisconsin. We met one of the park rangers. His grandmother was from Luxembourg but he didn't know her full name. I am using historical documents in Luxembourg but also good information here. There's a newspaper in Chicago called *Luxembourg News of America* and Luxembourg Heritage Society clubs for descendants. They deal with Luxembourgish manifestations and history.

175

We just visited one such club in Dubuque, Iowa.'

I was aware of the Norwegian and Swedish heritage of the region, and had been reminded, driving through Michigan, of the great migrations from Germany, but Luxembourg had never crossed my mind.

*   *   *

'Get caught in that rain?' asked Dudley Do-Right, a young, broad-shouldered, square-jawed, majestic-as-the-river park ranger. 'Hope you weren't in a tent. Nice doggy,' he said, eyeing Macy working the picnic ground at the top of the high limestone bluffs—the source, for you trivia-lovers, according to my AGS *Minnesota Guide*, of the limestone used for the interior of the Cathedral of St John the Divine in New York City.

'Got a leash for her?' he asked.

Park regulations, as everywhere, stipulated that dogs must be kept on a maximum six-foot leash. I showed him her leash.

'Good. How long you staying?'

I explained it was but a stopover and asked him if he had come across the Luxembourgers.

'I'm a Luxembourger,' interjected his driver.

'I'm Norwegian,' Dudley remarked. 'All my grandparents came from there.'

And I thought, what am I? Here were a couple of Americans defining themselves by their grandparents' heritage. Am I Canadian, the country of my birth and upbringing? Am I English, the country I now live in and hold a passport from? Am I Scottish, the land where my father was born, or Lithuanian, where his father was born? Am I

176

Ukrainian or Galician, the origins of my mother's parents? In simple terms, am I North American or European? I'd lived in the former for the first half of my life and the latter for the second.

Years ago, when offered an opportunity to move to Boston I used the chief as an excuse. 'Sorry, she sings "God Save the Queen" at sunrise and sunset. Paints herself blue and runs naked around Stonehenge at the vernal equinox. She could never live anywhere other than England,' I told my prospective employer.

But Julia surprised me when she said it was my choice. She'd go where I wanted. I had to make an active, not a passive, decision, and I decided to stay in Europe. I'd grown accustomed to the satisfaction of easy travel, to friends in Venice one month, Stockholm the next. I'd come to understand Britain's curious amalgam of respect for authority and underlying anarchy, its nonconformist streak and its admiration for eccentricity. I savoured its regard for the citizen's right to anonymity, that you were not compelled to carry identification with you, even your driver's licence while driving, and if you did—a photo ID licence was still but a new option—that existing licences were quaint, fold-up documents. I opted to stay, and embedded myself by acquiring a country home in coastal Sussex by the English Channel. I bought myself green wellies. There's a difference between roots and heritage, but for me the difference has become misty and musty.

Have you noticed the main cultural difference between flying business class and peasant class? Of course, only those few of you on expense accounts or preposterously rich enough to fly business class will know what I'm talking about, but it's not the foot massage the stewardess gives you in business class, or even the knitted pink cashmere socks they give you as a going-home present. In steerage you naturally talk to your neighbours but in business class that's just social suicide. What I really like about North Americans is that, regardless of the size of their motorhome, they have retained a tourist-class mentality and happily enter into conversation with anyone. In Britain, the natives find it easier to converse with my dog first then me later.

While walking Macy, I met an older couple, dressed for winter. Last night's storm had brought with it the first premonition of the cold to come. They'd moved from Lake of the Woods up on the Canadian border to a nearby small town. 'Where we lived we were famous for hockey, snowmobiles and the coldest spot in the nation,' the man explained.

This was my chance to ask about something that's always puzzled me. If you look at a map of the United States and Canada, there's a curiosity at the border of Minnesota and Ontario, at Lake of the Woods. The border between the two countries, for over a thousand miles from the Pacific in the State of Washington, through the Rocky Mountains of Idaho and Montana, and across the prairies of North Dakota and Minnesota, is the 49th Parallel. But at Lake of the Woods in Minnesota, the border takes a sharp left turn up into Canada for 25 miles, then turns right for an equal distance, then south to meet the 49th Parallel once more. This tract of the United States is cut off by Lake of the Woods. It can only be reached from Canada. I asked the man if he knew the history of this anomaly.

'Ah, the north-west angle. A surveyor's mistake. Most of it is State Forest. You can get there by Skidoo from Arnesen in the winter without going through Canada.'

Merv, fit and healthy-looking in an American Legion blue satin bomber jacket, a half-finished cigar in his mouth, joined us. His rusty Chevy Camping Van was parked nearby. I learned later that Merv had terminal cancer. 'I'm on reprieve,' he said confidently, when I met him again for some photos. 'Not s'pposed to be here, but on my last check-up, doc said don't come back for two months.'

Merv wanted to talk turkey.

'Look'n' forward to the hunt'n' season,' he exclaimed as he joined us. 'This time next month I'm turkey hunt'n'. In the spring, you should see those guys dance when I call 'em. You can only hunt males in the spring. Gobble like a hen and they come runn'n'. You should hear me. Next month it's hens. If I get a turkey, I take 'em home and put 'em on the smoker. Damned delicious.' I asked Merv if, as in New England, wild turkeys had been reintroduced.

'DLR captured them in the wild in Missouri, then released them here.'

I moved our conversation over to politics. I was curious to hear a veteran's opinion.

'I'm a military man and I don't mean to belittle my President,' Merv said, 'but I said from the very beginning, get the United Nations behind him, fine. He's got a big head that man has. He thinks he can just go ahead and force anything he wants,

179

and that's wrong.'

The emigrant from Lake of the Woods concurred.

'I shouldn't belittle him either but I'm not happy with his decision to sort of unilaterally make decisions that affect the world. He's made enemies of our good friends. What for?'

Their comments reflected my thoughts too. I didn't see, and still don't see the logic of invading secular Iraq and overthrowing Saddam, as part of a war against a reactionary, fascist brand of Islam. I didn't like the idea, I didn't believe Saddam was an immediate threat to us, but my bottom line was this: the Americans were there when Britain needed help. Now they have asked us for help. Try to convince them they're wrong, but if you can't convince them we're obliged to help them. At least if we're involved we can influence what happens.

Now, six months later, I'm no longer sure. Ham-fistedly, the American government has, as my Lake of the Woods camper honestly said, made enemies of its best friends—Canada, Germany, Sweden. Where's the moderating voice of pragmatism?

*   *   *

Stockholm was founded in 1851 by Eric and Jacob Petersson. That's Stockholm, Wisconsin, across choppy, mean and green Lake Pepin. The AGS *Wisconsin Guide* gives it a population of 205 in 1941. The road sign today says 97. Back then, it was the site of several carp ponds that supplied live fish to kosher markets in large cities. Clams were dredged locally from the river and sold to mother-of-pearl button factories.

This little town faded gently away until it was rediscovered in the early 1970s by artists and professional craftsmen. While other places this size are fortunate if there's a convenience store, Stockholm has a museum, antique shop, two restaurants, three galleries, and speciality shops selling merchandise ranging from toys to pottery, to quilts, to locally produced furniture. Following my nose, I visited the antique shop first. Gib, blue-eyes, brown hair going grey at the sides, wearing oval rimless glasses and a fisherman's cap, greeted me like a long-lost friend. We talked about the locality and about what Macy and I were doing, all the while with Gib attending to other customers.

I asked Gib about commercial fishing on the upper Mississippi. The Frontenac Park information leaflet had advised not to eat too much local fish because of PCB contamination. He told me he had once been a commercial fisherman.

'We used to fish for carp for Brooklyn. A rabbi used to come up from New York to bless truckloads of fish, all white meat, none of the inferior red meat. You could make steaks from those carp, but it all went into the best *gefilte* fish in the country. Now, with the PCB level so high, the only carp you can take from the lake are called racehorses, skinny little five-pounders. Rabbis don't come up to bless them.'

I learned that freshwater mussels and clams were no longer harvested for buttons. Zebra mussel infestation, as in Lake Chemong in Ontario, has destroyed much of the habitat for the former residents.

'If you want a good fish meal, I'd suggest the Harbor View Restaurant in Pepin,' Gib continued.

'My wife Judy cooks there. It's mostly fish they serve, but nothing local. King Hussein went there three times when he was receiving treatment at the Mayo Clinic in Rochester. He loved Judy's beet borscht. They usually have lamb on the menu, which was good for his bodyguards, but he wanted steak so they got that for him. You know, the news spread pretty fast in Pepin when he first went there for lunch.'

Gib asked where I was staying that night, and offered his place, explaining there was plenty of room for the GMC. As an alternative he suggested the Stockholm Village Park and Campground, across the road and railroad line, down at the river's edge. As I drove down to this small campsite, the sun broke through the clouds. Macy raced to the river and went wild with ballet leaps in the warm water. In the shallows she found a rubber boot in an advanced state of decomposition and pranced proudly with it. She watched intently as a freight train hooted and passed behind us. On the shore she found a couple of clam shells, deftly picked them up and carried them to the grass behind. I kept them as souvenirs.

For lunch at the Harbor View Restaurant I had tomato and rice soup with pesto and lots of grated cheese, followed by Alaska halibut in a black butter caper sauce, with sugar snap peas and rice. This was extremely good. Even better, from the table beside me, I overheard a family talking about cancelling a baseball game in Sedgwick, Deer Isle, because the fog was so thick you couldn't see second base. I asked if they were talking about Deer Isle, Maine. They were.

The Petersons moved from Stockholm to Deer

182

Isle two years ago. Bjorn, ten years old, was back to play fiddle with his father, Jay, at a public event next day in Pepin. We talked about Deer Isle. Jay explained there was no police presence in town and that the local eighteen-year-olds, making great money working on lobster boats, had a tendency to zoom around town in souped-up pick-up trucks. 'But we take care of things.' Stonington, I learned, has the second largest lobster catch in Maine, exceeded only by Portland. Jay's father, the image of the comedian Ronnie Barker, told me about his twelve-year-old golden retriever recently dying, then shook his head in disbelief and said he still couldn't talk about it, adding 'Socially here in western Wisconsin and Minnesota, we're very much like the Swedes.' I took that to mean you don't let your emotions hang out.

Back in Stockholm, Macy and I walked every street of the village. I bought freshly pressed apple cider and a warm loaf of cracked sunflower bread from the Bogus Creek Bakery, and a turquoise inlaid breadboard, made in Arizona—incongruously—from Amish Country Quilts. The owner winters in Arizona when Stockholm shuts up for six months. Mace did her Darcy Bussell ballet walk around the store and enchanted everyone, who smiled and commented how girly she was.

That night, opening night at the Lone Star Cafe, once the local Texaco gas station, then a hardware store, I met Gib, Judy and Lucy, the antique shop owner, for a few beers. It seemed inauspicious to be opening a restaurant as summer breathed its last gasp and the locals planned their winters in Arizona and Florida, but this was a relaxed crowd.

183

Gib and Judy introduced me as a writer. 'You're not Jonathan Raban?' one asked, hopefully.

I met the mayor, and the fact that Stockholm, population 97, had a mayor, struck me as quaintly attractive. We talked about the region. Rochester, Minnesota, less than 40 miles away as the crow flies—the nearest city—was suffering because it was now so difficult for Arabs to get visas. 'The Mayo itself is coping by opening a branch in the Middle East,' Judy explained. 'Hotels can't do the same.'

The crowd in the Lone Star were open and affable. Everyone table-hopped. Everyone knew everyone. University graduates or local mechanics, they looked at ease with life. Earlier, Gib had said the region was 40 years behind the rest of America. This was intentional. Many of the people I'd met had opted out of city life. They were here to live a life doing what they wanted, not what urban expectations compelled them to do. They had created a community they were familiar with from their youths. I envied that, their ability to live with a constancy to life, with the ever-familiar. The Lone Star shut early and I walked back down to my water-level campsite by the Mississippi. The night was chilly. Hundred-car freight trains rumbled past every half-hour. I was content. This was a good place.

*   *   *

Laura Ingalls Wilder was born in Pepin in 1867 and moved with her family to Kansas, Minnesota, and then Iowa, before finally settling in South Dakota. In the 1930s, when she was in her sixties, she achieved national and international recognition for her books on frontier life. *Little House on the Prairie* became a 1970s TV series. *Little House in the Big Woods* was set in Pepin. Today and tomorrow in Pepin were Laura Ingalls Wilder Days: pancake breakfasts, spelling bees for second-to-fifth-graders, tomahawk throws, craft demonstrations, a petting farm, local folklore music, horse-pulled wagon rides, quilting bees, an old-time fiddle contest, local talent shows, a Pepin-Laura lookalike contest with additional categories for 'Little Sisters' and 'Big Sisters'. There would be an evening bonfire, a grand parade, and an essay contest: 'How Laura Ingalls Wilder Influenced My Life'.

As I walked down the main road through town, an older man, unshaven that day, in the local uniform of plaid shirt, suspenders and jeans, eyed Macy. 'Goddamn woodchuck living under my porch. Can I borrow your dog for a few days?'

At the traditional crafts market, set up by the road between Locust and Elm Streets, there were demonstrations of blacksmithing, spinning, quilting, basket-weaving and wood-turning.

'Hi. Saw you at the bar, at the restaurant, yesterday. Nice dog. What is he?' said a stranger, as Mace and I milled in the crowds.

'Hi, Bruce. Get a good night?' asked another diner from the Lone Star.

At the petting farm, farm children had chickens, piglets, sheep and goats for others to touch and ask questions about. Most of the girls, all dressed as Laura Ingalls Wilder, crowded round a very pliable and self-satisfied Macy. 'She's so soft.' 'She's so gentle.' 'May I hug her?' They did, probably reminding Mace of what she was missing in the chief's absence.

There were 200 Laura Ingalls Wilders entered in the Pepin-Laura contest. There were also prizes for the best period costumes for men and women. The men won by a mile. Not that the women weren't well turned out for the event. It was obvious they'd diligently cut and sewn for weeks before. The guys won because the beards and clothes they wore were their own. This was their lifestyle. I knew these people. I'd met them before—in San Francisco, where I worked in a veterinary clinic in Haight-Ashbury in 1968. They were university grads, corporate lawyers, paediatric surgeons, guys who'd made lifestyle decisions to return to what they considered a more real way of living. Here, for our education and also for their own personal satisfaction, they turned wood, squared logs and hammered iron.

I liked it. No, that's not strong enough. I envied them. There was a warmth, a sweetness, an innocence to what I was seeing. There was a feeling of community as there probably was in Laura Ingalls Wilder's days, but this was a new community. Listen to this list of businesses thanked for their sponsorship of the festival. Alma Veterinary Clinic, Beth's Twin Bluff Cafe, Bogus Creek Cafe & Bakery, Dad's Place, Dan's Pepin Marina, Dan's Service, Deb's Nu Look, Dick's RV & Sport Shop, Great River Roasters, Harbor View Cafe, Heike Pharmacy, Hill's Hardware, Lynn's Barber Shop, Paul & Fran's Grocery, Ralph's Bar & Mary's Kitchen. See what I mean?

Chance. Serendipity took me off Steinbeck's route down to this part of the Mississippi. Now I didn't want to leave, but decided that if I stayed I might miss other places further on. At noon I shared a quarter of a barbecued chicken with Mace, as we sat on the grass listening to music, including Bjorn and Jay. I bought some locally grown musk melons and a watermelon, Red Barrow and Honey Crisp apples, and headed north up the River Road. Before I left, Gib caught up with me and gave me a bag of beefsteak tomatoes Judy had picked from their garden, the old Heritage variety. He's a potter and he also gave me a pottery dog made of charcoal grey, 'Gibsonite'. It sits. It stays. It lies down. It ups onto its haunches and begs. It even cocks its leg. And, if you blow through its mouth, it whistles. Gloriously goofy. It sits on my mantelpiece at home.

*   *   *

Leather-clad bikers are one of the white tribes of America. Over the years they have evolved from iconoclasts to rebels to outlaws to drug dealers to OAPs. The new generation of bikers are wealthy, middle class and still white as driven snow.

I'd noticed a seemingly large number of Harley Davidson-riding bikers, young and old, almost equally men and women, in Pepin, and now driving north there were more, at scenic overlooks above the Mississippi, having picnics, holding hands. Do you know how incongruous it is to see leather-clad bikers holding hands? North of Stockholm, their numbers noticeably increased, Willie Nelson lookalikes in squadrons of ten to twenty, red bandanas over balding heads, grey stubbly beards, all dressed in leathers, riding serious Harleys. Not all the bikers looked like Willie Nelson. Some looked like drop-out urban rabbis. The women were uniformly blonde, even the one African-American I saw.

Approaching Maiden Rock, on the road's narrow terrace between the river and the almost 700-foot-high bluffs to the east, traffic slowed to a crawl and there, parked on the highway and streets, filling the lawns of the riverfront park to shiny metallic capacity, surrounding a flagpole flying the Stars & Stripes like rows of gleaming hornets, were thousands of glistening, pristine Harleys, their black-clad riders milling in groups, drinking beer, eating pizza. I had to drive a mile north of Maiden Rock before I could find a place to park and, leaving Mace in the home, walk back past rows of Harleys two or three abreast on the road, all belching and farting in the traffic, slowly moving towards their destination. The bikers nodded, smiled or waved as they straggled past.

In town was a milling throng—eating, drinking, listening to music. If a biker bumped into me, I heard a gracious 'Excuse me'. The local church invited visitors to 'Bikers Breakfast on Sunday'. At Ole's Bar & Grill, bikers, all in shades, men with Zapata moustaches, women in chrome-studded leather, sunned themselves drinking Bud Light from plastic cups. A tanned couple—he with blond, highlighted, razor-cut hair, sporting a West Coast Choppers T-shirt, she in a small, strapless halter top and jeans, both wearing matching fringed black chaps—paraded as if it were Venice Beach, California. Walking back, now against the traffic, I was bombarded with constant questions and chatter.

188

'Is it like this up ahead?'

'Something happened up ahead?'

'Walked all this way and you didn't bring a guy a beer?'

This wasn't what I expected. In my long absence from America bikers had become gentrified.

Before leaving on this trip, I didn't know what to expect from Wisconsin. I'd never been here before and my image of it was much like south-western Ontario—dairy country. Parts are but it's gloriously more: a pleasing and, in an old-fashioned way, a pretty place where, it seems, nonconformity, ploughing your own furrow, still exists. The AGS *Wisconsin Guide* tells the story of a French Canadian trapper, Louis Massey, living near where I now was, who built a dugout and married an Indian woman. 'After quarrelling with her for 25 years, Massey built a separate dugout for his mate, and for the remaining 15 years of their lives they lived in close separation'. 'Close separation'. That's a brilliant description. Like the well-behaved bikers, unexpected.

*   *   *

I got lost in Minneapolis St Paul, as Steinbeck did, befuddled by 35W and 35E and I-694 that was part of I-494, and ring roads that overlap each other and a landscape which, wherever you looked, seemed the same as where you were. I was looking for Mall of America, to visit the Apple Store for computer supplies, but took I-94 by mistake. I think I should have taken the south branch of I-494, near 35W, or was it 35E? If I got to I-394, I knew I'd gone too far. I'm still not sure where I went wrong, but at least my route gave me the chance to pass Cretin Avenue. It felt like my spiritual home. Just outside the Twin Cities, a turtle had hunkered down halfway across the fast lane on I-94. No one was risking their own life to save it.

On a grey, showery, London-type of day, 50 degrees and damp, with arrows of Canada geese pounding the air, heading south, I drove to Sauk Center. Steinbeck had made a virtual pilgrimage here, to the birthplace of the novelist Sinclair Lewis, the first American to receive the Nobel Prize for Literature. Lewis wrote of the tribulations of life of the common man, a vein that Steinbeck mined equally well, leading to his Nobel Prize for Literature. It was too early on Sunday for me to visit the Sinclair Lewis Boyhood Home and Museum. Nor was the Sinclair Lewis Interpretive Center, sited between a Hardees and a $32 per night motel, open. I parked on Original Main Street, near its intersection with Sinclair Lewis Avenue, put on a jacket and tie and attended Sunday service at the local Lutheran Evangelical church. I sat near the back looking over a sea of blonde heads in front of me. After the service we gathered for donuts and coffee. I didn't start a conversation, nor did the congregants with the outsider. Nary a hello. Like the Amish children in Wisconsin.

Rather than follow Steinbeck's exact trail I drove a few miles further along I-94, to Alexandria, site of the Kensington Runestone Museum. I wanted to see this stone with runic inscriptions.

The runestone story, according to the AGS

190

Minnesota Guide, goes like this. In 1898 Olaf Ohman—one of the two million Swedes and Norwegians who emigrated to North America between 1850 and 1930—a farmer from Helsingland (a province in northern Sweden that produces old furniture that Julia much admires), while clearing a field for planting, found a stone tablet with a runic inscription carved on it, among the roots of a poplar tree stump. No one then knew what the marks were, nor could anyone read them. Ohman used the stone as a doorstop for one of his sheds.

Years later another Swede, Hjalmar Holand, chanced on the doorstop, recognised that the marks on the stone were 'runes'—old writing—and had the inscription translated by Nordic scholars:

Eight Goths [Swedes] and twenty-two Norwegians upon a journey of discovery from Vinland westward. We had a camp by two skerries (islands) one day's journey north of this stone. We were out fishing one day. When we returned home we found ten men red with blood and dead. A V M [*Ave Virgo Maria*] save us from evil.

On the edge of the stone was inscribed:
Have ten men by the sea to look after our vessel fourteen days' journey from this island. Year 1362.

Historians acknowledge that Scandinavian explorers visited North America almost 500 years before Christopher Columbus. For example, a Norse settlement has been excavated in

Newfoundland. Other Norse sagas recount visits further south on the Atlantic coast, to Vinland, but if the Kensington runestone were to be genuine, it would mean that by the fourteenth century Nordic explorers had penetrated to the heart of North America.

Now, there are quite a few Americans of Scandinavian descent rooting for this story. The museum—also a superb local heritage museum— not only exhibits the runestone, but also other ancient artefacts that would suggest a Nordic presence here almost seven hundred years ago. I spoke with the curator who, with some excitement, told me that the runestone was travelling to Stockholm in a month's time, to the Historiska Museet, the Museum of National Antiquities, and that hundreds of dignitaries, including the American ambassador, would be present for the opening of the exhibit. Just outside the museum is Ole, a statue of a Nordic lumberjack that adorned the Minneapolis pavilion at the New York World's Fair in 1964. Ole's presence reminded me that the Scandinavian sense of humour is broad and dry. If the runestone is an early practical joke, it's an extremely erudite and knowledgeable one.

*   *   *

When I was a veterinary student living in Guelph, Ontario, I enjoyed skipping lectures to attend farm auctions in nearby Mennonite country. The unique rural culture was fascinating and the items that came up for auction always unexpected: veterinary notebooks from the mid-1800s, public school texts from the same era, hand-cranked, wooden, wall telephones, cast-iron wood-burning stoves, drop-leaf tables. At the end of each auction quilts were sold for 'two bits'; that's twenty-five cents. I didn't have the eye to buy them. Just north of Pelican Rapids, listening to the urbane Minnesota sounds of Garrison Keillor's *Prairie Home Companion* on National Public Radio, I chanced on a roadside auction that reminded me of those auctions I attended forty years earlier.

Macy and I had hot dogs and mingled with what were mostly local farmers, studying, feeling, testing the lots to be auctioned. An attractive young woman—round-faced, make-up-less, long blonde hair parted in the middle and clinging to her charcoal-grey fleece—gave Macy a smile and a pet, felt burrs in her fur, sat her down between her legs and spent a quarter-hour picking out every single burr and seed. A wasted-looking bald man, with weedy, lank brown hair hanging over his ears, came over and asked if his dad could see Macy. We walked to a parked car where an unshaven, old, liver-spotted, bald man, with uncut, random white hair, untrimmed sideburns and a caterpillar moustache, sat. The son opened the door and his dad smiled, gently and thoroughly stroked Macy, and uttered unrecognisable gibberish. Dogs can be so good at unlocking closed doors.

Prices were good for buyers. A mounted 12-point mule deer head went for $60, white-tailed deer heads for $30 each. A fat pickerel, mounted on a backdrop of polyurethaned birch branches, cost a buyer $30. Scoped rifles went for an average of $300–$350, a cart wagon for $1250, and a fully restored doctor's buggy, complete with a fringe on top and a back isinglass window, for $1750.

There was an old home-made cedar canoe with pontoons—I guessed it was from the 1920s; and a perfect, small, early 1950s Evinrude outboard motor. If I lived in North America, other than the rifles, I would have bought them all.

*   *   *

Detroit Lakes, Minnesota, was more of a destination point for me than it was for Steinbeck. This is where Steinbeck spent a night and mused over failing to bring his American Guide Series guides to the states with him, 'the most comprehensive account of the United States ever got together', he called these volumes.

I'm embarrassed to say that I didn't know about this Roosevelt Administration project to provide work during the depression to unemployed writers. It's been called everything from 'the finest contribution to American patriotism that has been made in our generation' to 'Commie propaganda'. Compiled anonymously by some of the best writers in America—Studs Terkel and Saul Bellow contributed to the AGS *Illinois Guide*—and some of the most mediocre, the results were detested in some states where the printing plates were destroyed. First editions from the Dakotas now change hands for thousands of dollars, but it's still possible to buy 'reading copies' for most states, almost always ex-library editions, for under $20, sometimes under $10.

What is so entrancing about these books is that they inspect the ordinary. They give regional advice, recount regional fiction, tell tall tales, give calendars of events, offer local travel advice, reveal regional attitudes. The *Alabama Guide* tells me how to kill a possum—stand on a plank over its neck and pull hard on its tail. The *Mississippi Guide* tells the reader that the Mississippi Negro has 'a severely limited vocabulary', but those who 'know him well enough to accept his deficiencies, find him to be wise but credulous'. The *Massachusetts Guide* shows brave sympathy for Sacco and Vanzetti, executed for robbery and murder, saying, 'the determining factor in the case from start to finish was the affiliation of the two men with an unpopular minority group'.

Over 7500 writers were at one time or another on the Work Projects Administration (WPA) payroll. In each guide, local writers cover the climate, geology, palaeontology, flora and fauna of their state, discuss archaeology and Indian history, cover settler to modern history, and present-day—that is 1930s—agriculture, industry, transportation, industry, education, religion, newspapers, radio, sports, recreation and the arts. Major cities are described in detail, then each book finishes with usually around 20 tours through the state. In some guides, there are National Forest tours and canoe tours. Here in Minnesota, 15 different canoe trips are described.

The tours themselves are in many ways as valid today as they were 60 years ago. Travelling, as I try to do, along the old US highways, bypassing the interstates, reading the guides' trifling anecdotes, quirky diversions, vivid descriptions, innocent details—all of these have helped me form a clear picture of where I was and why it was as it now is. In other ways the guides are quaintly, sometimes embarrassingly, outdated, not just in fact but in

195

state of mind. African-American America is, to the writers, if referred to at all, a separate world, and that separation is taken for granted. 'Every Saturday is "Nigger Day" in the cotton regions,' states the *Alabama Guide*, 'when the week's store-buying is combined with much social small talk, courting and "funning".' Not just in the guides to the Deep South states, the text is often chilling.

These guides were, in a way, mass-produced, an epic undertaking lasting the better part of a decade. The results, however, are anything but. They are standardised only in that each covers the same subjects. How the topics are covered differs dynamically from state to state.

Detroit Lakes? Steinbeck was right. If he had had his guides with him, he would have had the answers to his questions.

The name of the town was derived from a word spoken by a French priest over 200 years ago. This missionary, standing on the shore of the lake with his French companions and Chippewa guides, commented on the distinct *detroit* (a strait or narrows). Henceforth, the Indians and white fur-traders employed that name for the immediate vicinity; 'Lakes' was added in 1927 as being characteristic of the district.

CHAPTER SIX

THE TRUE WEST

 There's nothing much now in Medina, North Dakota: Rose's Attic and a general store with signs in the window offering shoes, clothing, groceries, meats. The Northern Pacific Railroad runs through the heart of the town but doesn't stop any more, as it did with me many years before. I'd travelled through Medina in 1943, a foetus with my mother, on a train passing through on her way to Mandan to visit her doctor brother Reub. It was illegal during the war to take currency out of Canada. To provide my mother with spending money while in the States, my father, a florist, had hidden an American hundred-dollar bill in a corsage my mother wore, the bill covered by green floral tape.

Back at Moorhead, Minnesota, I hadn't realised that the little stream I crossed over was the mighty Red River and that I had arrived in Fargo, North Dakota, where Steinbeck felt the True West began. Beyond was a flat, dry landscape extending to the horizon, endless, symmetrical fields of sun-dried sunflowers, their heads drooped like millions of straw dolls all in mourning. Roadside signs advised, 'REDUCE OUR DEPENDENCE ON FOREIGN OIL. USE ND ETHANOL'.

The wide verges of the highway had been cut, raked and bound into round bales waiting to be collected. Thirty miles beyond Fargo, the road entered a 150-foot ascent out of what was once the continent's largest lake bed. Glacial Lake Agassiz, as it's called, was larger than the Great Lakes

198

combined. It formed at the end of the last ice age and poured its torrential waters down to the Gulf of Mexico, creating what would one day become the relatively small Mississippi River. Beyond the lakebed I drove onto the Drift Plain, into rolling terrain with, surprising to me, lots of lakes. I learned later that evening from Herb in the Decoy Bar that these lakes were created for duck hunters.

At Medina, I made a concerted but unsuccessful effort to rid us of the Amish horse auction houseflies that had been hitchhiking with us for over a week. I was unsuccessful, but Macy was pleased I hadn't eliminated her only interesting diversion while I was driving. The town has a campground with electric hook-ups. Two other vehicles were parked, hunters from Wisconsin and Minnesota.

There were no signs of life in Medina, not even a car on the solitary road. I went to the Decoy Bar, the only place open. The customers—men in their thirties to fifties, eating pizza, drinking beer, watching football on TV—stopped and looked as I walked in and sat at the bar.

'Here huntin'?' asked the bartender.

'Jes passin' thru,' I drawled, as I pulled the peak of my camouflage baseball cap down over my eyes, cracked my knuckles, flexed my shoulder blades, shifted to break wind, stretched my legs, and ordered a beer and a pizza.

Herb, sitting to my left, was slouched over the bar. He looked at me with bloodshot eyes and talked to me incomprehensibly, with translation provided by the bartender.

'He wants to roll you for the next round,' the bartender explained. I rolled the dice.

'You do it again. Three rolls. The most of the highest numbers wins.'

I rolled again, then again. Five fives. Herb couldn't beat that. He bought me another beer.

We talked, though I didn't much understand anything Herb said. Then he picked up the dice and we rolled them once more. Five fours. I won again and he bought another round.

We talked some more and now I was picking up a bit of what he was saying. Herb farmed 4000 acres; cattle and wheat. He offered to roll again. I'd had more than enough to drink, especially on an empty stomach. My frozen pizza was still unthawing and cooking on a rotating contraption behind the bar. Beside that contraption were handwritten signs. 'Bar bills now due'. 'Fried steak on Thursday 6.30–9.30'. There was a ceramic penis, dollar bills taped to the walls with messages written on them, a truck calendar and an old, dinging cash register.

'What do you do in the winter, Herb?' I asked, and Herb performed an experienced wanking motion with his right hand. The bartender dropped the dice in front of me. 'Herb, I owe you at least one. Let's roll for the next round.' I knew the odds were now on his side. So did the bartender. We rolled the dice. Four sixes. He bought me another. The pizza arrived, but it was either inedible or I was already too full on four beers. I ate some and asked the bartender to offer the rest to her other customers. They nodded their thanks and we rolled the dice again, and again I won.

Now I was getting to understand what Herb was saying. My age and married, with his wife back at the ranch, Herb has one son pig-farming in Iowa and another working in Bismarck. There's no one but Herb to look after the ranch.

'Them that irrigate'll survive. Them that don't, don't.' Maybe he said 'won't'.

'You irrigate, Herb?' I asked, but I can't remember his answer or much more after that.

We rolled for another beer, and then another and each time he lost. Some time before closing I must have left the Decoy Bay and found my way back to Macy. I'm not sure, but I think I slept that night on her bed, nuzzled up to my hot dog.

Next morning was sunny, fresh, cool and invigorating. There was a heavy dew on the windows. I showered, ate and departed onto a stretch of old US 10, heading west out of Medina. This was a truly wonderful road, rolling with the landscape, the thinnest of ribbons over an endlessly undulating landscape of tawny, golden fields. Flights of Canada geese passed above. Three squadrons flew at a chance angle, making a perfect VW symbol, a lofty advertisement but with no one but me to see it. The old road ended in a flooded coulée less than fifteen miles out of town. I backtracked a few miles to an interchange and joined I-94. Macy loved I-94. Straight as a pool cue.

In Bismarck, the state capital, on the reeded banks of the Missouri River we chanced upon a pet cemetery, unmarked but for the small concrete slabs in the grass, imprinted with either the outline of a dog or a cat, labelled with aluminium tag markers and epitaphs. 'LadyBug—1969–1979. She was a Lady'. 'Keoh, 1976–1985. Although you are beyond our sight and touch you are never beyond our love'. 'Jet, 1967, Rev. D.R. Cochran'. 'Snoopy,

1967–1984'. Beside two graves, each marked with fifteen-inch-high crosses made of white and pink plastic flowers, on the sun-dappled grass, among the willow and oak trees, Macy found a stick, lay down by the banks of the mighty Missouri and chewed.

*　　　*　　　*

Across the Missouri was flinty Mandan: railroad yards with a red brick station house still as it was 60 years ago, where Yanktonai Sioux performed native dances for the benefit of passing tourists and where my mother bought an Indian beaded handbag with her contraband dollars, a bag she gave to me on a recent birthday. On the other side of the long Main Street is a row of red brick stores and buildings, some with false fronts. I'd moved from my third time zone to my fourth and also back in time, to Gene Autry, Hopalong Cassidy and Roy Rogers. To me, this was the real West, the true West. Why on earth had my urban uncle, a Mayo Clinic superstar, headlined in 1920s newspapers throughout North America for his groundbreaking new tonsillectomy technique, ended up here? How did he even know that 'here' existed?

I was curious to see if there were vestiges of Uncle Reub's stay in Mandan. This favourite uncle of mine was, ultimately, a self-made failure. At five foot three inches and with thick glasses, he lacked the presence of a bigger man but his intelligence and charisma were Olympian. A serial monogamist—his marriages and loves were countless—he had an endearing, enduring and

202

enchanting ability to make you think you were the only person in the world who really mattered to him. As boys—he lived with us after one of his nervous breakdowns—he'd told my brother and me he had deeded land he owned near Mandan to us. We assumed it eventually had been confiscated for non-payment of taxes.

I visited the library at City Hall but their records only went back to the 1960s. The librarian suggested I visit the Monroe County Tax Equalization Bureau, across the road, where there was a register of land deeds. I explained to the receptionist what information I was looking for.

'I'm sorry, we don't have records that old. They've gone to the archives of the State Historical Society in the state capital, but Dr Wheeler, he's the county coroner, he might be able to help.'

I asked why she thought a coroner might be helpful and she explained, 'Well, Dr Wheeler's 95 years old. He's been a doctor here since the 1930s. He might have known your uncle.'

She gave me his telephone number and address and, as he lived only minutes away in the hills rising behind Main Street, now covered in 1950s homes, I decided to make a cold call. I drove to his home, parked outside and knocked on the door where there was a sign, 'In case of fire, save the cat first'. A bald, cadaverous, liver-spotted, stern-looking man, in slippers, pyjamas and robe, answered the door.

'I'm sorry to arrive unannounced,' I started, but he was already opening the screen door and beckoning me in.

'Come in. Come in, young man.'

He shuffled into the living room with me following and I explained my visit. 'My uncle, Reub Breslin, practised medicine here during World War II.'

'Yes, yes, I remember him well. I don't believe we ever actually shared cases. A good doctor. A fine man.'

As we spoke, his cat inspected my legs. Dr Wheeler was impressed that his cat had not gone to hide.

'Tammy's usually leery of strangers. He was left in our backyard. We went to Alaska for a week and when we got back home we were told we'd have to change his name to Tommy. The woman who looked after him noticed his true vocation. He rules this roost. He gets me up at least once a night to feed him.'

Before I could say anything, and I can be reasonably fast on the draw, Dr Wheeler pressed me with his unquenchable curiosity.

'Where do you live? Where are you going now? Are you going to visit Medora? What is your profession? What is your speciality? Are you alone? Is your wife a vet too? Are your parents alive? What does your father do?'

When I answered that my still-alive father, at 96, was still driving he replied, 'Good for him. Don't interfere with that. Have any of your children followed you into veterinary medicine?'

When I answered in the negative, he responded, 'I don't advise kids to go into medicine. Medicine isn't fun any more. Too much government interference. Too much messing around from the insurance companies. Mind you, at my age, the only medicine they allow me to practise is on dead people.'

Dr Wheeler's wife joined us. He turned to her.

'Call Ange to come over to meet Breslin's relative.'

While waiting for Ange to arrive, Dr Wheeler told me—as a vet I might be interested to know—that so far this year there had been 780 confirmed cases of West Nile Virus in people, in North Dakota, including one death.

'The mosquitoes carry the virus in their saliva glands and transmit it to birds while feeding on their blood. The birds remain viraemic long enough before they die to pass it on to other mosquitoes. Of course, we're just dead-end hosts, no use to the virus. Horses are the same. Do you know how many horses have been infected?'

I answered that I didn't.

'Neither do I.'

Dr Wheeler mentioned that he drives up to Duluth, Minnesota, to go fishing.

'Still fishing?' I said, impressed with his vigour.

'Do you mean, do I "yet fish" or "still-water fish"?' he responded.

'We have good salmon fishing, when they're biting. As a vet you know that each stream has its own chemical composition. It comes from minerals, plants and chemicals. We can't smell it but salmon can. They learn that odour soon after hatching. At the hatcheries the fingerlings are exposed to morpholine. Seven years later they return to streams where the DLR has added morpholine to the fish ladders. That means they can take the eggs and milts, hatch them in the hatchery and train salmon to return to chosen streams.'

Angeline arrived, a small, composed, white-haired, perfect prairie Presbyterian. She was married to Reub's dry cleaner, Barney, who had a store at the Lewis & Clark Hotel where, I learned, my uncle lived during his years here.

'Oh, Dr Breslin, such a good friend of ours years ago. He married Frankie, the bank owner's daughter. (I knew his second wife only as Francis.) After he left, we kept in touch. When my husband and I attended a Presbyterian meeting in New York, Dr Breslin came down from Toronto to see us. I tried to keep in touch. I spoke to his sister. That must be your mother. But I lost contact with him. Can you tell me what happened?'

My favourite uncle's eventual decline was painfully sad. His last wife, Cynthia, a stunning blonde 40 years his junior, suffered from an intermittent and overwhelming death wish. It was an unexpectedly happy and successful marriage— perhaps his best—but on many occasions Reub's psychiatric abilities were called upon to prevent suicide attempts or to revive his wife. One day Cynthia succeeded in killing herself and Reub disintegrated. He chose to live the remaining decade of his life in a psychiatric home. I spared Ange the detail.

'I have few regrets in life,' she told me, 'but I regret losing contact with your uncle.'

I understood her feelings. I asked if any of them knew how he came to live in Mandan. None had an answer to my question. Even as a vibrant young man, already his demons were chasing him to this most empty corner of America.

*   *   *

For weeks I'd been meaning to service my rig and have the faulty generator checked.

'Hey, that's the Cadillac of motorhomes, even today,' said the knowledgeable man on reception at the Chevrolet GMC service centre.

While the oil was changed and other fluids checked, Mace and I climbed a nearby hill topped with a high transmission tower. On the steep descent, she developed a severe limp. She'd punctured her paw with a cactus needle. Her first cactus needle! I was thrilled for her.

Back at the service centre, the receptionist was making countless calls, trying to find someone in North Dakota who understood 30-year-old generators. She found Clarence, who explained over the phone that my problem was either a fuse or a circuit board. We found the fuses. They were OK. That meant I needed a new circuit board and that would have to wait until I found an Onan generator specialist. They checked and the nearest, in the direction I was heading in, was on the Pacific coast, in Portland, Oregon.

'Going to Medora?' Clarence asked.

We left Mandan on County Road 139—what was once US 10. The sky remained cloudless. The road, another linear beauty, was deserted. I stopped for a walk through the tawny fields near an isolated and abandoned 'little house on the prairie'. We strolled down a long track to the train line, arrow-straight, cutting through the hills from east to west. We walked along the two parallel bars of iron extending to the eastern horizon, reflecting sky-blue in the afternoon sun, hopping from tie to tie. In the distance, to the north, a lone cowboy rode his horse along a ridge. I blinked but it was real, not a mirage. County 139 eventually became a dirt road. I didn't want to kick gravel and damage the paintwork on my home, so I headed back to super-straight I-94, tied the steering wheel to the driver's seat, set cruise control at 65, went back, lay down on the sofa and read. All right, I lie. But you couldn't imagine a straighter road. Nodding donkey oil wells sat on the horizon. There was scarcely a tree in sight. I passed bale-lifters and flatbed 18-wheelers picking up round hay bales from the verges. What are the economics of cutting, raking and baling an unending narrow field over 300 miles long? I watched the headlight of an oncoming freight train snake around bends on the horizon, heading back east to where I'd been. It was a cinemascopic, David Lean moment. And, I was heading for Medora, because that's where everyone in North Dakota expected me to go.

*　　　*　　　*

Three hundred and thirty-two miles from Fargo, the expansive, gently rolling prairies of the Missouri Plateau end—abruptly, malevolently, frighteningly—in a conflagration of seared gorges, bare ridges and grotesque buttes. Down the buttes' sides, exposed by years of erosion, are coloured strata—taupe, muddy-brown, brick-red, salmon-pink, fire-ash grey, bilious yellow—sandstone and shale seabed deposits, a visual recapitulation, before my eyes, of Cenozoic, even Mesozoic times.

The highway makes a 300-foot twisting descent, through ravines and valleys, to Medora on the east

A 'LITTLE HOUSE ON THE PRAIRIE', NORTH DAKOTA

bank of the Little Missouri River, the entrance to Theodore Roosevelt National Park.

While sitting, drinking a beer, watching the colours of the canyon walls change from brown to indigo to black, Larry—bearded, roly-poly, gregarious—walked over from a neighbouring campsite and joined us. I'd noticed the Alaska plates on his van and knew from the tag he was a veteran.

'Veteran'. That's an oddly American word. In the States I have to be careful when I introduce myself as a vet. 'Where did you serve?' I've been asked, more than once. In Britain, people, when asked, call themselves 'former'. I've worked with a colleague who is a 'former Marine commando'. He served in Korea. Others use the word 'retired'. I've employed a career army man, now 'retired', as a veterinary practice manager. The words used in Britain signify the past, that you 'once were' but now you've moved on. Here, in the States, the word 'veteran' has an amplified meaning, so much so that Larry's licence plate tells the world that, at some time in his life, he was in the military. You 'once were' but 'forever are'.

I asked Larry where he served and he told me Vietnam.

'I'm a farm boy from Ohio. I was drafted into the army. In Vietnam I was good at what I did. I liked it.'

Larry explained that he liked it so much, when his time was up and he returned to the States, he asked to go back to Vietnam.

'When I got back here, I didn't fit in. I looked at people and thought, it's not them I'm killing for.' I needed to get back. That's where I felt at home. It was the most intense experience of my life. I didn't know you could live with such intensity. The problem was I could never equal that intensity, the camaraderie with Tom and Ed and Mike. I moved to Montana, got married, but my marriage failed. How could it succeed when nothing equalled the love I felt for my guys in 'Nam? I moved on to Alaska. Do you know there's more vets in Alaska per capita than in any other state? Got married again and got interested in hunting. I killed good. One day I was out hunting and saw a bear and I couldn't kill it. I went back, told my wife I'd killed my last bear, and gave her a list of all my guns to sell on the radio. I had counselling. Now I shoot with a camera.'

What type of shell shock—post-traumatic stress disorder—Gulf War Syndrome—call it what you like—is going to affect the kids in Iraq? Vietnam veterans like Larry served in an unpopular war. They got scarred—seeing mutilated bodies, being shot at, knowing healthy buddies who got maimed or killed—as exposure to any war scars. They returned to a country embarrassed by defeat in Vietnam. There was no Heroes Welcome. And that scarred them too. What's going to happen to the kids in Iraq, where the expected popular uprising to plant democracy in the heart of the Middle East, the reason they were given for going to war, has become a think-tank pipe-dream?

*   *   *

Late September, but it was a surprise how much autumn flower was still in bloom. Among the blue-grey, silver sage were purple blazing star and

211

purple asters, but they were dominated by the yellows of snakeweed, gumweed, golden asters and ever-present goldenrod. Macy and I had the park to ourselves. We went where we chose.

We yomped over white ground encrusted with small bits of brick-red shale, eroded by rain and wind from a nearby butte. This was scoria, clay burnt into brick-red shale by centuries-old, burning coal veins. Macy nosed the ground, rolled and ran, then sighted movement near the base of the butte. She raced up its almost perpendicular side, chasing a ground squirrel. Seconds later she was at its top, 120 feet above me, standing alert on a promontory. I envied her view and wondered how she'd get down. She did, slowly and carefully.

On we walked, past stumps of petrified trees, over petrified logs. A hawk floated above us. There were no trails, but the ground was hard and the sun on the horizon told us where to head for when we turned back towards our home. This was a perfect time of year to travel. If we had come here during the summer season, we would have been restricted to approved parking and been accompanied by throngs of other tourists. Macy found a rib bone and, tail held high, tossed it in the air, then carried it back to her home, dropping it on her bed inside. I moved it away and was surprised by its weight. Looking closer, I saw it was petrified wood in the exact shape of a beef rib.

There's a burning coal vein a mile or so off the paved road and I drove there, but its parking area was occupied by a herd of milling buffalo. There was no way I, let alone Macy, could leave our vehicle. I parked and gazed at the grazers. One stood out, separate from the rest, a massive male, who looked like he weighed a ton. The first French explorers, seeing these magnificent creatures, called them, *'les boeufs'*, 'the beefs', or 'the oxen'. Over the years that word got modified. An 'l' was added and it became 'buffle'. Then it got Inspector Clouseau'd into 'buffelo' and, finally, 'buffalo'. Plains buffalo got wiped out in the great hunts of the late 1800s. Their hides made good insulating coats. Traffic cops in Winnipeg, Manitoba, still wore them when I visited there in the 1960s. By the twentieth century less than 300 wild bison remained on the American plains. These, before me, were descendants of bison reintroduced into the badlands.

Back on the main park road I saw a car, the first all day. We walked a ridge above a deep, narrow canyon, leading to a broad elbow in the Little Missouri River. I munched on slices of watermelon and, as I was about to throw the rind over the edge of the precipice, I remembered that (a) Mace likes watermelon; (b) Mace retrieves. Walking back to the GMC, I noticed there was fresh buffalo manure splashed in its wheel arches. That reminded me the vehicle needed a good wash. It hadn't been cleaned since Toronto.

*   *   *

Steinbeck says he could have stayed forever in Montana. I'd never been here before, but was soon to learn that what he fell in love with still exists, what he called the 'time to pause in their occupations to undertake the passing art of neighbourliness'.

I stopped in Wibaux to tank up my home. As I

paid, the gas station woman, white-haired, grandmotherly, a woman who would have been in her thirties when Steinbeck passed through this town, said, 'You're a nice-looking young man. You know, visitors say, "It's beautiful here in Montana, but how do you live here when there are so few people to talk to?" And I tell 'em, "That's just the way we like it. You can be your own good company." So, you've had French vanilla cappuccino. You know that's our favourite here. You like it? A day like today makes you feel good, doesn't it. Sunshine. Fresh air. That's quite a vehicle you've got there. Restore it yourself?'

Personally welcomed to Montana I continued on the intermittent vestiges that remain of Steinbeck's old US 10, often renamed Frontage Road, paralleling the newer highway.

Just before Miles City, US 12 meets old US 10. The AGS *Montana Guide* describes a horse abattoir at this junction.

The horse abattoir was established to make profitable use of the thousands of horses that cluttered the range after farm mechanisation and other causes had reduced the market for horses. It was fully equipped with modern slaughterhouse machinery. Horses were driven in from large corrals, shot, skinned, boned and converted into a kind of inspired corn beef, much of which was shipped to Belgium.

'A kind of inspired corn beef'. I wish I knew who wrote that. I drove past the site, now an auto dismantler's.

214

Old US 10 into Fort Miles is lined with dereliction, motels and businesses all boarded shut. Some motels have been converted into long skinny homes. Downtown, at Ray's Second-Hand, I met Ray, 85 years old and still a big, erect man. Jeff, his son, sells second-hand furniture next door. I wanted to buy a needle and thread to sew a split seam in my trousers.

'I don't sell needles and thread,' Ray explained, 'but I've got needles and thread if you want to use them.'

Ray's Second-Hand is on the respectable north side of Main Street, where buffalo-hide buyers, bankers and pawnbrokers once kept shop. The south side was devoted to saloons, brothels and gambling joints. While I sewed, I learned that Ray had cattle-ranched in Iowa and South Dakota.

'They told me to go to the bank. I could have been bigger, but I didn't want a banker nosing around my business. My neighbour had to hide his boat at my place when the banker called. After I retired, I still ranched. Small. Twenty pair. Never liked to sell 'em. Gentle animals, specially the heifers. Even the bulls. Beef bulls are gentle, not like dairy bulls.'

Ray asked where I was heading and I explained I was travelling with my dog.

'Best dog I ever had, she was a blue heeler. She was trained to leave the turkeys alone, but one night she accidentally got locked in the turkey shed. They were all dead next day, every single one of them. I beat that dog with a dead turkey until I regretted what I was doing, but that dog never bothered a turkey again.'

I asked how he moved from ranching to the

215

second-hand business in Montana.

'My wife. She got interested in flea markets, in collectables. Just went from there. Collecting to selling. A few years back I couldn't give oak furniture away. Now it's all they want. Ranching's changed. It's different now. Californians are buying up all the land. Ted Turner buys everywhere, then just puts buffalo on his land.'

'Not much wrong with that,' I replied.

' 'Cept neighbours' taxes go up because their land is now taxed at what Turner paid for his.'

Ray had racks of deer antlers in his front windows and on the walls. My daughter Tamara asked me to bring back moose antlers but those I'd seen in Maine were too pricey. A few bucks here would make both Ray and Tamara happy. I bought four racks but then couldn't resist the 76-inch-long longhorns, leather-wrapped at the bone, mounted on oak. I bought them too.

*   *   *

What a difference there is, travelling on the interstate or taking the old road. On the old, narrow highway, a pencil thin line with no shoulders—the mildest incursion into nature— you're part of your surroundings. Mailboxes, rows of starlings on telephone wires, buildings both used and derelict, rough tracks into fields, beehives, scrubby shrubs, livestock lying or grazing in fields near the road, graveyards for people, graveyards for pick-up trucks, it's all part of a human landscape. On the nearby interstate you see wonderful vistas, but there's no human element. You're abstracted from life as it's lived.

Near Reed Point I stopped and we hiked over the railroad tracks to the fast-flowing, clear waters of the Yellowstone River. Mace rolled on the remains of a dead deer, then apple-bobbed in the shallows. I skipped stones. A turkey vulture wheeled in the air above. It was another clear, blue, cloudless day. Across the river, the aspens were touched by autumn, their leaves an almost sulphurous-yellow in the morning sun. And beyond, suddenly, unexpectedly, majestically, were the Crazy Mountains. Traces of snow dusted the peaks. I'd reached the Rockies.

At Big Timber I decided to give my big buddy a shampoo. A couple of trucks were already occupying the two wash slots at the truck wash, but there was a vet's clinic, the Big Timber Veterinary Clinic, next door, so I wandered over to say hello.

Bill Langford, the vet, was off on calls. His mother, a diminutive, deeply tanned, sprightly, grey-haired woman in small, oval, gold-framed glasses, wearing a turquoise sweat shirt with an image of a running wolf on it, was holding the fort. The charm with which she simply said 'Hello' made me want to spend the day with her.

Bill's clinic was a Western-American variation of James Herriot's 1950s Yorkshire Dales veterinary surgery, a Hollywood version of what a lone, Western livestock vet's place should be: a bulletin board with horses for sale; posters on livestock diseases; chairs piled high with cardboard cartons holding more boxes containing ropes, gloves and other paraphernalia; glass cabinets containing old cardboard medicine boxes, and a front desk display cabinet with boxes of large syringes and varieties of horse and livestock wormers. Macy was invited to investigate the clinic and she did so with aplomb. She reappeared from a back room, ears perked. 'Smells like home. I like it.'

Bill was expected back in an hour, so I washed the GMC, then drove down to the river for a walk. A white pick-up truck arrived and I just knew the driver was a vet. Bill was a rumple-faced, ruddy-faced man in work jeans and work shirt. He'd been in rural practice in Montana now for 25 years, almost twice as long as the average for work in such a harsh climate. 'It ain't easy. More than once I've been knocked unconscious, and you know what the rancher says when you come to? "OK, Doc? We've got some more cattle to do."'

It was a busy day for Bill, but his last call was to his brother Greg's, back near Reed Point, which I'd passed through earlier in the day. He asked if I'd like to come along. Bill's father, Bill senior, was there then we arrived, a leathery, lined, stooped man. I was surprised when Bill told me he was only 79. Like most livestock farmers or ranchers, he limped from a lifetime of physical injuries. But he stooped as well because he'd developed COPD, chronic obstructive pulmonary disease. Hay dust. I must have looked startled when Bill told me his dad's age and he continued, 'We've got a saying here. "Montana's a beautiful woman but she's hard on her men."'

Greg's daughter, Joan, hopped off the yellow Cat tractor she was driving, pulled off her work gloves, shook hands and said, 'Hello.' Here was another Hollywood image, an athletic, blue-eyed, blonde cowgirl—no make-up, fresh and beautiful—in jeans, hide work gloves, sun visor and zipped sweat top, here to punch cows.

218

Greg and his wife Vicky arrived and Bill set to work pregnancy testing. He rolled up his right sleeve, revealing an arm the width of a fire hydrant. 'It wasn't this size when I first started this work,' he said. I was surprised he wore soft-toed slipper-like shoes. 'Steel toes are dangerous. Cow steps on them and they can cut your toes off. If I get stepped on in these, it all just spreads out.' While Joan and Grandma punched the cows down the wooden chute, I operated the metal 'squeeze', the 'crush' as it's called in England, catching each cow by its neck as it tried to run through, then pushed a wooden plank behind her to prevent her backing out. Bill, gloved and lubricated, then got to work. Most of the cows were pregnant. Bill's massive arm made checking spring heifers a bit trying for both the heifer and the vet. I offered to help. I had the longest, thinnest arms in my class and was the only male student who could do pregnancy checks in sheep. Bill politely thanked me and explained he wanted to get through this herd as fast as possible.

When Bill found a dry cow, one that wasn't pregnant, he had me cut a straight line of hair off the bottom of its tail. These cows were separated from the rest and would go to auction. I threw the matts of hair away, where each mass was pounced on by the white, fluffball ten-week-old-pup Joan had brought with her. The pup's mother, Tammy, a Maltese-poodle-Yorkshire terrier-shih tzu cross, was relaxing nearby. While I wondered how all these little dogs got to meet in the mountains of Montana, Greg walked over and said, 'Wanna go fishin' t'marrah?'

During the last weeks I'd been gradually

219

reverting back to North American, but there was still that part of Britain in me that made me, in my mind, take a step back and say, 'But we've only just met.' I controlled that urge and took up his offer.

Like my summer cottage in Ontario, their house was a very personal home. Greg had removed the bark from each of the foot-thick logs it was constructed from and Vicky had sanded and varnished each one of them. With the help of a professional log building specialist, they had constructed their home log by log. Inside, Macy investigated each room until she met one of the cats, One-Eye, who told her to piss off.

The first freeze had set in weeks earlier. On chairs were cardboard boxes filled with green tomatoes, chillies and squashes from their garden. On other chairs were baskets of folded washing, piles of books, heaps of cushions from outdoor furniture, dog blankets, road atlases, stacks of magazines. It was a warm, welcoming home. Vicky grated red potatoes from the garden, grabbed a ton of meat from the fridge and cooked up steak, hash browns, vegetables and garlic bread for dinner.

Still with his sun visor on—he never took it off, inside or out, during the days I stayed with his family—Greg had questions. He wanted to know where I'd been, what the land was like. He seemed itchy, thinking about moving. Vicky was more forthright. She wanted to move where the growing season was longer. Here, she told me, you were lucky to see much more than a hundred days between the last frost of spring and the first frost of fall. Greg had other interests. Without sounding like he was prying, he asked me what Britain thought of the Iraq war and I explained that while the majority opposed British participation, they acceded because the United States asked for help and when it came to the crunch, the hearts of Britons are with Americans.

'I just don't think it's right that the vice president's old company gets all those contracts,' Greg said. Later, discussing the war itself, he said, 'You hit somebody. You knock him down. And he gets angry at you and so does his son.'

Mace and I were offered a room in their home, but we opted to sleep in our own home. That night a strong, warm, Chinook wind descended from the eastern slopes of the Crazy Mountains. I slept with the windows open and my throat turned to caustic sand as the dry, hot air blasted through the screens. Macy got up and drank from her water bowl repeatedly. Next morning Vicky made pancakes and bacon served with home-made chokecherry sauce, followed by tea. Grandpa Bill arrived and while he and Joan collected grasshoppers into Mountain Dew and Dr Pepper cans, Macy and I walked the fields around their home. I learned later that day that if you're trout fishing in Montana, don't forget your grasshoppers.

I'd thought we were going to fish in the nearby Yellowstone River, but Greg wanted to take me somewhere special, high in Gallatin National Forest, to his favourite spot on an isolated portion of the Boulder River. Joan, Grandpa and I drove into the great forest on the Montana side of Yellowstone National Park. Tammy sat on Joan's lap, leaning most of her body out the front window, occasionally shouting instructions. We passed hot

221

springs and Grandpa explained they were still fine, but all closed by public health people. He told us of climbing as a youth to the top of the highest peak in the Crazy Mountains, with only a lariat rope to help him. We passed a field of sheep, guarded by two llamas, and he reminisced how he used to run cattle in these mountains, how he trailed sheep in and trailed sheep out. Today, he explained, those sheep would be rounded up by four-wheelers and brought out by truck.

We passed a 'Posted' sign and Grandpa commented, 'Private land now. That was good fishing.' Then he regaled us with great fishing stories. He said he and his buddies used to give the Norwegians a hard time but they were good-natured about it, that the Finnish girls were real good-lookers but they'd only look at Finns, and that 'That guy we've got in Washington could sure use Thatcher right now.' He told us his best horse was so fast and so strong, he could hunt from her and tie a deer over her. We passed a field and he told me that's where he lost Freckles, his dog. 'Brought a colt back and tied her down and next morning there were Freckles and the colt together.' He told me that old-timers working up here might not see anyone for 60 days. 'They'd get lonesome, real lonesome.' He talked about cutting trails through the forest using jackasses to carry supplies, how he always carried a .22 rifle for bear and moose, and that today there were more predators than ever.

'There's lions in the brush next to the forest. Bears too. Neighbour lost seven calves this spring to bears. Drought's forced bears down from the forest. But it's those wolves in Yellowstone. That's the problem. They're s'posed to stay in the park but there's more out, in Montana and Idaho, than there are in, hundreds of 'em. Them and the drought drove white tails and elk out of the park. The lions and bears just followed.'

When I was at veterinary college, just after Steinbeck travelled through Montana, Ontario still had a $75 bounty on wolves. They were numerous in the province and were thought to be troublesome. Here in the American North-West they'd been extinct for some time, but in the early 1990s it was decided to reintroduce wolves into Yellowstone Park.

In Ontario, people eventually took against the wolf bounty. The *Toronto Daily Star* should claim credit. That paper gave front-page photo coverage to a story of teenagers on their snowmobile chasing a wolf for over an hour on winter ice until it could run no more, killing it by repeatedly running it over with their machine, and then claiming the $75 bounty. Listening to wolf howls is now a summer tourist attraction in Algonquin Park, just north of our summer cottage. It's the same here. Yellowstone tourists love it. They don't see the local ranchers' dead stock.

'See them lodgepole pine? Covered in resin? That's a defence. Mountain pine beetles killin' 'em. You see sawdust around the base of the tree and you know it's infected. The beetles carry a fungus. Plugs the water gettin' up the sapwood. Tree fades and the needles turn that red colour. See them over there? Needles fall off and the tree's dead. Beetles like old trees like these, over a hundred years old. Ones more than eight inches wide. Better food. Better bark. More protection.

223

But they got low resistance.'

Grandpa Bill's father left school when he was eight. He'd left school at twelve. Uneducated in the classic sense, here was a wise and knowledgeable and curious man. If he lived in Japan, where people with personal skills can receive national acknowledgement, he'd be designated a Living Monument.

At a bridge over the narrow rushing waters of the Boulder River, Grandpa Bill practised casting, while Joan broke out our lunch. His arthritis compelled him, with a little reluctance, to fish in nearby waters and so, using his fluorescent pink plastic cane for support and with a wicker fishing box strapped over his shoulder, he descended to an open bank on the river just below the bridge, while Joan took me through the light-dappled forest, over fallen trees, through spongy deer moss, up river.

This stretch of the Boulder River is narrow, with heavily forested riverbanks making it hard, sometimes impossible to reach the river. The river itself is, as you'd expect, littered with boulders from the size of footballs to automobiles. They're slick and the river runs fast over those that are submerged. This is a tough stretch of river to wade into to fish.

Joan knew where she wanted to go. She cast her line a few times into deep shaded pools below rapids by the far bank, then didn't hesitate to walk further upstream to other stretches of water. I was always downstream and seeing her standing on a boulder in the river, in an oversized quilted shirt, her hair pulled back in a simple ponytail, lodgepole pines behind her in a backdrop of sun-speckled variegated greens, turquoise-blue sky above, her cast line catching the sun's light, drifting slack above the sparkling water, Tammy sitting by her side, I thought it one of the most serenely beautiful sights I'd ever seen.

We gradually moved upstream, Joan ensuring I baited my line carefully so that the 'hopper disguised all the hook's metal. When she found a deep and accessible pool she suggested I fish there. I hooked a grasshopper on my line, cast, and felt a hit. The 'hopper was gone. I hooked another, and felt another light hit. I left the line slack then as I felt the slightest tension, I had a fish on my line, played it, landed a ten-inch rainbow trout and proudly took pictures, all of which I accidentally deleted when I dumped the day's photos in my laptop computer that evening.

We fished for a good part of the afternoon, then returned to the car where Grandpa, who'd caught a Yellowstone cutthroat, was talking with Greg and Vicky. Ranch needs had delayed their joining us earlier. We sat by the road and talked farming.

Greg has 6000 acres, and a California buyer wanting it. 'He says we can stay in the old house, he'll buy me a new Dodge Ram each year and we'll keep the fences painted and the grass cut. No stock. He don't want stock.' Greg's neighbour sold out to a California buyer who wanted a Montana ranch. The buyer privately paved the local county road past his ranch. Greg was unhappy. 'Cars drive past fast now. They're a danger to my cattle if any get loose.'

Greg explained he wasn't alone with the same problem. 'Joan wants to ranch but there's no future in ranchin'. What do you do when the value of your

THE BOULDER RIVER, MONTANA

land shoots up so high you make more by sellin' it than you do by usin' it? The government don't help. They don't work for the farmer like they do up in Alberta. They work for big business.'

Vicky's family had moved across the border to ranch in Canada. 'They've had the same drought. Seven years. They took the compulsory government insurance and got paid $40,000. Then the rain came and the rape could be harvested for silage, and they sold it for $30 a ton and the government let them keep that. My insurers refused to pay and we had no crop to harvest.'

I asked whether NAFTA, the North America Free Trade Agreement, helped.

'Everyone knows that's for big business. I could buy a new Dodge pick-up in Canada for 30,000, Canadian, but I can't 'cause the American car dealers lobbied Washington. Big business can import Argentinean cattle into Halifax, keep 'em there for ten days, get Canadian papers for 'em, then bring 'em cross the border. No taxes. Just undercuts the ranchers.'

All the while, fishing or talking, Macy worked the woods and riverbank, drinking its sparkling water, rolling on moss, chewing on sticks. As the sun moved behind the trees we headed back to the ranch. Lower down, white tail deer were in abundance, grazing alfalfa in irrigated fields. Grandpa saw antelope in a distant field. Joan went all wistful, 'I like antelope. They're so pretty . . . They're real good eat'n'.' Later on she asked, 'Do you cut your own Christmas tree? I love Christmas. It lasts here from December to February.' I'd noticed the fairy lights were still in their windows.

The family took me to Big Timber for a dinner

of burgers and fries, then back to the ranch. Macy took off after 'giant squirrels'. Some white tails had been grazing only yards from where we parked at the ranch house, but she returned within half an hour. We talked more. Vicky was enamoured by information in the AGS *Montana Guide*, calling Greg and Joan to look at sections. She read the populations of the local towns in 1940—300, 300, 400. Today, there weren't enough kids to populate a single school in the region.

'Yep, Canada sounds good,' Greg said. 'I like dry cold. Don't like the wet. Those Canadians sure are tough. Twenty below and the kids are out there in T-shirts play'n' hockey.' Greg's mind was wandering north. Vicky wanted a longer growing season. Whichever way they went, I was a passer-by seeing a way of life gently winding down.

*   *   *

Steinbeck had entered Yellowstone Park from Livingston, then backtracked out when Charley cursed and snarled and growled and screamed and shrieked and screeched at park bears. It was 'a shocking spectacle, like seeing an old, calm friend go insane'. Rather than follow his southerly dogleg I continued due west.

This is a serene landscape, fields of grazing Charolais that look like alabaster statues in the morning sun, groves of aspens in their full strength of autumn yellows. In Bozeman I stopped and phoned Julia. I could hear the smile in her voice, now that Jean was well on the road to recovery.

'You're in Montana?' she said cheerfully. 'Buy sapphires!'

I often follow the chief's commands and on Main Street, right across from where I was parked, was the Gem Gallery. Macy and I went to investigate. 'Pretty puppy,' I heard as we entered. She was on friendly territory.

I learned that Montana has three deposits of sapphires: Rock Creek and Dry Cottonwood Creek, in the direction I was heading; and Yogo Gulch here in central Montana. While the first two deposits produce yellow, gold, green, blue and some pink stones, Yogo Gulch produces only blues and purples. Yogo Gulch was discovered around a hundred years ago, on a gravel bar in the Missouri River, near Helena, the state capital. And while in other countries, blue sapphires are 'created' by heat treatment to boost the colour, Yogo Gulch sapphires are cosmetic-treatment-free. They're naturally cornflower-blue.

I bought a pair of double AA unmounted stones for the chief, then headed on past Butte and at 6369 feet of altitude crossed the Continental Divide. I stopped for Mace to have a scamper, then scatter trout as she drank from a still stream. It suddenly dawned on me that the mucoid stools she'd had for a few days were caused by Giardia, an intestinal parasite potentially present in virtually all streams in North America.

Heading towards Philipsburg on State Highway 1, there's a sign, 'Granite Ghost Town', and an arrow pointing right. I took a levelled dirt road, forked right onto a narrower road then came to a tight left switchback. I rounded it, grounding out and spinning the GMC's wheels as the vehicle strained around the corner and up the steep, rugged gradient. Unexpectedly, I was on a deeply

229

rutted narrow dirt track now, clinging to the side of the mountain. Two more tight jackknifes quickly followed. There was no alternative but to drive forward, no place to turn around, no place to even come to a halt and think about what to do. I climbed, in my 27-foot-long, 27-year-old motorhome a thousand feet, then another thousand feet, and now the road went even narrower, cut into the side of the mountain. Another 600 feet up and finally I reached the ghost town of Granite, over 7500 feet above sea level, over a thousand feet above the heights of the Continental Divide I passed over on the interstate earlier in the day.

At a crest above the remains of this old silver mining town, I found a flat area to park on. Macy and I got out and wandered. A notice board provided by Montana State Parks gave some history. The town once had a population of 3000. There was a Miners' Union Hall and across from it many of the eighteen saloons in town. The red light district was in the gulch behind the saloons. There was also a library, a hospital with five doctors, a school, four churches, and, I find this hard to comprehend, a roller rink. There was no cemetery. The ground here on top of the mountain was too rocky for internments.

Now, all that remained of the wooden structures were heaps of timbers, although some walls of buildings were still standing. The stone buildings, the bank and the superintendent's house were still recognisable structures as was the two-storey red brick Miners' Union Hall. Its rusted iron facade still held the structure rigid, although the front wall and roof were now long gone. Also on the notice board was a newspaper story about Granite. 'It's best to visit in a four-wheel-drive. *Under no circumstances attempt to take a camper or RV up Granite Mountain.*'

*   *   *

Is there anything better than bacon and eggs, buttered toast and dark coffee, all by yourself on a cloudless morning, on a mountain top under the big blue sky of Montana? While Mace squirrelled and chipmunked, I read my AGS *Montana Guide*.

> Of 88,000 ounces (of sapphires) annually recovered, about 86,000 are used in watch and meter bearings and for other mechanical purposes.

Suddenly, my dog was yelping high-pitched, painful squeals. These were the sounds I'd heard in Ludington, Michigan, when I lost her. I saw her in the distance by a pile of weathered planks, which had once been a building. Rattlesnakes hide in places like that. So do black widow spiders. Had she been bitten? Her shrieks continued and she pranced around, tail high, nosing first here, then there, then digging urgently at the woodpile. I watched, and she shrieked and yelped again. Bitch! It wasn't pain. These were sounds of frustration, at losing her quarry.

I packed up and started the four-mile descent from the mountain, no more than five miles per hour max, in the lowest gear and with my foot on the brake all the time. The GMC weighs 13,000 pounds loaded; I vaguely remembered the mass, momentum and velocity physics equation and knew that to control my descent I had to inch my way down.

The road seemed even narrower today. Washouts forced me close to the edge of the precipice, but now that the drop was on the driver's side I could see how close the tyres were to the edge—never less than ten inches. Slowly, at a walking pace, I descended. After fifteen minutes and around a mile of travel, I started to worry about the brakes. The GMC is an Oldsmobile Toronado in strange attire. The brakes are Toronado disc brakes, circa early 1970s. I'd had my foot on them for over a quarter of an hour. I stopped, put the GMC in 'park' and pulled on the handbrake, but felt no tension in it. It wasn't working. I went out and smelled the brakes. There was a smell of burn.

The GMC took up the full width of the track. I was blocking the way for anyone wanting to drive up, so I decided to move on, and continued to crawl down the mountain. Ten minutes later the steep, twisting descent got bad—I mean real bad—and I could feel through my foot that I was losing the brakes. I was pressing the brake pedal to the floor, but all that was doing was preventing her from gaining speed. She was rolling at a steady five miles per hour and ahead of me was the series of sharp jackknifes. Ascending yesterday, I'd seen three rusting old cars over the edge at one switchback. I smelled burn and saw smoke rising from both front wheel wells. I pressed on the brake pedal as hard as I could, but the GMC continued to slowly roll forward. I pulled on the useless handbrake but it was pointless. I put both feet on the brake pedal and stood with full force and that slowed us down to two miles an hour. I knew it would shear the pin, but I threw the gear lever into 'park' and my home came to an abrupt stop. No sound of metal snapping. I'd managed to stop just before the steepest switchback to the right. Ahead and to the left was nothing but descent off the side of the mountain.

Now what? I got out of the GMC and the smell of burn was intense. Dense smoke poured from both front wheels. Sharp crackling sounds came from both discs. The only thing to do was walk down the mountain to Philipsburg, two miles away, and get help. But what kind of help? What type of vehicle could get me out of the stupid situation I'd got myself into?

Macy and I walked the remaining mile down the steep trail, to the dirt road leading further down to Philipsburg. We met a pick-up heading up to Granite, a husband and wife who prospected for gold as a hobby. I liked that. It was a bit like Julia and me, searching for gold in Scandinavian antiques. They made room for us in the cab, turned around and drove us down to Philipsburg, dropping us off at the wrecker's where the sign on the door said, 'Open'.

It wasn't. I sat there on the back of a parked pick-up truck for half an hour before I realised it was a permanent sign, never changed. It was Saturday and the garage was shut for the weekend. We walked further down the hill, along Sansome, past the Granite County Museum and Cultural Center, once the Courtney Hotel, to the main street, Broadway. In both directions the road, wide as an eight-lane highway, was lined with attractive red brick buildings from the late 1800s. At the bottom of Broadway, to the west, were the Sapphire Mountains. Looking up the street, to the east, was the Flint Range. It was perfection, another Hollywood image, this time of a classic Western town. To the right, I saw someone come out of a store and headed there, to Doe Brother's Soda Fountain and Toy Shop. I walked through the screen door. Seven men filling all but one of the stools at the soda fountain, and the woman serving them, turned in unison, stared at us for a couple of seconds then, like a choir, sang, 'How are ya?'

'My dog and I are great, but I can't say that for my vehicle. I burned out my brakes this morning, descending from Granite. Doesn't seem to be anyone at the wrecker's.'

'Let me phone and find out,' offered Sally, the soda fountain owner. She dialled the wrecker's home number and handed me the phone, but there was only a recorded message that he was away.

Dan interjected, 'Phone the sheriff. He'll know where he is.' Sally phoned the sheriff but no luck there.

Big Mike said we should call the wrecker's in Anaconda because they had a bigger rig. Sally got me their phone number and gave me the phone. Anaconda sympathised, but I was told their wrecker wasn't heavy enough to touch a motorhome. Dan, Rich, Donnie and Clyde smiled and shook their heads at the Anaconda wrecker's unwillingness to make a considerable cash killing by coming to help. We called the wrecker's in Butte, 60 miles away. Same story. Clyde told Sally I should call Drummond. 'They're always pull'n' sem-eyes off the interstate.'

I phoned and explained my position. 'Granite Mountain, huh? Yep, I know that road. No way my wrecker can git up there. I'll check with the boss and call ya back, but maybe you should call the sheriff and see what he says.' He did call back. His boss had told him there was no way he'd send his wrecker up Granite Mountain.

Sally had given me a cup of coffee and brought out her four-month-old Basset pup, who was playing hide and seek round the soda fountain with Macy. I'd become the biggest excitement to hit Philipsburg since the Northern Pacific railroad branched here in 1887.

'Cool 'em down and give 'em a chance to peel off,' suggested Rose.

This is the land where the song 'A Boy Named Sue' came from. I wasn't going to ask Rose how he got his name.

I was, putting it mildly, up the creek. What to do? I looked at these guys, then together they arose from their row of red soda fountain stools, turned to me, hooked their thumbs in their jeans and in unison said, 'We'll rescue you from Granite Mountain.'

Not actually. But that's what it felt like. The men at the bar continued to discuss what to do, when the oldest—early seventies, tallest and quietest—Pat, wearing a green baseball cap, thin gold-framed glasses, buttoned, long-sleeved, striped cotton shirt under a dress Black Watch tartan wool hunting vest, got up and came over.

'You say you're from Ontario? That's where my family came from. Best dogs in the world, golden retrievers. Always had 'em.'

Then Clyde, bearded, bear-shaped and ruddy-faced, climbed off his stool and walked over, 'I think we can get you off the mountain.'

'Let's go,' said Pat. Mace and I followed.

'I'll get some gear and meet you there,' offered Clyde, and he was out the door.

Pat cleared the front cab of his Dodge Ram 4 x 4 pick-up of everything but his scoped rifle. I pushed a box of cartridges over towards Pat and Macy and I climbed in. Pat MacDonald's family was from Scotland. 'Run out. Moved to Ontario in the 1790s,' he explained. With the name MacDonald, his family was probably from the Isle of Skye, removed in the Clearances that dispersed his clan to Cape Breton, parts of the Eastern Townships of Quebec I'd passed through and also to places like Fergus in south-western Ontario. I had a descendant of a half-Norse, half-Gaelic king rescuing me.

In the late 1800s Pat's family moved on, from south-western Ontario to Montana. Pat's was one of the oldest ranches in this part of the state. Like Greg's, Pat's father had been born here in Montana. He ranches Herefords. 'My son tried those new breeds, Charolais and Limousines, but they're not good converters,' Pat said. I asked whether he was retired, a foolish question. Men like Pat retire when they die. From talking with Sally afterwards, he was also perhaps the most respected man in the region.

'If ever anyone needs help, Pat is willing and he has the equipment,' she told me.

Driving back towards the road to Granite, we talked about the problems in ranching that the Langfords had told me about. He smiled an acknowledging smile. 'They want trophy ranches.

236

Places where the grass is always cut and cedar fences. There's one man buying up land here, we call him the Flying Wallet. From Microsoft.'

As we drove up through the steep switchbacks, Pat, looking straight ahead, said, 'D'ya mind my askin'? Why'd ya come up here?'

Lamely, I answered that I was curious to see Granite and hadn't realised the ghost town was at the top of a mountain.

Pat could remember the Miners' Union Hall when it was still active. 'The dance floor on the second floor had crystal chandeliers. When the manager left, the hall got vandalised. Lots of homes in Philipsburg have hardwood floors from that building.'

We reached the GMC, squeezed past and continued to a point in the road, with trees on both sides, where Pat could do a three-point turn. Riding his Ram the way I bet he rode a horse, Pat deftly swung his pick-up round and descended until he was behind the GMC.

'Get some rocks in front of those tyres and check your brakes,' he told me, and I did.

After two hours of cooling, the brakes were holding. Pat checked the rear of the GMC, seeing where he could attach his towing strap. He looped that to the GMC, then got a chain out of his pick-up, crawled under his front fender and threw the chain over the chassis bar. 'It's only Dodge that doesn't add a hook at the front,' he explained quietly.

Pat tied the towing strap to the chain, got in his truck and reversed to give the chain and strap tension. 'OK, start 'er, put yer foot on the brakes and take 'er out of gear.' I did. The brakes held. I

237

put the shift into low gear and gently eased up on the brake pedal. With Pat's foot on the brakes in his truck, acting like an anchor behind me, we began the steep descent, through the switchbacks, past the first, then the second, and finally the third—the steepest and tightest. Ten minutes later we were off Granite Mountain. Clyde had just arrived. It had taken more time than he'd expected to get his gear. 'Good work, Pat.'

I thanked them both for doing something no wrecker in western Montana would risk and asked if they'd like a coffee, but Pat wasn't someone who stuck around.

'Got a function to go to,' he explained.

They departed and I drove back to Philipsburg to thank Sally for her help. As I walked in, a woman at the now empty bar said hello and asked what part of England I was from. Word had spread. We were the day's news.

*   *   *

Dan was a deputy sheriff but got pensioned off when he broke his back in a car accident. 'Not much money in law enforcement unless you're on the take,' he told me. Now he helped out Sally at the soda fountain.

Cold bothered Dan's back and he wasn't looking forward to winter but with a son on tour in Afghanistan and his 97-year-old frail mother living nearby on the 22,000-acre spread he grew up on, New Mexico, where he wanted to live, would have to wait. I was heading for New Mexico and I asked him what he'd do there.

'I'm a good rattlesnake catcher. Get $9.97 a

238

pound. Some weigh over ten pounds. Once harvested four dens, caught 13,000 rattlers.'

I asked more.

'You gotta know what you're doin'. Average brood's a dozen or more. Males' tails are longer. They like rough ground where rodents are. That's what they eat, mice 'n' stuff. Bigger ones eat young cottontails and jackrabbits, squirrels 'n' rats. When a rattler strikes, its fangs unfold from the roof of its mouth. They're hollow, like doctor's needles. If a rattler looses a fang, it jus' grows another. Some folks think rattlers spit venom, but that's not so. Never got bit once.'

I was worried about Macy's natural curiosity once we got to the deserts of the warm south-west and asked Dan's advice.

'An experienced dog knows how to evade a rattler's strike. Can't strike far. Not so much as half its body length. Dogs get bit on their legs when they step too close or on the snout when they nose too close. Hard to see a fang mark but it swells pretty fast and goes dark blue. If yer dog's vomiting and lame, she's been bit. Keep her quiet and get to a vet or a hospital. They all got anti-venom. If yer climbing anywhere jes watch where yer putting yer hand. If a rattler senses any warmth, it strikes first, no questions asked. They're active at night, so listen hard and take a flashlight when yer walkin'.'

*　　　*　　　*

Before leaving England I'd packed a full medical kit for Macy: stethoscope, auroscope, tourniquet, sterilised surgical pack, needles and syringes, wound dressings and cleansers, suture material,

239

scalpel blades, antibiotics, anaesthetics, anti-nausea injections, skin, eye and ear creams and lotions. I had everything except Flagyl, the most common medicine to treat the most common form of rural diarrhoea.

By the time I got to Missoula, where I knew I'd find a vet, bugs had once more splatted themselves onto my best line of vision. I chanced upon The Western Montana Small Animal Emergency Clinic where Mace trotted into reception, inhaled and once more felt at ease and at home.

I filled in Macy's admission form, giving both her name and mine. Bruce King, the vet on duty, working at the emergency clinic while he built his own place in Coeur d'Alene, Idaho, 150 miles west, looked at my name and said, 'Don't I know you?' I asked where he'd graduated, which was Washington State University, and said I'd known his dean, Leo Bustad, but had never visited Pullman, Washington.

While we mused on where we'd met, Bruce's receptionist brought over two books, kept in reception for clients to leaf through, the *Encyclopedia of Dogs* and *Know Your Dog*. Bruce had a eureka moment. We bartered, from my perspective, an extremely reasonable exchange. I signed my books and Bruce, concurring with my diagnosis, supplied me with Macy's needed tablets. He also told me where the nearest brakes specialist was and I drove over.

I parked outside one of the inspection bays and Wayne—tall, laconic, chewing tobacco—walked over to the driver's window that I'd slid full open. 'Howdy.' He paused and chewed. 'How can I help?'

240

I explained that I'd gone up to Granite Ghost Town, the handbrake didn't work, I'd burned the brakes coming down, and asked if he could check how bad the damage was, if it was safe to continue.

Wayne stood there. He took another wad of Skol chewing tobacco from a pack in his shirt pocket, tucked it in his cheek pouch, looked down the length of the GMC, then he turned back to me.

'You've got balls the size of turkey eggs. Took this up Granite Mountain? Balls like turkey eggs. I gotta phone my wife and tell 'er. I chickened out two weeks ago in my camper when I came to that first jackknife. Went back next week in my Chevy S-10. It was a hairy climb in that. Damn! Turkey eggs you got.'

Wayne looked at the front wheels. 'Now. Let me think about this.'

He reached through the driver's window and, with arms even longer than mine, tightened a nut on the handbrake. That's all that was needed. The brake still worked. Then he checked the front discs with a penlight.

'RVs today are built on truck chassis. You got an Olds 455 Toronado engine and Toronado brakes. Yer safe but if yer doin' a lot a mount'n' drivin', it's best you get new ones.'

Wayne had told me what I needed to know. It was safe to continue. We moseyed on through the western Montana forests of evergreen, yellow and golden aspens and alders, and I thought, turkey eggs, that's just about the best compliment anyone's ever given me.

*   *   *

241

Ask me what I think when I hear 'Idaho', and I think 'potato'. This is unfortunate. Spuds have given Idaho a faulty image. I wasn't prepared for the state's compelling beauty. This is a great place to visit. From Lookout Pass in the Bitterroot Range, the interstate descends from Montana into Idaho's upraised thumb, passing on stilts over vestige settlements in the densely forested coulées below. In pristine wildness, in one of the finest, most isolated, sparsely populated parts of the United States, people live with constant traffic noise directly above them.

The interstate continues through pure stands of dense Douglas fir. The bark on young trees was smooth and grey, older ones looked darker and furrowed. I could have left the interstate and travelled on parts of old US 10, now signposted as 'Scenic Byways', but didn't because of the brakes.

At a rest area, two kids with two pit bulls, a broken-down car they had abandoned and a freshly written sign, 'Home to California', hoped I'd give them a lift. Their dogs tried to eat mine so I didn't. Near the top of another pass, I stopped at Mullan Tree Historic Site for a walk and noted that Macy's stools were back to normal after just two tablets. Like all dog owners, the quantity, quality, even texture and consistency, of dog poo is a daily observation. In my circumstances, as a vet, it's also my livelihood.

The Mullan Road, built by the federal government before the Civil War as a military and emigrant route from Fort Benton, on the Upper Missouri, to Walla Walla, near the Columbia River, was carved through this pass. Here the conifers were more majestic, mostly tall, lean, thin-barked lodgepole pine. The gravel trail of the original US 10, built in 1916 over the trail broken by the Mullen Road, is still visible—just—cutting through the forest, and along it were huckleberry bushes, covered in ripe blue berries. The shrub's evergreen leaves are browsed by deer and elk, while its berries are eaten by bears, birds and, on this occasion, a dog and me.

Back on I-90 semis were parked at the top of the pass, their drivers checking their brakes before the four miles of uninterrupted six per cent gradient descent into the Pacific time zone, the fifth of our travels. I hesitated for a moment, then remembered Wayne in Missoula. I'd taken my rig up Granite Mountain. 'Turkey balls'. A few minutes later and suddenly I was driving above the cottages, boathouses and boats of Lake Coeur d'Alene. It was like the heartland of beautiful British Columbia.

I was unprepared for the sidewalk cafe culture and lakeside parks of Coeur d'Alene itself, a residential and resort town where pick-up trucks pull skijets and boats rather than horse trailers. The name Coeur d'Alene means heart of an awl and was bestowed by French Canadian trappers upon the tribe of Indians inhabiting the shores of the lake. Apparently, the trappers found these Indians so inhospitable and so difficult in their fur-bartering, that they declared their hearts were no bigger than the point of a shoemaker's awl. The name stuck—first to the tribe, then to the lake, then to the river, then to the mountains it drains, then to a fort and finally to the town. The AGS *Idaho Guide* explained that the town stands on the site chosen by General Sherman for Fort Coeur d'Alene, built in 1878 and abandoned in 1901. In 1884, it was the site of the lower 48 states' last gold stampede.

In 70-degree sunshine, I stayed in town long enough for a huckleberry shake for me, a huckleberry cone for Mace and some huckleberry preserve for future breakfasts.

Steinbeck was too preoccupied with concern about Charley to notice the grandeur of northern Idaho. Noble, dignified, Charley had prostate problems and couldn't pee. 'I lifted him into the cab and drove hell for leather for Spokane.' The vet he found wasn't much help, but that encounter provoked Steinbeck to write about 'dog lovers'.

> 'Such people, it seems to me, in what they imagine to be kindness, are capable of inflicting long and lasting tortures on an animal, denying it any of its natural desires and fulfilments until a dog of weak character breaks down and becomes the fat, asthmatic, befurred bundle of neuroses. When a stranger addresses Charley in baby talk, Charley avoids him. For Charley is not a human; he's a dog, and he likes it that way. He feels that he is a first-rate dog and has no wish to be a second-rate human.'

We've certainly got an ambivalent attitude towards our dogs, a rational understanding that dogs are not furry people in disguise, yet an almost helpless inability not to humanise them. My clients do it. My family does it. I do it. Like Steinbeck, I know that in our desire to comfort and protect, unwittingly we can create canine basket cases.

244

Where I disagree with him is that I see a whole lot of dogs, and the great majority are simply delighted—over the moon—to be treated as people, to eat our food, sleep in our beds, take charge of homeland security, become top dog in the human family.

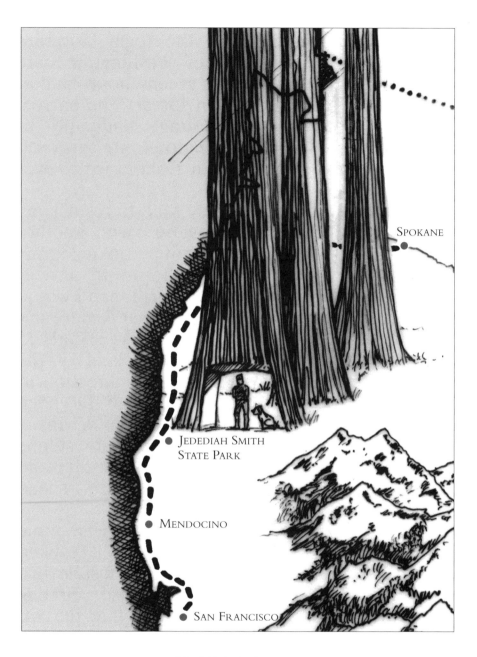

SPOKANE

JEDEDIAH SMITH
STATE PARK

MENDOCINO

SAN FRANCISCO

CHAPTER SEVEN

THE PACIFIC NORTH-WEST

I've travelled the foggy, forested pacific coast of Washington State before, a grey, green, mossy land of temperate rain forest. The barren, brown undulating landscape of eastern Washington State surprised me. It reminded me of North Dakota with fewer trees.

I stopped at Spokane Valley Mall to restock my blood vessels' cholesterol reserves with another batch of hot Krispy Kreme donuts. Looking at my map, I saw I was now much farther north, at near 48 degrees, two degrees further north than I was at the apogee of my travels in the east, at Rivière-du-Loup, Quebec, on the St Lawrence River. Only 75 miles north was British Columbia, land of the pecan butter tart. I pondered which direction to choose, then remembered the advice I'd been given about my brakes: avoid mountain driving. I headed south-west through sagebrush steppe towards the Columbia River, while the local radio station offered music 'to smooth off life's speed bumps'.

The day was still and the sky clear. Ahead of me I saw, in a field to my right, a plume of what looked like smoke over 400 feet high. It was a dust devil, a whirlwind, 30 feet wide at its base, circling clockwise, sucking yellow-brown soil into the air. Further on there were three more, all in one field, their bases in brown torment. I continued through empty, desolate stillness. This land's major product is dust. The empty old highway I was on, paralleling its four-lane replacement, runs for

248

almost 30 miles, through a grey, sandy landscape dotted with grey-green sagebrush, dried riverbeds, slabs of igneous rock, sandy hills and withered, deserted farms. It seems almost incomprehensible that settlers tried to farm this godforsaken region. The road traverses the town of Connell's three blocks of baked Main Street, goes past old grain elevators, through land where the tallest plants you see are low, wiry, sagebrush.

My old friend, Leo Bustad, when dean of Washington State University's veterinary school, 60 miles east of here, introducing himself at scientific meetings, used to show a slide of tumbleweed rolling against a barbed wire fence in a backdrop of nothingness. 'This is the Washington State University campus where I teach,' Leo would explain. There'd be an intake of breath. He'd lean forward, peer over his half-glasses and say, 'It's not the end of the world . . . but you can see it from there.'

Leo was a class act as a public speaker, but more—one of those remarkable people who gentle you out of your contentment with the *status quo*, who make you question your unanalysed thoughts on life, your preconceived or preconditioned way of seeing things, who help you think and, in helping you think, refresh your mind, and help you see a new you, a new way, a new outlook. Best of all, he helped you make that leap without your even realising you were doing so. Leo's gentle humour, his twinkle, his smile, his patent, uncomplicated dog-like honesty, was how he hooked us, how he transmitted his real message— celebrate life, revere life, use your moral sense, your scientific knowledge, your gut feelings to create a sense of wholeness, a sense of purpose. Without resort to religion, Leo made us appreciate how we're inextricably linked to all living things that share this world.

Now, here I was in the land you could see from Leo's university campus. This land is in a rain shadow created by the Cascade Mountains. Rain falls on their western slopes. None gets this far east. Nothing grows but sagebrush and bunch grass. The AGS *Washington Guide*, published in 1941, says that, 'Water supplied from the Grand Coulée reclamation project will soon give new life to this area.' True. Amidst the aridness are patchwork fields of green and gold, each with massive, wheeled, field irrigation units, each the length of a football field.

At an abandoned farmhouse I pulled off the road and Macy created her own dust devils running demented figure eights, disappearing from view in explosions of powdery-dry earth on what looked like a just-seeded field. I drove on, parked in the middle of the road, knowing no cars would pass, and took pictures of this parched landscape. A whirlwind crossed the road ahead of me, then, like Banquo's ghost, disappeared.

*   *   *

During the past weeks, place names and peoples across the northern reaches of the United States have reminded me of the dramatic historical consequences of small, far-off events. I've travelled past Fond du Lac and Eau Claire, Wisconsin, and St Paul and Detroit Lakes, Minnesota. In North Dakota I passed lands once occupied by Sans Arc and Brulé Sioux, in Montana, past Cheyenne, Gros Ventre and Pend d'Oreille tribal lands. I was enchanted by Coeur d'Alene, Idaho. Here in Washington are the Quinault and Nez Percé tribes and the Grand Coulée Dam. Directly across the Columbia River in Oregon is The Dalles, 'The Flagstones'. Elsewhere in Oregon are Deschutes, Willamette and Malheur National Forests. Lewis and Clark may get credit in the United States for their travels to the West Coast. William Lyon Mackenzie may get credit for his travels across Canada a decade earlier, but true credit for the first Europeans to explore North America must surely go to the anonymous *couriers de bois*, the adventurous French trappers and hunters who first blazed trails across the continent. Were it not for a single bullet inflicted upon the French General Montcalm on the Plains of Abraham, where Macy had kicked the sky in glorious sunshine only weeks ago, this vast region, from Nova Scotia to the Pacific, from Hudson Bay to Louisiana, would have been French.

The sun's blinding glare off the Columbia River made driving west along its northern shore an act of concentration. This thin road traverses dry, desert lands of burnt bunch grass and black rock until Roosevelt is reached, where there are irrigated fruit farms and vineyards. Across the river, the interstate snakes out on a great causeway, arcing into the river, creating a lagoon under the brown bluffs above. Rows of eighteen-wheelers, like earnest chains of soldier ants, moved back and forth in slow, double-file procession. Near the eastern edge of the Columbia River Gorge National Scenic Area was a full-scale model

251

of Stonehenge, a World War I memorial site, complete with 50 RV hook-ups.

Beyond The Dalles, buttes turned into hills and they turned into mountains: the Cascade Range. Near the river were massive tablets of stone, black in the setting sun, some over 30 feet high. Surely these were the inspiration to create the nearby Stonehenge Memorial. At Hood, suddenly, I was in flourishing, dense vegetation, out of the Cascade's rain shadow. We walked the banks of the Columbia, and camped overnight overlooking the river.

*　　　*　　　*

In 1778 an English captain, John Meares, set out in search of the Columbia River. He entered its broad mouth, decided it was no more than a large bay and departed, naming the entrance Deception Bay and the promontory on the north, Cape Disappointment. The 'half-empty' Meares missed it. Fourteen years later, a Bostonian, Robert Gray, sailed into the bay and up the river, naming it after the boat he sailed on, the *Columbia*. Called the 'Ouragon' by local tribes, that river name, 'Oregon', was given to the vast territory on both sides of the river where I now was, from the Rocky Mountains back east, west to the Pacific Ocean, where we'd arrive later today, and from the 42nd Parallel, the northern limit of present California, to the 49th Parallel, the southern boundary of British Columbia. Out of this area would be carved the states of Washington, Oregon and Idaho, and parts of Montana and Wyoming. And it was down this river that Meriwether Lewis and William Clark travelled in 1805, the first white men recognised to have crossed the vast Oregon Territory. What history seldom reminds us is that Lewis took his dog with him on his momentous travels.

It was at the Cascade Rapids, where Macy and I spent the morning, says the AGS *Oregon Guide*, that local Wahclellah Indians stole Captain Lewis's canine buddy.

> Three men, well armed, were instantly dispatched in pursuit of them, with orders to fire if there was the slightest resistance or hesitation. At the distance of two miles they came within sight of the thieves, who, finding themselves pursued, left the dog and made off.

Lewis, enraged that his dog had been dog-napped, gave orders that if this were to happen again the thieves should be instantly shot. He spent two years travelling to the Pacific and back. After spending only a month of 24 hours a day in intimate contact with my dog, I understand his feelings. Anybody does anything malicious to my dog and I'll hang 'em by their goolies. Don't mess with my Macy!

It had been a hot night and I was pestered by Harrier jet-sized mosquitoes sounding like wind generators, as they buzzed me in bed. Hundred-car freight trains passed every half-hour. At Lac Megantic, Quebec, their distant air horns were sonorous, soothing, reassuring. At Stockholm on the Mississippi, the sound of freight trains rumbling by in the night gave a feeling of contentment. Here in Home Valley, the railroad track passed less than twenty yards from where we were camped. And those drivers, they just knew I was there. I swear they blasted their air horns when they saw my motorhome through the trees.

Beneath the crumbling cliffs of Table Mountain, we walked along the Columbia River. The air was damp. There were mosses everywhere, bleached elk moss clinging from every branch of every tree and ferns growing luxuriantly from the moss-covered black rock. We left the path and chanced upon an old railroad line on a raised bed, still with its iron tracks but now with ferns and trees a foot or more in diameter growing from between the wooden ties. I assumed this forgotten line in the forest had once transported people and goods around insurmountable Columbia rapids.

Highway 14 became more tortuous as it twisted through the Cascade Mountains, but I'd already found speed-sign religion. If a sign said 45 mph, I slowed down to 40, if it said 30 mph, I slowed to 25. It was morning. I soon had lines of cars and semis behind me, but that was their problem, not mine.

Logging trucks reappeared, the first since New England, but these carried not hundreds of small logs as in the east but eight to ten full-length trees: spruce, western cedar and lodgepole pine. Eastern logs were turned into newspapers and books. These were destined to become homes.

A road sign warned me to check my brakes. There was a five per cent descent. Chicken shit. I was the conqueror of Granite Mountain. Abruptly I was back in the boonies, flat but productive agricultural land. It was 9.00 a.m. and 54 degrees F, 30 degrees cooler than eighteen hours previously in the parched south-west of Washington State.

In the drivers' lounge at the Onan repair centre, a fellow my age, a Ted Turner lookalike—neat grey hair, fit, trim, bushy moustache—in a short-sleeved Hawaiian shirt, khaki shorts and trainers, put down his paper and beckoned Macy over. She relishes intimacy from total strangers and pressed her head against his bare knees, as he expertly tickled and rubbed behind her ears. 'What a calm dog. Good-looker too,' he volunteered.

Jeff explained he was visiting his daughter, that, in fact, because there's no sales tax on RVs in Oregon he's a paper resident there, although he and his wife had been on the road for several years. 'I drive and my wife navigates. I have no idea where we'll be next week. This time it was, "Let's visit Sue Ellen." That gave me a chance to have the generator serviced.'

When I'd taken Macy for a walk earlier, Jeff had had a good look at the GMC.

'She's in great condition? Did you restore her?' I couldn't lie to such a nice guy and explained our story.

'I lived in one for three years, from 1974 to 1977, counselling Vietnam veterans,' Jeff told me. 'GM donated thirty GMCs, some of the first off the production line. It was good for them, to help iron out wrinkles, and good for us because we had state-of-the-art Cadillac homes to travel the country in. That's what turned me to RVing.'

Jeff explained that the Department of Veterans Affairs recognised the relationship between mental trauma and the nature and character

255

of war. Psychiatrists within Veterans Affairs anticipated that the nature of the Vietnam War would lead to substantial numbers of men suffering from complex feelings of guilt, anger and grief. They knew, too, that most of these men would be too 'manly' to talk about their problems, so psychologists and psychiatrists like Jeff hit the road in a fleet of gleaming new GMCs and visited veterans in their own homes. I never knew that.

Listening to us was Roger, same age but double the size, a cherubic Santa Claus wearing a black T-shirt with a fluorescent motorcycle on it. Roger smiled at Mace and me, and said, 'May I?' I thought he was asking whether he too could have a tickle but he wanted to share his McDonald's with her. She took an instant liking to Roger. So did I.

Roger was from Arkansas and drove a 53-foot rig. He had an army disability pension. 'Agent Orange,' he explained. He also had a cat, but didn't have her with him because he was travelling with a trainee driver. Roger had that tone and inflection, and level, easy, relaxed way of talking that makes you feel comfortable and good. Shut your eyes and you'd swear you were hearing Bill Clinton speak. He smiled naturally when he talked. Life sounded better just listening to him.

Roger had been in trucking for 35 years. He settled down once because his wife 'got tired of me being gone', ranched beef and chickens but, he said, his wife left him anyways so he went back to what he enjoys. 'You know, if you and yoar dawg are enjoyin' doin' what yo'are doin', why not do it full tam? The company ah work foar lets you take yoar dog with you. They encourage you.'

Roger used to deliver tankers of orange juice

from Florida to Alberta, Ontario, and Quebec in Canada. 'There are no baffles in those tankers. If you don't concentrate, that orange juice will take you straight through a stop sign.'

Alberta in winter was the trickiest trip. 'Paps from the engine circulate through the juice and keep it from freezin', but if yo'are not careful, even though yo'are delivering it insad a heated building, it turns to sludge and won't flow. The only tam I ever got lost was in Montreal, Quebec, but I learned the important words. No'ard is no'arth. Sood is saouth. Est is east. And ouest is west.'

The people I'd been meeting on our travels were easy to talk with and happy to talk about almost anything, but there was one subject I've had to tease out of them—politics. Almost universally people felt uncomfortable talking politics, but when I raised the subject with Roger he was happy to give his opinion.

'There are two reasons I don't really lak Bush. The first is, when he was the Governor of Texas and the speed limit was 55 miles per hour, he never changed it. There's almost 900 miles of desert when you go across the bottom of it. At 55, it's an all day job. The second thing is he's an oil man. They're puttin' money in their own pockets with this oil thing. Look at what Halliburton's doin'. That's not right.'

Roger asked me where I was heading and gave suggestions on routes to take. He'd travelled old Route 66 through Texas, New Mexico, Arizona and California, and had a suggestion that would take me back to old Route 66 in California.

'Second rest area past Ludlow, get off of that road, take the second ramp to the left, you go down through rollin' moguls. You know what moguls are? They're not mountains. Go all the way 'til the road comes up to a railroad track. Watch for trains!' He smiled and laughed. 'One train about every three minutes comes through there. You got to get between them. And if it's rainin', it's a flash flood area 'cause it comes off the mountains. Get over the tracks to the stop sign. And now you go all the way through to Goff, G-O-F-F. You'll be goin' around the Needles Mountains. It's not any further, but it's a lot easier on your vehicle than climbin' those mountains. If you climb those mountains, turn your air conditioner off or you'll overheat your engine. At the sign that says Las Vegas North and Searchlight South, take 95 saouth. That'll bring you raght back on 40.'

Roger smiled and I replied, 'Thank you, Mr President.'

Jeff's RV and my piece of American heritage were both ready at the same time. After a two-hour inspection, it was decided that the phone diagnosis I'd received from Clarence in Mandan, North Dakota, was right. I needed a new circuit board. Problem was, Portland didn't have one. I paid an enormous bill and arranged for a circuit board to be sent from Ohio to their San Leandro, California, facility. Jeff's 45-foot bus conversion, towering beside my GMC, made my vehicle look like a dinky toy. On the other hand, he was driving a bus and I was driving a dream.

His Hungarian Viszla barked from the bedroom window as we approached our respective vehicles. 'Like clockwork, he's got a routine. Eleven o'clock and he wants us in bed. We climb in, then he does too, noses under the sheets, heaves a deep sigh and settles in. Look at me, Bruce. Do you see a sensible guy? People think we're nuts, but we love it.'

Before departing Jeff gave me a little advice. 'Always keep Macy on a leash. We were checking into Yellowstone last year and a couple like us were filling in a report. Their Rottweiler was off his leash when they saw a bear. They stopped, hunkered down and slowly turned away but their dog challenged the bear. Dead in thirty seconds. I won't ever let my dog off his leash in a place like that.'

*   *   *

Travelling from Stockholm and Pepin, on the eastern banks of the Mississippi River, through to where I was now, near to the Pacific Ocean, had been a short journey in time but a timeless passage of discovery. Somewhere, I'd resolved my guilt for absenting myself from family and business responsibilities. Somewhere, I'd eased back into the natural openness of North Americans. Europeans sometimes call this national personality trait naiveté. If it is, why consider it a pejorative? What's so bad about innocence? What's wrong with open, unaffected guilelessness? What's so unsophisticated about good neighbourliness, about revealing that most profound aspect of the human condition, that buried within we have a natural capacity to be innately decent? Somewhere along the way, in the concentrated variety of events and people and vistas, I'd relearned what I once knew. Selflessness and sentimentality are inherent parts of human nature. People are intrinsically good.

In Marion County, outside Portland, just past a road sign—perhaps aimed at overweight America—announcing, 'Overweight? Oversized? You need a special permit', I turned off the highway to Nicholas and Natasha Dubenko's Berry Empire. Emigrants from Russia, the Dubenkos produce 15 varieties of berries, but they had frozen their last crop the day before I arrived. Nicholas assured me that his flash-freezing technique locked full flavour into his berries. He disappeared into the hanger-sized freezer and returned with boxes of frozen berries. 'Try this. It's my Marion berry. This one is my Emperor berry. You like them?' I did, and I bought a freezer-full of Marion berries and a jar of Emperor berry jam. As I was leaving Nicholas stopped me, passing a container of frozen blueberries through the window. 'Have these. They will make your journey even more enjoyable.'

That evening Mace frolicked in the Pacific Ocean, scavenging kelp on the empty, broad, sandy beach, throwing each mass gloriously in the air, catching it, running with it trailing from her mouth, somersaulting and high-stepping in canine abandon. It was low tide. A sunken barge was just visible near the low tide mark, waves eddying around its metal deck. Dense grey cloud merged anonymously with the ocean. The few people walking the sands were accompanied by their dogs. Back in the dunes, not unlike those at Climping Beach in Sussex only immensely deeper in depth, my dog raced and rabbited until commanded to return to her home for the night. It was good to be by the sea once more.

As a white cotton sea fog hovered over the ocean, the sun burst like sparkling amber above the horizon, streaming shards of flaming yellow light over the flat wet sands. Macy and I walked the deserted beach, our footsteps the only marks in the sand. Well, that's not completely true. I walked. Mace careened. She blazed her way to the distant surf, arced through the breakers then, like a cannonball, fired herself back to me and past me, turning in a wide arc and repeating herself once more. To the north, Newport Bridge glinted in copper light, like a piece of ageing Meccano against a dark green mountainous backdrop. As the sun rose above the distant trees, my dog's body was mirrored in perfect reflection on the glistening sand.

In crisp, clear sunshine we headed south on coastal US 101, a road that literally hugs the sea. Soon a sea fog enveloped us and the temperature dropped back into the fifties. Trees on both sides of the highway were sculpted by ocean winds into mile upon mile of seemingly perfect bonsai. This was nature's topiary. Poodle owners must love visiting here.

We stopped at Seal Rocks for an hour on the narrow beach. Massive pinnacles of black rock, eroded by millennia of storms, line the coastal waters, like gigantic, upturned, fossil shark teeth. The high water line was littered with bleached-white deadhead logs. Macy found a small one shaped like a thick, fat femur and paraded triumphally. She carried it back to her bed in her home.

A PINNACLE ROCK, TRADEMARK OF THE OREGON
COASTLINE

Emerging from the car park I saw a rare GMC motorhome, with California plates, towing a jet ski, heading north. I've read that there are more GMC motorhomes in California than in any other state. Now there were also lots of small convertibles driving in both directions, all with California licence plates. I drove past Driftwood Beach but it had been denuded of driftwood, and with good reason. Pieces of driftwood, as I was seeing here on the Oregon coast, are sold in English garden centres as garden sculpture. A large piece can cost thousands.

At Cape Perpetua, the forest plunges down to the beach. Where land had been logged there was no timber regrowth, only low ground cover. I stopped at Seal Lion Caves where a sign told visitors to bring binoculars and money to see Stellar sea lions, but I couldn't get myself to pay to see wildlife. I've got a great reason. Ten years ago, when my son Ben was teaching English in Quito, Ecuador, during a gap year, he invited me to join him and his friends for a two-week journey on a fishing boat through the Galapagos Islands. Within minutes of our entering those Pacific waters for a swim, curious young sea lions would glide over to investigate. They were followed by adolescents and eventually by their mothers. Within twenty minutes we would be surrounded by inquisitive sea lions, their large, luminous, innocent-looking eyes peering into our face masks. They torpedoed towards us, then at the last possible millisecond veered to either side, above or below.

In fact, the most exciting encounter I've ever had with an animal occurred while swimming in the Galapagos. Our guide permitted swimming after he was sure no mature males, especially beachmasters, were present. While our group was swimming among a group of adolescent and female sea lions, I surfaced to defog my face mask. As I took it off and rinsed it, in front of me, six feet away, was the head and shoulders of a mountain, a male sea lion who'd been abusing anabolic steroids. This animal made Arnold Schwarzenegger look like Kate Moss. He was looking me in the eye and by instinct, confronted by overwhelming authority, I averted my gaze, held the mask to my face and started to drop my head into the water. As I did so I was swamped by the tidal wave he produced, as he launched forward to give me a Glasgow kiss. It was fortunately only a threatened head butt. With my face now in the water, looking beneath me, I saw him pass, first his head, then his massive scarred shoulders, then, like the spaceship in the opening scene from *Star Wars*, his massive body glided beneath me.

We stopped for lunch in pretty Florence. Overlooking the harbour, sitting at a table on the sidewalk, I had garlic French fries and thinly sliced beef and salad on a Hogie with dipping gravy, while Mace was offered a large bowl of iced water. Our waitress told me of the cat she'd rescued from her neighbours, a skinny five-year-old female, now drinking and urinating excessively. I told her to go and get her cat, but she couldn't leave until late afternoon. A passer-by, walking her German shepherd, stopped to talk and greet Macy. I couldn't help but notice the dog had a swelling in one of her mammary glands and almost absently felt it to determine its margins. After so many years of vetting, certain needs are permanent. It

264

just doesn't feel right to meet a dog or cat and not check how fit it is.

Travelling down the Pacific coast, at each beach we stopped at there was a sign, 'Tsunami Hazard Zone. In case of earthquake go to high ground or inland'. Along the road were signs showing 'Tsunami Evacuation Routes'. Now at Reedsport, a manufactured homes town, was a sign, 'Leaving Tsunami Hazard Zone'. Azaleas replaced coastal rhododendrons, then myrtle trees, their bark wind-blasted away, exposing shiny, chestnut-red to blond-coloured wood beneath. Almost every hair colour that Revlon sells is seen at its best on myrtle branches and trunks.

Beyond Bandon, past a series of dune-sheltered lakes, I turned west to Cape Blanco Lighthouse, the most westerly point in the lower 48 states, and climbed down a steep track to a deserted beach, laden 30 feet in depth with beached driftwood. Mace blazed new trails through the deadheads and sand. Now, among the bleached logs, there were darker redwoods, glistening fire-red in the late afternoon sun. More than once, surf pounding through the most recently beached logs caught Mace unawares. At the base of the hill we had descended, a small trickling stream emerged just above the beachwood. There were myriads of animal tracks leading to this uniquely located drinking hole. I would have stayed here for the night but there was a prominent sign back at the road, 'No Camping'.

Mace's agility continued to astound me. If she thinks she can leap and at least gain purchase with her front claws, she'll do so, successfully. She has no self-doubt about her physical abilities, no fear.

Her scent-trailing seems perfect. She retraces her tracks perfectly, now climbing back up the cliff, following her exact trail down, last night trailing and retracking through the dunes to and from the beach. I hadn't realised until this trip how 'doggy' she really was.

*   *   *

George Gist was the son of a Cherokee mother and a Dutch-Indian trader. He was raised as a Cherokee, became a skilled silversmith and had his name written by a friend so that he could fashion a die to stamp his silver. This simple act led him to ponder the white man's 'talking leaves'. Over twelve years he devised an 85-character alphabet, each letter representing a monosyllable of his Cherokee language, preserving each symbol on sheets of bark. It was only when he showed he could communicate with his six-year-old daughter by means of these symbols that the Cherokee chiefs approved of his work.

When the Cherokees were moved from north-west Georgia and Tennessee to Indian Territory, to what would become the state of Oklahoma, Se-quo-yah, as he was now called, moved with them. He became interested in lost tribes of the Cherokee nation and travelled on to California in search of a tribe of Cherokees that had moved further west.

Se-quo-yah's perfection of a phonetic alphabet for his tribe is a feat long forgotten. Equally forgotten is that it is his name that was honoured in the naming of the world's tallest living trees, the coastal redwoods, *Sequoia sempervirens*, the ever-living giants of northern California, and the giant sequoias, *Sequoia gigantea*, of the western slopes of California's Sierra Nevada mountains. From seeds the size of tomato seeds grow trees taller than the Statue of Liberty. From buttressed bases their thick cinnamon-brown trunks rise, free of branches for a full third of their height, crested in a taper of short branches, dressed in small, stiff, sharp-pointed, deeply, brilliant yellow-green, evergreen foliage. These alone are reason enough to travel to southern Oregon and northern California.

'Welcome to California', the sign said. '$1000 fine for animal abandonment', warned the next. This is excellent. I was back at the latitude of the most southerly portion of Ontario, back in a state I had lived in for a few months, 36 years ago, and back in a land where animal welfare was on the political agenda. Driving through a pea-souper of a fog, it took me a while before I realised the majesty of the surrounding forest, the humbling power of the coastal redwoods.

Jedediah Smith State Park gives a perfect introduction to the coastal redwoods. Local roads, snaking among groves of giants, give right of way to the trees. Those abutting the road are 'protected' by light reflectors. On one right curve on US 199, a tree has been worn back several inches by semis shaving it, leaving a technicolour selection of their paint.

Redwood groves are given names and the Simpson-Reed Grove on US 199 is daunting in its grandeur. I drove into the grove, and we walked through the dimly lit forest, surrounded my lush ferns, elk moss dripping from lower vegetation. On the trunk of one redwood, captured in a shaft of

267

sunlight, were two almost fluorescent orange-peel mushrooms. Beside the giant trees Macy looked like an insignificant being, a field mouse pausing by an oak tree. Back at Sag Harbor I was told it was 'awesome' that Macy had travelled from England to America. Here, in northern California, is the true definition of the word 'awesome'. I took countless photos: Macy beside redwoods, Macy inside hollows in redwoods; but later, when I looked at these pictures, none captured the feeling of being among them. I don't think that feeling can be captured in words either.

Steinbeck felt the best word was 'respect'. I imagine Leo Bustad would have felt the best noun was 'reverence'. To walk among these imperious mammoths, to go almost dizzy looking to their heights, to hear the deep silence and feel the comforting solitude is something you can experience only by being there, not by being told about it. Steinbeck says he hadn't told Charley about redwoods, that such a tree would be the highlight of his travels, and chose carefully one that Charley would anoint. 'Look, Charley. It's the tree of all trees. It's the end of the Quest.'

But Charley wasn't interested and Steinbeck was crestfallen. Good dog-man that he was, Steinbeck cut a small willow branch from a tree at a nearby creek, sharpened the butt end and stuck the little willow in the earth so that its leaves rested against the redwood's bark. Charley cruised over. 'He sniffed its new-cut leaves delicately and then, after turning this way and that to get range and trajectory, he fired.'

I'd planned to ease my way through the redwoods—to meander—and let me apologise now to any California State Park official who might read this: I apologise for letting my dog walk on park trails. Good God, have you ever read such annoying hokum as the park diktat that says, 'Dogs may not be on any trails. Dogs can be on paved roads only'? Are my dog's paws going to compress the ground and damage the redwood root system more than I am? Why on earth is it forbidden for dogs to be walked on their leashes on trails? I was annoyed, really annoyed. The standard national and state park regulation—'Dogs must be on a leash no longer than six feet long at all times; there are no areas in the park where dogs may be off-leash, except in your tent or vehicle'—was also listed in the dog rules. I broke the law. I apologise.

There are few towns on the coastal highway, but each has the same accumulation of gas stations, drive-through restaurants, motels and mini markets. Lots of spooky-looking guys walk the road. Many have grey-haired ponytails. Back in Oregon, carvers were making trolls and Vikings; here, in California, the wood-carvers were still making the types of long-haired, tormented faces they painted in psychedelic colours when I worked in San Francisco in 1968. They cooked their brains then and they haven't cooled down yet.

The coast remained fogged in. Logging trucks, with four trees making a complete load, passed in both directions. We ascended into Del Norte Coast Redwoods State Park, where a low fog sat on the road but the sky above was blindingly blue. I stopped at the Harry C. Grove Grove—I liked that name—and we ambled around, again on our own. The park was empty. Leaving the park there's a two-mile, seven-degree decline. Of course, this was no sweat. What did that mechanic in Montana say? Ostrich eggs? Balls the size of ostrich eggs. While other RVs stopped and prepared, I slipped into second gear and just floated down from the heights. At the bottom, women, wearing orange boiler suits that read 'CDC Prisoner', were working on the road. I found the word 'prisoner' on the women's California Department of Corrections workclothes surprisingly shocking.

Just beyond Prairie Creek Redwoods State Park, I stopped by a meadow where Mace rolled on elk droppings. Instantly, a park ranger arrived.

'I see you have a leash, so I won't cite you. An elk was chased here by a dog a few years back. Broke its leg. Had to be put down.'

Walking over a bridge, with Mace now on her leash, I saw three, antlered elk browsing under willow trees. Turning onto the main road, a harem of twelve females were browsing on the road's verge.

In Eureka I tanked up on Patriot-brand gas and bought some more Homelands-brand salami, both—I thought—commercial indicators of post-September 11 America. I'd been buying my food from farm stands and highway stores for weeks now and found supermarket shopping difficult. The fruit was waxed to a mirror-shine and stacked to symmetrical perfection. Vegetables looked like they'd been grown hydroponically; had never seen soil. Everything else was packaging, not food. Past Eureka, the road left the fogbound coast and headed inland. Late-blooming California poppies lined the roadside and in the distance I saw a helicopter, like a giant dragonfly, hovering low to the ground.

270

MACY ANOINTS THE REDWOODS, JEDEDIAH SMITH
STATE PARK, NORTHERN CALIFORNIA

Mace and I went for another prolonged walk, this time through Founder's Grove in Humboldt Redwoods State Park. We circled Founder's Tree, on its recently added root-protecting platform: 346 feet tall, 40 feet in circumference, millable to over 125,000 feet of lumber—a single tree large enough to build at least ten houses. These trees transpire huge amounts of moisture. Each of the trees surrounding us could produce perhaps 500 gallons of water per day. They're actually capable of producing their own fog. This tree and its nearby relatives would probably not be here but for the actions of the Save-the-Redwoods League. In the 1920s, individual members and groups of league members personally bought redwood forest and eventually convinced the State to create a park system. Today, only four per cent of the redwood forests that existed 150 years ago remains. Prairie Creek was established in 1923, Del Norte in 1925 and Jedediah Smith in 1929. In 1968, these parks and other lands were joined in the creation of Redwood National Park.

We camped in the park that night, in a campsite that had been logged out in the late 1800s. Throughout the campsite were thriving examples of why these trees are called *sempervirens*, ever-living. Coastal redwoods don't have taproots. Instead their shallow roots, only four to eight feet below ground, radiate outwards up to 100 feet or more, interlinking with the root systems of other trees, creating a mutual support network. New trees can grow from the 100 or more seeds contained in the unexpectedly small cones but seed-germination is not the redwood's preferred method of reproduction. It favours cloning,

272

sprouting new trees from a root collar, an area just above its root system that encircles each tree. Looking carefully, it was apparent that the impressive trees in the campsite, now over two feet in diameter and up to 100 feet tall, all formed circles around flat-topped eight-foot-wide stumps. These relatively young trees, clones of their parent trees, used their dead parent's root system to absorb nutrients. These rings of trees carried genetic codes unchanged for millions of years.

Unlike the empty groves I had visited during the day, the campground was well occupied. 'Always busy since September 11,' commented the portly, young, blonde park ranger. 'In season we're now turning away three for every space we have. Mostly dog owners, right now. It's always more sedate when we've got dog owners.'

I commented on the low helicopter I'd seen earlier in the day and she told me there was an 11,000-acre forest fire just up the road. The helicopter was picking up water from the river. Another 12,000-acre fire, also started by curtain lightning, was burning down the road by Myers Flat. Fire-fighters from Oregon and Arizona as well as California were on hand.

'Lots of smoke jumpers brought in. These guys are just nuts. They parachute into the fire and hack fire-breaks with just the tools they carry. Scary!'

*   *   *

At dawn I awoke to the sounds of Vietnam. Helicopters everywhere. While I wrote, Mace entertained herself by throwing what looked like green olives up in the air and then pouncing on

273

them. They were tight redwood cones. Over breakfast with a retired cop from San Diego, on a month-long camping trip on his new Yamaha, we talked GMC motorhomes. 'Six miles to the gallon?' he asked.

'Nope,' I responded. 'Driving easy. Getting eight.'

We touched on the War on Terror. 'I was in favour of killing Saddam but this Halliburton thing, there's something wrong about that,' he commented.

Before moving on, I took Mace across the road for a long walk through a grove of battle-scarred, old-growth veterans, most of them scorched up to 30 feet or higher. It was a living lesson on how fire-resistant their resinless fibrous bark is. Poison oak climbed everywhere. Driving south, I had the 'Avenue of Giants' to myself. To my right, occasionally I saw smoke. Signs told me not to stop. Legally and safely stopping for an espresso at Myers Flat, my coffee maker told me that this fire, the Williams Grove fire, was the first in living memory. Two thousand seven hundred fire-fighters from as far away as Montana and eighteen helicopters had been drafted in to 'monitor' the fire, to let it burn.

'It's a low fire in the underbrush,' he explained. 'It was an acre when the first fire-fighters arrived a month ago. They came to monitor it, not put it out. That's the policy for natural fires. Lightning fire? Allowed to burn. Campfire fire? That's put out. There's a ranch over there, 3000 acres. Over 80 per cent of it got burned out by the fire. Sparks flew a mile and torched out their place. They lost so much timber and are real mad at the Parks for not

274

containing it when then could of. Unless they've got their own fire insurance there's no compensation because it's a natural fire, not a man-made one. It's a fight between the environmentalists and the landowners. The environmentalists have the government on their side, so there's no real contest.'

In a field beside us, a gizmo with snorkels and cups had been set up and I asked my coffee maker what it was. 'Smoke detector. Kids burn straw beside it at night because if it detects too much smoke in the air, school's out. Right now, school's out for the next week.' While we talked, Macy cantered down to the grassy field where the smoke detector sat, met a local dog, play-bowed and raced circuits. Just behind her, less than 400 feet away, the forest on the far side of the river was lost in smoke.

'What happens if the wind changes?' I asked.

'The fire-fighters really get to work and I get out of here.'

*   *   *

Sam—lean, lanky, elderly, black—travels everywhere with Lucky, his bullet-shaped, beagle-sized, old smelly rag of a dog. I met them at a drive-through redwood, the Chandelier tree, where Sam took a photo of Macy and me walking through the tree. Afterwards he stroked and nuzzled Macy. 'Lucky is a good dog and does everything to please, but I'll never get over Tommy.' His eyes welled with withheld tears.

Sam was travelling in an old pick-up truck with a camper unit attached. There was no rust on the pick-up, a good indicator that it had spent most or all its life where snow doesn't fall and salt isn't used to grit highways. He pulled a couple of dog biscuits from his windbreaker and now Macy was happy to abandon me and align herself with Sam.

We talked small talk. Sam was born in Louisiana but grew up near Los Angeles. He never married. He'd been a waiter, a dancer, a soldier, a garage mechanic and now he lived in Oakland and did odd jobs. 'I'm a handy man,' he explained, emphasising the word 'handy'. And a sad one. As dignified and as erect as he was, Sam's rheumy, red eyes were filled with sorrow.

'Who was Tommy?' I asked and Sam explained that Tommy was his previous dog, the best friend he ever had.

Those who've never had a dog find it difficult to understand how this can be, how someone can consider a dog to be a better friend than a fellow human. It's really quite simple. Dogs don't judge you. They accept you for what you are, who you are, how you look, how you walk, what you wear, even what you think. They're honest—totally, irredeemably honest. The emotions they feel are the emotions they show. There's nothing false or fake about dogs. What you see is what they really are. Their truthfulness makes them the easiest of companions. An affiliation with a dog is a simpler union than we can ever have with another human. It's this honesty, simplicity, integrity that we mourn when we lose the companionship of a good canine buddy. I looked at Sam and, somehow, 'Mr Bojangles' came into my mind. Remember 'Mr Bojangles'? He danced at minstrel shows and county fairs and spoke of travelling with his dog for

276

fifteen years. But then his dog died and he grieved for twenty years.

*   *   *

Weather-worn Fort Bragg spreads over a sloping coastal shelf at the southern edge of this wild and rocky coastline. Once the site of a redwood sawmill sending hundreds of thousands of board feet of redwood lumber a day to where it was needed, now it's an army town sending Andrew, Ross, Jesse, John, Molly, Jimmy, Angelo, Josh, Jamie, Rich, Kelly, Mark, Clint and Jesus off to war. Hand-painted red, white and blue signs in front gardens, empty lots and fields, dedicated to these kids said, 'Thank You', 'Come Home Soon', 'Freedom is the Reason', 'We Love You', 'We are Proud of You', 'We Are With You', 'Your Family Loves and Misses You', 'United We Stand', 'God Speed', 'God Bless America'. These are the innocents, serving their country.

This land is united, unflinching in its determination to root out terror. But under this visible resolve, I've been confounded and surprised by the unease that people I've met have expressed about how America is going about this task. I've been meeting middle Americans, church-going, mostly rural, retired Republicans. They voted for the present administration. They don't talk about their feelings to their neighbours. They don't want to be thought unpatriotic.

To me, a foreigner, but also an ally, they express their concerns, their reservations, their worries. They're united in the belief that something must be done to contain international terror but worry about how secular Iraq fits in. They're united in their belief that only America has the military might but worry about an administration that, ham-fisted, has made enemies of its friends when more than ever it needs the moral support of its friends. They worry about the morality of how America is going about this. They worry that friends of the government are financially profiting from war. They know that Andrew and Ross and Jesse and John and Molly and all the other kids are serving their nation 'to put things right', to make the world safer, and they rest uneasy, knowing the perils these kids face so far from home.

In 1967, Americans were not fearful of raising their concerns about the Vietnam War. Those who were opposed to that war were active and vocal in their opposition. In 2003, Americans are more tentative. Their concerns are muttered *sotto voce*. What, I thought, will it take, for opponents of their government's war policy, to give them the confidence to speak out, as they have so hesitantly spoken out to me?

*   *   *

Forty years ago, when I last visited here, Mendocino, ten miles south of Fort Bragg, was a jumble of New England-style, gabled, weathered, wooden buildings on a low bluff over a half-moon-shaped bay, at the mouth of Big River. When I worked in a veterinary clinic in Haight-Ashbury, San Francisco, in 1968, this faded but well-preserved village nestling in the surrounding pine-clad hills, had been discovered by drop-outs and had evolved into an artists' colony. I came here with the hippy vet I worked for and had been enchanted. It's still a beautiful village, but now a middle-class destination-town where a single room in a bed and breakfast starts at $150. The homes, stores, churches and halls are all freshly painted, the gardens lush with early autumn flowers and ripening vegetables. It was chilly and damp, 55 degrees F and foggy, but guys in wide-brimmed straw hats, cotton Hawaiian shirts, beige Bermuda shorts, and boat shoes with no socks, strolled through the village before returning to their Volvo SUVs and Range Rovers. I checked into a private RV park, hooked up and settled into a site surrounded by towering rhododendrons. It took Doug and Barb only minutes to find me.

'We saw your GMC in Fort Bragg and followed you, but lost you in Mendocino. Hello, I'm Doug Bodine and this is my wife, Barb. Restore it yourself?'

The Bodines were GMCers from south of Fresno, near Sequoia National Park, on their first long trip in their GMC. Of course, they were as interested in inspecting mine as I was in checking out theirs. Doug was a true GMCer, retired, in his sixties, a natural mechanic. He and Barb had personally replaced their gas tank the week before embarking on this trip. We talked GMC talk—it's a bit like train-spotting talk—and I explained Steinbeck's route I'd planned to take through southern California, from Salinas where I was to visit the National Steinbeck Center and over the Diablo Range into the San Joaquin Valley, through Fresno to Bakersfield, where I'd hook onto the remains of old US Route 66.

'If you're taking that route, you shouldn't miss

the giant sequoias. The GMC is too big to take up into the park, but if you'd like to stay with us, we live in Three Rivers, just outside the park, we can take you there in our car.'

Next morning, after Macy was chased and almost run over by Bogey, a Harley Davidson cap-wearing, paraplegic, silver-grey miniature poodle in colour-co-ordinated diaper, slung in a wheeled chariot to support his paralysed hind limbs, we left in a pea-souper fog and climbed the tortuous highway over the Coast Range, returning to US 101. The closer we got to urban centres, the higher the cost of gasoline. In North Dakota it was as little as $1.39 a gallon. In Oregon it was $1.69. Now it was $1.99, and when you've got a 50-gallon tank in your vehicle those cents really mean something!

The highway droned with frenetic traffic. Oppressive heat had returned, 85 degrees compared to 49 degrees on the coast only hours earlier. And I had no generator, no air conditioning for the vehicle itself, just the dashboard unit. I sweated. Macy panted. Fifty miles out of San Francisco, at Santa Rosa, traffic heading north was at a standstill, a depressing, unending line of people carriers escaping the city. I was back in urban America.

*   *   *

Paul and I grew up together in Toronto. We went to hockey games each weekend in winter and baseball games each weekend in summer. We squabbled about statistics, swore never to see each other again, then met on the subway the following weekend for another match. Paul moved to

California to attend Stanford University and stayed. I moved to London. Forty years on and 8000 miles apart, we still know how to gently wind each other up. We'd both like to spend more time together and I'd upped speed in the last week to catch him before he travelled to China with one of his many daughters.

The following days were family days. I went with Carole and Paul's daughter, Carrie, her husband Dave and their delicious Australian shepherd, Bailey, to a park in Moraga where dogs are actually allowed off their leashes until 9.00 a.m.! Golly gosh! We went to an antique fair where I met a displaced, laconic, ponytailed Mancunian, a specialist in South-West American Indian silver and turquoise jewellery. We visited Berkeley for a scrumptious fish meal. Each night I slept in a sumptuous bed, and dreamt of returning to my own home, parked at the bottom of their drive.

Paul took me to Candlestick Park to a football game, the San Francisco 49ers vs the Detroit Lions. I learned later that earth-mother Carole felt concerned about Macy. My dog and I hadn't been apart for over a month, and after I'd left Macy stared at the door long enough to convince Carole to take her, along with her floosy bichon, Bean, to Bailey's for the afternoon.

Carole had packed deckchairs, cushions and a massive picnic for Paul and me, and we joined the thousands of tailgaters in the parking lot, cooking barbecues, mingling, singing, schmoozing before the game. This wasn't Oakland, or Millwall. This was a quiche-eating crowd. Yes, there was beer, but mostly it was white wine accompanying barbecued asparagus drizzled with olive oil. Twenty minutes before the game the trestle tables, chequered red tablecloths, Thermoses, picnic hampers and sound systems returned to the pick-ups, SUVs, RVs, people carriers or—in our case, a 7-series BMW with personalised licence plate—and the crowd, all in jeans or chinos, red 49ers polo shirts, boat shoes and SF baseball hats, trooped cheerily into the stadium. There wasn't a black or Hispanic face in sight. The game's opening entertainment began and then a tenor from the San Francisco Opera sang the national anthem:

And the rockets red glare,
The bombs bursting in air,
Gave proof through the night,
That our flag was still there.

The crowd was standing silently, some with hands on heart, but as the tenor sang 'that our flag was still there', it broke into a profoundly euphoric, incessant, exhilarating roar. These were actuaries, lawyers, secretaries, accountants, dentists. This was middle-class white California and their patriotic surge of excitement was spine-tingling. This was a new expression of patriotism. My middle-class, 1960s generation was ambivalent about outward shows of patriotism. The national anthem, whether in the United States or Canada, was something to get through before or after the game. 'It ain't over 'til the fat lady sings,' they said of Kate Smith's rendition of the national anthem at the end of the game. There was no mention of what she was singing.

The night before I moved on, after recounting to them my travels through Montana, Paul told me

282

a story about a luxury bus trip he and Carole once took from Yellowstone in Wyoming to Mount Rushmore in South Dakota, during which the bus broke down near the Montana state line in the middle of nowhere.

'We were milling around at the side of the road and a lady drove by in a four-door Ford. She stopped to ask what she could do, told us there was a restaurant six miles up the road and offered to start ferrying people there. 35 of us, OK? So we adopted the sinking-ship principle of women and children first.

'While we were waiting our turn, another car came along the road, then another. We didn't flag them down, they just stopped and asked what they could do to help. They started ferrying us to the same restaurant. In the meantime, the first lady, when she found the restaurant closed, knocked on the owner's door and he opened the restaurant for us.

'Next along the highway was a grizzled outdoorsman in a Ford pick-up truck. He saw our problem and said, 'No sweat. I'll tow you to the restaurant.' He set up a towing rig at the front of the bus. Remember, this is a full-sized Greyhound-type bus. He had a regular-sized pick-up truck. He got the rig set up, then told the rest of us to get in the bus which we did. He then proceeded to have this small Ford pick-up truck tow a fully loaded bus with fifteen passengers and everybody's luggage, six miles up the road. And he was pulling uphill.

'Now all 35 of us were sitting in a Wyoming roadhouse. Given the delay, the tour operator decided to host the bar bill, and we all got sloshed along with whatever locals dropped by. The replacement bus from Helena was late. We were in that roadhouse for six hours. If we'd broken down near San Francisco, you could stand on the side of the road for days without anybody stopping to enquire. We marvelled at the generosity of the locals. Every single one of them stopped, not to find out what was wrong, but to help, to assist. We joke about frontiersmen, but there's a generosity of spirit right across America that we forget about when we live in cities for too long.'

There was a generosity of spirit here, too, in suburban California. That evening, Carole presented me with perfect piles of neatly folded sheets, pillow slips, T-shirts, trousers, socks and underwear. There was a food package for me and one for Macy, toys for Mace and gifts for Julia, who would be joining us in Houston. Tomorrow, hopefully, the generator would be repaired and we'd have air conditioning for our travels through the desert. I was itchy to get back to nowhere.

CHAPTER EIGHT

SOUTHERN CALIFORNIA

'I cannot agree that it should be declared public policy [wrote Adlai Stevenson, Governor of the State of Illinois, commenting on proposed legislation that would restrict the movement of cats] that a cat visiting a neighbor's yard or crossing the highway is a public nuisance. It is in the nature of cats to do a certain amount of unescorted roaming. The problem of cat versus bird is as old as time . . . In my opinion the State of Illinois and its local governing bodies already have enough to do without trying to control feline delinquency.'

It was Adlai Stevenson, the best President the United States never had, who encouraged John Steinbeck to travel once more around the United States, as he had done in the 1930s, to canvass opinion, and to gather impressions for another book. Stevenson was Steinbeck's contemporary, a friend and like the author, born here in California. Once a journalist for a family-owned newspaper, he later served one term as Governor of Illinois and then twice ran for President, failing hopelessly on both occasions. He liked cats. He was wise and gifted, but didn't understand that it's totally impossible to become President of the United States if you're perceived to be a cat lover.

While Stevenson encouraged Steinbeck to travel, Steinbeck's wife, Elaine, concerned about her husband's health, discouraged the thought. I look at the photos of Steinbeck on various editions of *Travels with Charley* and see why. He was an old man, yet he was younger than I am, still in his late fifties, when he embarked on his journey. It was Elaine who volunteered that Charley should accompany her husband and who also provided the title for his book. Steinbeck bought a new Ford pick-up truck with automatic transmission and an oversized generator and had a camper body, provided by the Wolverine Camper Company in Michigan, mounted on it. He christened his mobile home, Rocinante, after Don Quixote's horse, probably because his wife, or friends, or even he thought the trip quixotic. Throughout my travels I've pondered giving a name to my home. For the first days it was certainly 'The Bitch', but once I was accustomed to her idiosyncrasies, once I felt secure with her, she simply became 'Home'.

Now, in early Monday morning rush-hour traffic, I was driving my home through Oakland to San Leandro, where I hoped my generator circuit board had arrived. I parked among fire trucks, buses and semis. Beside me, two silvering, chocolate toy poodles in a semi's cab barked proprietorially. The driver told me one had lost all his front teeth when he fell out the door. It's a long way down if you're a flyweight. My engineer entertained me with stories of how useful cooking-oil spray is to make burr-removal from cocker spaniels easy after hunting. He proudly announced he'd been in a saving scheme for his daughter's education since the day she was born. He'd saved $350,000 and hoped she'd go to Kansas State and become a veterinarian. I didn't ask if he considered that a good investment. In the drivers' lounge truckers were talking about Iraq. 'Hard to go sunny

287

side up when the yolk's broken,' said one.

It was mid-morning and already 80 degrees. I was out of pocket another $500, but with a circuit board and renewed air conditioning, I set off down US 101, arriving at lunchtime in Salinas and the National Steinbeck Center. The 'museum', 'learning centre', call it what you will, is sited in the derelict centre of Salinas, Steinbeck's home town. Affiliated with San Jose State University, it contains over 40,000 items of Steinbeckiana. Active Steinbeck researchers must also look elsewhere, however. Stanford University and the University of California-Berkeley both have Steinbeck archives, as do Princeton and Columbia in the east and the University of Texas in Austin. The Pierpont Morgan Library in New York also has a Steinbeck archive. What I'd come to see, however, was Rocinante herself.

After his travels Steinbeck immediately sold his truck and in the following decades it was put to steadfast use on a farm in Maryland. Remarkably, decades later Steinbeck's original buyer still owned it and in 1990 donated it to the National Steinbeck Center. Fully restored, it's a highlight of the centre. Mace had a roll in the grass under a massive photo of Steinbeck receiving his Nobel Prize for Literature. Then I paid my entrance fee, examined the selection of T-shirts, book markers, paperweights and ties, all with Steinbeck quotes on them, available from the gift shop, bought a copy of *Travels with Charley* and wandered through a friendly interactive facility where, at the push of a button, Henry Fonda in *The Grapes of Wrath* appeared on screen, uttering arresting Steinbeck lines.

I listened to a recording of his Nobel Prize commendation.

> . . . his sympathies always go out to the oppressed, the misfits and the distressed. He likes to contrast the simple joy of life with the brutal and cynical craving for money. But in him we find the American temperament also expressed in his great feeling for nature, for the tilled soil, the waste land, the mountains, the ocean coast, all an inexhaustible source of inspiration . . .

The Steinbeck Center makes no mention of the assassination article published in the *New York Times* on the day Steinbeck received the Nobel Prize for Literature. Like Ernest Hemingway, Steinbeck is criticised for being too obvious in his symbolism, too emotional, too sentimental. In Arthur Mizener's *New York Times* knifing, Steinbeck's more or less accused of being comprehensible to common people, people like high school students, people his biographer, Jay Parini, deliciously calls 'actual voluntary readers'. I'm one of those actual voluntary readers and I tell you this. Read *The Grapes of Wrath* again. Are his descriptions of the dust, the people and the roads poetic? Does he love his characters? Does he catch the rhythm of their speech, their cadence, their tone? Does he not care for them? Does he not involve us? Is his anger not real and true and heartfelt?

I moved on to what is the highlight of the centre, the *Travels with Charley* section. May I be sacrilegious and say I don't think *Travels* is a particularly good read? True, it's his best-selling book. In 1962, the year he was awarded the Nobel Prize, it was paperback of the year. It was one of his greatest commercial successes but, honestly, do you think it comes even remotely near the anger, the integrity, the poetry, the humour of *Cannery Row*, *The Grapes of Wrath*, *East of Eden*, *Of Mice and Men*, *Tortilla Flat*? I watched a looping edition of NBC's TV 1968 re-creation of *Travels with Charley*, aptly narrated by Henry Fonda, and was faintly embarrassed by its banality.

On one wall is a ten-foot-high reproduction of the original edition's endpaper map of Steinbeck's route, appended with quotes from the book and highlighted by tracking lights travelling along his route. There is a wall-sized picture of Steinbeck sitting uncomfortably in a folding deckchair, Charley standing with his front feet on the edge of the chair. And beyond, surrounded by glass like a teller in an old bank, is Rocinante, a dark green pick-up with a white camper unit, looking vaguely like a gypsy caravan. The wooden interior looks warm and inviting. Before leaving, I listened to a recording of his Nobel Prize acceptance speech:

Furthermore, the writer is delegated to declare and to celebrate man's proven capacity for greatness of heart and spirit, for gallantry in defeat, for courage, compassion and love. In the endless war against weakness and despair, these are the bright rally flags of hope and emulation . . .

I wondered, in America's present state, what Steinbeck would write about today? How would he see America's international role? Would he be pleased with the way America uses her power? After Steinbeck's friend Adlai Stevenson died—in London in 1965—the political commentator and columnist Walter Lippmann delivered a eulogy, in which he asked what course America would have followed under Stevenson.

> On one course we shall plunge ourselves into the making of a ramshackle empire . . . and we shall wave the flag to cover our spiritual nakedness . . . or we shall, as Adlai Stevenson would have done, remain true to our original loyalty, and, transcending assertiveness, vulgar ambition and the seductions of power, we shall make this country not only great and free but at peace with its own conscience.

I imagine Steinbeck's ambitions were similar to those Lippmann attributed to Stevenson. They certainly are mine.

*   *   *

Joaquin Murrieta was a bandit. In the mid-1800s, he terrorised stage-coach routes and mining regions throughout central California. The newly formed state offered a $5000 reward for his capture 'Dead or Alive', and in 1853 a posse of twenty State Rangers, led by Captain Harry Love, left San Jose to find him. Murrieta's former wife told them he might be in the Priest Valley of the Cholame Hills. The valley had acquired its name a few years earlier, after a priest and 100 Indians were encountered there, resting after rounding up

291

wild horses. Murrieta and his gang were surprised in an arroyo in the valley. Murrieta's lieutenant, Three-Fingered Jack, scrambled away through the underbrush, but Love gave chase and shot him between the eyes. Murrieta jumped on an unsaddled horse but Henderson, one of Love's rangers shot the horse, then, with two more shots, killed Murrieta. His head, together with Three-Fingered Jack's hand, was cut off, packed in salt and taken back to San Jose—proof that the bandits were dead. For the next 50 years, in jars of alcohol, they were exhibited throughout the state, disappearing during the San Francisco earthquake and fire of 1906.

Down US 101, I travelled past mile upon mile of flat irrigated fields filled with equal parts salad greens and migrant pickers until, just beyond King City, I turned east, up into the Cholame Hills towards Priest Valley. It took only minutes to drive above the dust and smog in the valley, into rounded, burnished golden hills. When these are green, during the rains of December to March, I imagine they look not unlike the treeless South Downs of Sussex. The road climbed further. At its height the air was fresh, clear and sweet. Below me the atmosphere was the colour of muddy water.

Over the range of hills, I descended into the warm air of Priest Valley. We walked through tinder-dry grass, climbing rocks covered in orange, yellow and black lichen. Macy squirrelled through fields of dry, silver-leafed, burgundy-headed wild flowers. A dead-end road, signposted Coalinga Hot Springs, beckoned me and I turned north onto it. After a few miles, the road hit a series of switchbacks. A jackrabbit popped up, waving a hand-painted sign, 'Hey, turkey brain. Really wanna try this?' Right, I lie. But you get the point.

I turned round and drove back half a mile to a flat pull-off by a smaller arroyo, to camp for the night. After parking, we started back up the road. I wanted to see what was beyond the switchbacks and, as we walked, I noticed that Macy, using her nose, was flipping bits of black tyre-tread off the road onto the verge. I looked closer. It wasn't tyre-tread. She was tossing tarantulas. I scanned the road. There were two, just-squashed tarantulas, still moist and gooey in the 90-degree heat. I'd scrunched them driving up the road. Around Macy and me there were at least a dozen more—two to three inches long, eight hairy legs, eight eyes on each head—all walking intently, obliviously, up the tarmac, heading for the switchbacks. I've handled tarantulas before, usually in my guise of the know-it-all TV vet, and knew their bite was venomless and mild. Macy continued tarantula-sniffing and I saw that one of them had its butt raised in defence. Tarantulas have tiny barbed hairs on their bellies and can fling them when threatened. I commanded Mace to 'Come,' which she did, and we moved off-road. Near the dry riverbed the ground was littered with pine cones the size of Macy's skull. I tossed one for her but she couldn't get a purchase on it, preferring to nose around looking for rodents.

The area looked desert-like, but only at this time of year. The Priest Valley gets over 20 inches of rain a year. London, England, gets 27 inches. The difference is that here it all falls in the winter.

Back at our isolated campsite I made us dinner, set up my chair, and as the night darkened, listened to the humming, buzzing cacophony of cicadas and crickets, softened by whistling birdsong. The moon was so bright that night I couldn't sleep. Neither could Macy. She whimpered to go out, to look, to listen. I told her to go to bed. She whimpered again. On the third occasion, when I told her once more to get in her bed, she jumped on mine and looked out the window. By 4.00 a.m. the moon had passed over the mountain range to the west and I got to sleep.

*   *   *

When I got up that morning my clothes, dropped on the floor last night, had changed colour. And they were moving, covered in a myriad of tiny red ants. I'd wondered, the previous evening, sitting outside and contemplating nature, trying to work out which trees the cicadas were in, why my ankles were so itchy. Now, walking through my home, I saw red ants everywhere—on the kitchen work surface, the floors, Macy's bed and bowls, even her feet. And there were a quadrillion zillion fruit flies hovering. I'd left the driver's sliding window open over night and peaches out on the counter.

After a cursory sweep, removing the majority of my visitors, I turned on the generator, made an espresso, then went for an hour's walk into the arroyo. This was Mace's first chance in almost a week to experience unencumbered freedom, to do as dogs wish to do. She urine-marked everywhere, so much so that I assumed she was coming into season. She raised uncounted birds, found an old femur to chew on, then urine-marked some more. We walked up through dry waterbeds, the routes of winter waters from the hills, through land broken

294

by occasional fork-trunked digger pine and smaller trees covered in pale green succulent leaves. Thin, papery bark hung in curled strips, like red tissue paper, from their trunks and major branches. These must be manzanita, I thought, the source of a bowl I'd bought at the Chandelier redwood. We moved on through chaparral until the arroyo became too narrow to climb farther. This was the land Joaquin Murrieta and Three-Fingered Jack retreated to.

When we returned to the GMC, there was a hummingbird hovering by the front window, staring hopefully at a red plaid cushion I'd left on the front passenger seat. I checked Macy for livestock, de-anted some more, and headed back out of the canyon towards the main road. I stopped by an abandoned 1940s pick-up truck, riddled with bullet holes, and tried in vain to remove its old black and yellow licence plate as a souvenir. Walking back to my vehicle, I saw I was still home to dozens of red ants but now also had tenacious burrs over my clothes, even on my socks deep in my boots.

I descended through the Curry Mountains towards Coalinga. All the road signs were pocked with bullet holes, all the men in pick-ups passing me wore cowboy hats. Another of Steven Spielberg's drivers tried to crawl up my tailpipe, so I sent Blondie to the back window to scare him. He backed off. In Coalinga, as almost everywhere else I'd travelled, the newest building was the self-storage site. Everyone in America, it seems, even in the most remote regions, has surplus. I drove into the Kettleman Hills, rolling hills covered in Chevron-Texaco nodding donkeys and circular oil

TRUCK GRAVEYARD AT COALINGA, CALIFORNIA

tanks. We passed a fresh, road-killed coyote. He was big, the size of a small German shepherd. That's why Mace had been urine-marking so frenetically this morning. She was anointing coyote droppings. Crossing in the distance, I saw an unending train of 18-wheelers. It was Interstate 5. Beyond, were cotton fields, peach and pomegranate orchards, vineyards and olive groves.

I let Mace out for a run in a parched, already harvested field. As she kicked up clouds of dust, I immediately regretted letting her do so. Valley Fever, I thought—coccidioidomycosis, as they say in the vet business. I hadn't thought of this infection, contracted by inhaling spores from dry soil, since I was at university.

A couple of months before graduating, my final clinical report was on a case of fungal infection, in a local hound, a disease called histoplasmosis. One of my classmates from Montreal had actually contracted this illness, when soil was disturbed during the construction of the Montreal Metro system. Another fungal infection that can affect deep organs in the body is called blastomycosis. Valley Fever is unique in that it's restricted almost wholly to the San Joaquin Valley and dogs are overwhelmingly the species most likely to be infected. Spores get inhaled into the lungs and travel to lymph nodes. If the immune system fails to kill them, serious but at first non-specific disease develops. A dog may have swollen glands, develop a cough, be depressed, run a fever, lose its appetite, develop swollen joints, become lethargic, experience pain, lose weight, even go blind. It often takes months for clinical signs to develop but, unlike when I graduated, today there are effective anti-fungal treatments. Even so, I ordered Mace back into the GMC.

Near Lemoore, I thought I was driving past a series of feedlots until I saw a 'Land O'Lakes' sign and realised these were massive dairy units. At one I saw around 500 cows, the next even larger—800 cows—and another equal or greater in size. The cows, restricted to an area only large enough to walk around in, ate from long rows of feeding troughs—high-energy fast food before another milking. Over dinner one night at Paul's, one of his daughters, Susie, had asked, 'What's wrong with the industrialisation of agriculture?' Here was an answer: cows converted to production units, crowded in unnatural numbers, stimulated by synthetic hormones, burnt out by high-energy feeds. The only thing natural about what I saw was that they were producing milk because they had calved. Were their young in veal crates somewhere near?

At least roadside shopping was good. Nibbling on grapes purchased at a roadside stand, I noted, with a wee bit of concern, a one-and-a-half-inch, pug-ugly spider crawling up my T-shirt towards my neck. This makes for an interesting situation. You're travelling at 45 mph with a mouthful of grapes. Your dog is seated beside you, looking mournfully up into your eyes. A spider of unknown pedigree is attracted to your warm neck. What do you do? I didn't want to anger it and tried to flick my T-shirt, but the arachnid clung like glue and continued its remorseless trail towards my jugular. Slowly I eased my home off the road onto the dirt shoulder, opened the sliding window, stretched my T-shirt beyond the limits of stretch and, with a forefinger flick, kicked the spider into passing traffic.

Incidentally, the local towns are well worth a miss. Visalia suffers the same infliction as the rest of small town America—a standardised sameness, a drab blandness, a self-inflicted anonymity of chain superstores and themed restaurants. Exeter was better. We stopped for a walk and an ice cream. 'Is she a Labrador-cocker spaniel cross?' a father and son asked. I looked at my dog and realised she had lost whatever fat she had arrived with. She was sinewy and lithe from her weeks of vigorous activity. She was as dogs should be, but rarely are.

*   *   *

My GMC struggled up the steep incline to Doug and Barb Bodine's home. Blue jays leapt from branch to branch in the trees by their home, while hummingbirds hovered around sugary feeders. Over barbecued chicken, meat loaf, courgettes, garlic grilled potatoes, sweet potatoes, salad, and home-made apple pie served with cheddar cheese—a perfect sweet and tart combination that suggested either Doug's or Barb's family had once lived in the east—we talked about their trip to Mendocino and my experiences of the last few days. 'Those tarantulas you saw,' Doug explained, 'they're all males out looking for mates. That's why they weren't interested in you or your dog. They're pretty docile. A bite's nowhere near as bad as a bee sting. Were they black?'

I answered in the affirmative and Doug explained, 'Females are more brown. They leave a scent by their burrows. That's what the males you saw were trailing after. They find it easier to travel on the road. Smoother. The males usually die after mating, but females can live for 30 years. It takes up to ten years for a female to become mature.'

Doug was the local Culligan Soft Water man before he retired and Barb a local teacher, although it was Doug who was now teaching me about the life-cycle of California tarantulas. He was just as good describing coyotes. 'They're a big problem here. Up to three-quarters of a million in the state and sometimes it seems they're all here. Take lots of house cats. You'll hear them howling tonight. You know, they call people who bring illegals across the border from Mexico 'coyotes'. Secretive during the day; active at night. Everything that's been done to control coyotes only makes them wilier and smarter. Same with people-smugglers. Our coyotes are mountain ones. Down in the desert they're small, maybe 25 pounds, but up here they're twice that weight. Darker in colour. Their song is beautiful.'

The Bodines typified the Americans I'd forgotten about after decades in Britain. A chance encounter in an RV park and I'd found myself with a warm, hospitable couple who not only were going to take me up into Sequoia National Park tomorrow, but this evening were my own personal, natural history, lending library. They offered Macy and me a room but we both preferred our own home. Throughout the night, coyotes howled. Macy stood up all night, peering out the back window, ears perked. Now I knew it was because she had distant relatives outside. Their yip-yip-yowls only ceased when the sky lightened the following morning.

*   *   *

The General Sherman Tree, the world's largest living thing, was originally called the Karl Marx Tree. And Sequoia National Park, America's second oldest park, was established and maintained by the military, not for its scenic and recreational values, but to protect this region from socialistic colonists who planned a co-operative utopia in the wilderness. Such is the strangeness of America.

In 1885, the land registrar in Visalia reported to Washington what he thought were suspicious applications for land above the Marble Fork of the Kaweah River. Just beyond Three Rivers, where I now was, branches the North Fork of the Kaweah. Further on by the entrance to Sequoia National Park, is the East Branch, and at what today is the Potwisha campsite in the park is the Marble Fork Branch. Above there is where the land applications were for. It's also the location of the Giant Forest.

The land applicants had visited this region, planned to harvest sugar and yellow pine and solemnly vowed never to cut the giant sequoias, naming the most outstanding trees after their heroes of the Paris Commune, American and international socialism. Wary of the colonists' motives, the government suspended all land registrations in the region. In response, the colonists formed the Kaweah Co-operative Commonwealth Company to litigate in court. In the meantime they worked on constructing a road. Four years later it had reached four miles beyond

Potwisha, but within another year an act of Congress had created Sequoia National Park. Troops were sent to expel the colonists and administer the region. One of their first actions was to rename the trees after American-government icons and generals. The Karl Marx Tree was named after the soldier native people called Great Warrior Sherman, the soldier who built Fort Coeur d'Alene.

Doug told me that even today Three Rivers is peopled by individuals of independent spirit. In the 1890s, the local paper wrote of 'Cossack Terrorism' and soldiers were booed in the streets. Over the next 24 years military administrators built roads and facilities. Locals say that one of the most industrious was Captain Charles Young who commanded a battalion of African-American cavalrymen, all mounted on coal-black horses. It was not until 1914 that the government felt it was safe to appoint a civilian administration for the park.

Macy and I were up before dawn for a walk in the dry chaparral. She found fresh bear scats to sniff and, just as quickly, a young chestnut bloodhound and a black Labrador-shepherd cross joined her in the dry grass. After an introductory bum-sniff and play-bow they rollicked and raced up the road, over rocks, through dried waterbeds and tinder-dry vegetation, as the sun rose to another cloudless day.

Barb had prepared a sumptuous breakfast, then we all walked outside, past their car to an open-top, silver-coloured, old, classic Jeep. Doug turned to me and smiled. 'You and Macy will have more fun on your own. You can do exactly what you like.

The Jeep's a little frisky. It's a V6, so you'll have to get accustomed to lightness on the accelerator.' He handed me the keys. I'd spent an hour with the Bodines near Mendocino, and another few hours last night over dinner. Now they were giving me their Jeep for the day. I was staggered by such warm generosity.

There was exactly enough room in the back for Macy's bed. She hopped over the back onto it, I leashed her to the side of the roll bar, turned the ignition, entered first gear, touched the accelerator and exploded out of the drive onto the steep road down the mountain. Under Macy's bed were two bottles of water and her water bowl. Barb had provided lunch for me. Doug was right about the V6 engine. The merest feather touch to the accelerator threw my head towards Mace in the back.

Heading up into the Sierra Nevadas, dry chaparral soon gave way to trees, western sycamores along the canyon floor below, yucca, buckeye and pine around me. At the park entrance I was given a map and written advice:

Rattlesnakes are common in the park. Always be sure you can see where you step or reach. Cougars live in these parks. Avoid hiking or running alone. If a bear approaches, scare it away. Park roads are steep, narrow and winding. Downshift even in automatics to prevent a burned-out transmission going uphill and burned-out brakes downhill. Giardia lamblia is a protozoan in natural water in the park. Boil surface water three minutes before drinking. When a

303

thunderstorm threatens, get in a vehicle or large building. If your hair stands on end, drop to your knees and bend forward with your hands on your knees. Don't lie flat.

Macy agreed to these terms and we continued, past wooded mountains from which protruded jagged scars of granite, stopping at Hospital Rock. From where I parked, Moro Rock towered 4000 feet above me. In 1856, Hale Tharp, a farmer from Three Rivers, ventured up here in search of pastures and a ranch site and met the local native people, the Yokuts. 'The Indians liked me,' Tharp said, 'because I was good to them. I liked the Indians too, for they were honest and kind to each other.'

The Yokut told him of the giant trees, so big that it took 25 men, hands clasped together, to encircle the largest of them. Two years later, Tharp discovered the Giant Forest. The Yokut asked Tharp to explain the meaning of the pictographs painted on the rocks at Hospital Rock—birds, dragonflies, wheels—drawn by people who had preceded them. Of course, he couldn't. In less than ten years the Yokut were decimated by disease and conflict with settlers. Their living presence remains in the multiple mortar holes in the granite rock, over which Macy was now walking, holes in which they ground acorns and buckeyes from the trees on the slopes up from the valley.

Beyond Hospital Rock is a series of hairpin turns. Macy hunkered down and, in her usual way, avoided looking at the scenery: yucca and buckeyes clinging to life in the limestone. At Ampitheater

Point scenic lookout a group of men and women, with FIRE emblazoned on the backs of their shirts, were peering south, some with their hands cupped over their eyes, others with binoculars. They told me they were monitoring a fire that was in the process of changing direction, threatening private land to the west. We climbed higher, over 5000 feet higher than where we began, and arrived at the Giant Forest. There were only a few cars in the parking lot and we were alone as we walked around Crescent Meadow surrounded by giant sequoias.

The aura of these trees is different to that of the coastal redwoods. In this open, sunny land they looked more like formal, massive Doric columns all painted in shimmering cinnamon-brown. In the coastal redwood forests, I needed to use a flash to take pictures. Here in the open terrain that giant sequoias need, their feet-thick bark is more three-dimensional, their stout branches—many of greater diameter than my six-foot height—more impressive, their breadth more arresting. Magnificent coastal redwoods have a tapered crown reminiscent of evergreens. These trees, with conical crowns in which each of their ten to twenty branches looks itself like a fully grown tree, are, to my eye, unique. Their shape reminds me, if anything, of soft, seductive Monterey pine. All the trees had blackened burn marks on their trunks. Some had fire-blackened cavities twenty feet high in their bases. Unlike coastal redwoods that multiply by cloning, giant sequoias only grow from seed and fire is needed for the egg-sized cones to release their flaky seeds for dispersal and to provide ash for fertiliser and growth.

We walked, mostly alone, but at the President Tree, two little girls joined us, their parents mildly irritated that the kids were more interested in a common golden retriever than in the glories surrounding them. Macy posed for pictures and we walked on, suddenly confronted with the blackened consequences of what must have been an enormous and very recent fire. The Congress Trees and all those surrounding them were freshly charred. All other vegetation was completely burnt out. Wood, burnt to a crisp, littered the ground which was covered by a vast and seemingly limitless bed of blackened, sooty sequoia cones. Fire-fighters had dug down at the bases of some of the burnt carcasses, leaving three-foot-deep holes. A woodpecker hammered on a nearby oak. A ground chipmunk hid under a massive piece of foot-thick bark buried in the soil. Ash was everywhere.

At the General Sherman Tree I stopped for lunch, joining Ross, an American-Irish tenor, and his wife, bicycling through the park. My own method of transport, the Bodines' Jeep, brought looks of envy. This is where the crowds were, gathered around the world's largest living thing, a congregation at a superlative. I sat on a bench beside a bickering elderly couple. She commanded, he shrugged his shoulders, their grown children looked annoyed. He turned to me. 'Sixty-five years!' he explained or exclaimed to me. I asked him to take our picture.

The General Sherman Tree, the park brochure tells me, is 274.9 feet tall—that's two and a half feet higher than the height recorded in the AGS *California Guide* published in 1939. Its circumference now, at 102.6 is also a foot greater. It is, however, younger. In 1939 its age was guessed at 3000–4000 years. Now it's estimated at a more conservative 2300–2700 years.

At Moro Rock there's a sign:

WARNING
AREA OF EXTREME DANGER
dark clouds nearby or overhead
thunder, hail or rain
hissing in the air
static electricity in the hair or fingertips

The sky was blue, not a cloud in sight, but there was another warning sign. It showed a dog on a leash with a red line through it. I took this to mean dogs on leashes are not allowed to climb Moro Rock, so I unleashed my companion who raced up and back down the 300 feet of concrete and rock steps perhaps three times, while I puffed my way to the top. There I met three Bureau of Land Management men monitoring the forest fire.

'It took some time before we learned the value of forest fires,' explained one of the men, a muscular, brown-eyed, possibly bottle-blond. 'It's a tough call. This one's part of the natural ecosystem. We didn't start it, but we're watching her. The forest needs fires, but they destroy property. This one's changing direction. See that helicopter? We've started dropping water.' In the distance a helicopter released water from a massive cylinder beneath it, a mere tear from heaven.

*   *   *

MONITORING A FOREST FIRE, MORO ROCK,

I've travelled extensively in the United States but never before through cowboy country. Heading west towards the Mojave Desert and Arizona, I got kidnapped and taken to a mountain-top eyrie by a wild-haired native. Earlier in the day, Barb had given me a care package of freshly baked biscuits and apple pie when I left. She wanted to fatten me up before I met Julia in Houston. I headed south through land that gradually evolved from pancake flatness to undulating hills, stopping at a hilly orange grove for Macy to have a wander. Returning to our home, I saw a coyote on a ridge across the road, loping along, tail down, staring unblinkingly at us. When I stopped, he stopped, ever staring. He was big, about two-thirds Macy's size, perhaps twenty inches at the shoulders, but long, pushing five feet from nose to tip of his tail. A slight breeze was blowing from behind Macy and me. He'd scented both of us long before I saw him. Doug told me that around Three Rivers coyotes work in packs and I looked for others but saw none. Always staring, he showed no fear, lolloped along and after little more than a minute was gone. I drove on, through crops of nodding donkeys on both sides of the road, through Bakersfield and, on its outskirts, past a grape vineyard with nodding donkeys among the vines. Was this how those really heavy, dark, rich California reds were made?

Somewhere near Keene, Julia phoned me and I pulled onto the hard shoulder. It was less than a minute before Pete arrived, driving a pristine white 1978 GMC. He thought I might need help and when he learned that I didn't, that wasn't going to prevent him from giving me lunch. Now some folks enjoy spontaneity and some don't. The chief is in the latter camp. She likes anticipating—the restaurant, the movie, the gift. Me? I followed Pete up a tortuous road, as steep if not steeper than the one Doug and Barb lived at the top of, to a spectacular home he'd built overlooking the valley below. To the north were the Sierra Nevadas. Looking east, far below, I could see Highway 58 and beyond it a train climbing towards a westerly mountain pass.

Pete was retired from education. With luxurious silver hair and moustache, wearing a denim short-sleeved shirt and khaki pants, he looked the prototypical, relaxed Californian. Masses of hummingbirds hovered at feeders by his front and side doors. One got inside when we entered and we had a heck of a time getting it back outdoors. Pete doesn't have a dog; he has cats, but he keeps Milkbones for neighbours' dogs who visit and gave one to Macy, who instantly made herself at home. Pete keeps losing cats; he thinks to coyotes although there are grey foxes in the area.

He guided me through an archway of natural stones, not unlike Stonehenge monoliths, forming a passageway through an eruption of land, to the Spanish-Colonial front door of his home. I entered a room, with full-length westerly views, filled with pre-Columbian artefacts. Pete had built his house for its mesmerising vistas but the views inside were equally intriguing. 'It's like a private museum in here,' I commented. 'A poor-quality museum,' Pete added. On one wall was an oil painting of Venice, on others vibrant oil paintings in primal colours.

Of course, we talked GMCs.

'GMCers are my age; I liked it and wanted one

310

when it first came out but couldn't afford one. They, or should I say, we, are mechanically minded and friendly people.'

I asked him for his ideas on what name I might give my GMC and he suggested 'Meno'.

'Depending who you are talking to, it can have two meanings. It can refer to the type of menopausal men who buy them, or to the temperamental nature of GMCs,' he explained.

Pete was a wry teacher.

Looking west to Bakersfield the atmosphere was orange-brown.

'Pollution gets drawn down into the valley by high pressure from the Bay Area. It combines with agricultural pollution and dust to produce what you see there. Just sits for months. That pollution you see will clear when high pressure lifts and a seasonal low moves in, perhaps later this month.'

I offered to make Pete a salad with Wisconsin blue cheese followed by local melon and stolen pomegranates, but he preferred a couple of TV dinners. As he popped them in the oven our conversation turned to politics. He became, not tense, but less relaxed, walked over to the work surface island in the middle of the kitchen, and leaned on it with both hands.

'I wonder whether there's a single politician in this country who can justify the moral contradiction we are revealing to the world. As an educator I have been proud to teach students that America is the true bastion of democracy; that democracy is of the people, by the people and for the people. That's the democracy my generation fought for. That's the democracy we planted in fascist Europe. How, then, do you teach students today that it's right to criticise the French and the Germans for doing what the people of those countries democratically willed—no involvement fighting in Iraq? This is a contradiction that is deeply disturbing.'

Pete was a fastidious man. I got the feeling everything about his home, about his dream come true on top of a mountain was of his making, rather than influenced by his wife who spent much of her time elsewhere. He was articulate and I would have enjoyed staying, but I had a Houston deadline to meet, the chief's arrival in little more than a week. Before I left, he took me on a tour of his garden to show me work in hand, work to do, and his pride, a deciduous Dawn redwood, *Metasequoia glyptostroboides*, found only in a remote valley in Szechuan province, in central China. Here was the third member of the redwood family, only ten feet high, browsed by foraging deer, but surviving in California.

*   *   *

I braked my way down the tortuous mountain, no problem for me—got balls the size of velociraptor eggs—and drove further into cowboy country. In the UK it's easy to forget that California is not only the San Francisco Bay Area and Los Angeles, that most of this most populous state in the Union is barren and empty, virtual wilderness. I'd spent longer here than in any other state or province and still there were hundreds of miles to travel before I reached Arizona.

Beyond Tehachapi Pass I entered the rain shadow of the Sierra Nevadas, the western rim of the great Mojave Desert. A sign warned: 'Campers—Gusty Winds Next 8 Miles'. Squat yuccas grew in abundance, then, unexpectedly, spike-leafed Joshua trees, the largest of all yuccas, in stands on both sides of the road. On a book tour years ago, on a free weekend in Los Angeles, I had visited Joshua Tree National Park, south of the Mojave Desert. Foolishly, I hadn't realised that these 'cactuses', up to 40 feet tall and three feet in diameter, long thought to be members of the tequila-producing agave family but now classified as part of the lily family, also grew in abundance here by old Highway 66. Those surrounding me were relatively small, but still over fifteen feet high. I took the bypass around the town of Mojave. Mojave Airport, on my right, looked busier than Heathrow in summer until I realised the tails of the planes were much too close together. Hundreds of parked 707s, even 747s, were mothballed, probably because of the drop in air travel since September 11.

At Boron, north of Edwards Air Force Base, I turned onto 20 Mule Team Road, part of old Highway 66, drove through town and stopped for gas. The station attendant admired the GMC's tyres. 'Sixteen-and-a-half-inch. Don't see them often. Hard to find, and when you do, they're real expensive. Bet the ride's good. Restore it yourself?'

Heading south in California I'd also been heading back east, and was now at almost the same longitude as Coeur d'Alene, Idaho. The sun sets early here, on the light side of 7.00 p.m. Before it got too dark, on a two-lane stretch of highway, I found an unmarked dirt road, drove south for two

313

miles and pulled off onto hard sand for the night. As I opened the door, Macy discharged after a jackrabbit, a hopeless waste of energy. I followed her, walking west towards mauve, blue and purple ranges of mountains. Frustrated at her inability to outrun the natives, she hared in demented arcs in the hot, strong wind that suddenly flared, then settled into ground-scent trailing. She found a lumbar vertebra, to my eye probably canine, probably from a coyote, and rolled on her relative.

As the sun set, the sky turned a fiery orange, then flaming pink and finally funereal mauve. Polluted skies do bring advantages. Behind me an iridescent harvest moon appeared, shrinking and whitening as it rose above the horizon, until it shone in the sky like an incandescent white ball. I got out my chair, made a chicken salad supper and sky-gazed until Macy implored me to return home for the night.

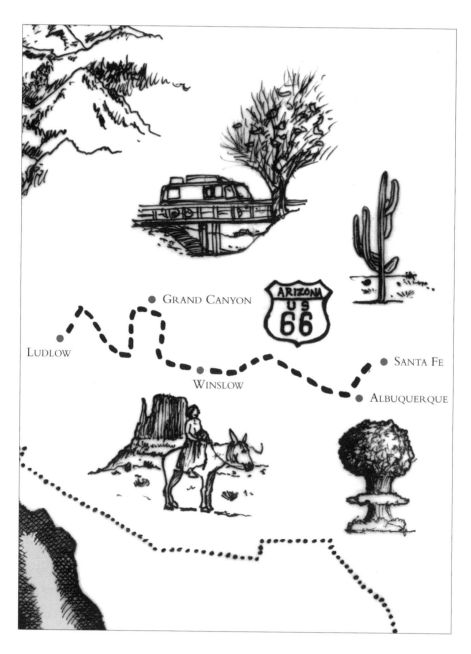

CHAPTER NINE

ROUTE 66

 Nine turkey vultures, bald-headed, black-bodied, with sylphic, silver-grey flight feathers, rocked on the morning wind directly above me. I could hear their wings flapping to catch rising thermals. A jack rabbit waited until Mace was almost upon it then jetted away, Macy following, like Baryshnikov, pirouetting gracefully over sagebrush and creosote brush, leaping and diving through mesquite root, yelping in frustration as she had yelped in Michigan, when she was carried off in the mouth of the hungry bear. In the surrounding desert, Mace found alternatives to her prey—an air filter, a faded, original-formula Coke can punctured with rifle shots, a vertebra, a gun powder container, sagebrush roots and branches. Just east of Ludlow, surrounded by lavender, blue, grey and beige mountains, I was on the first remnants of old Highway 66.

> Sixty-six is the path of the people in flight, [Steinbeck wrote in *The Grapes of Wrath*] refugees from dust and shrinking land, from the thunder of tractors and shrinking ownership, from the desert's slow northward invasion, from the thrusting winds that howl up from Texas, from the floods that bring no richness to the land and steal what little richness there is there. From all of these the people are in flight and they come into sixty-six from the tributary side roads, from the wagon tracks and the rutted country roads.

Sixty-six is the mother road, the road of flight.

To Steinbeck's dust-bowlers this Californian end of Highway 66, through a silent, dessicating desert of eternal emptiness, must have seemed a cruel joke. Was this the California they were escaping to? But for me the narrow undulating, empty ribbon of road I was now on, rising and dipping with every nuance of land, was comforting. I felt part of the land, part of history. Almost everything made by man along the road, Steinbeck's 'mother road' was closed or abandoned—gas stations, auto courts, restaurants, homes. Rusting cadavers of cars dating back to the 1930s, long stripped of anything useful, littered the landscape. In *Travels with Charley* Steinbeck says only that he knows this road well, but makes no mention of the fact he was now traversing the road he was responsible for making so famous. Today there's an annual Steinbeck Award for the person who has done most to capture the spirit of 'Route 66'.

Over 210,000 dust-bowlers escaped from the poverty and despondency of Oklahoma and Texas in the dirty 1930s, moving along this road to the promised land of California where work was available for migrant pickers. What the myth of migration doesn't tell us, is that only eight per cent, less than 17,000 individuals, remained in California. Highway 66 was a two-way road. Most returned.

A Federal Highways Act in 1921 had created a numbering system for America's highways. Those going north and south were given odd numbers. I travelled up US 1 on the East Coast and down US 101 on the West Coast. Those going east and west

317

were given even numbers. I journeyed on parts of old US 10 across the northern reaches of the country and now was on old US 66 returning to the east.

US 66 was unique in the angled route it cut, from the upper Midwest to San Bernadino on the Pacific. It evolved in part from a pre-Civil War, government-sponsored, wagon road programme roughly following the 35th Parallel across New Mexico and Arizona, linked to other wagon roads through Texas and Oklahoma, then up through Kansas and Missouri to Chicago. There was a time when the road hardly seemed needed. In 1925, an average of only 207 cars a day travelled from Albuquerque to Gallup, New Mexico. Ahead of me, at Needles on the Arizona state line, trucks and automobiles were loaded on railway flatcars to cross the Colorado River. By 1930, there were still only 64 paved miles in all of Arizona, New Mexico and Texas.

Steinbeck wrote of the road's value for 1930s migrants, but Highway 66 probably affected more Depression Americans by supplying federal work relief through the Work Projects Administration and the Civilian Conservation Corps, than it did by offering a route to California for migrants. Tens of thousands of otherwise unemployable men worked constantly on the road until 1938 when all of its 1648 miles of gravel and dirt, 'over the red lands and the grey lands, twisting up into the mountains, crossing the Divide and down into the bright and terrible desert and across the desert to the mountains again and into the rich California valleys', as Steinbeck wrote in *The Grapes of Wrath*, were finally, continuously paved.

Heading east, this rutted old road curved south under its hectic replacement, I-40, and cantered through shot-up, virtually abandoned Bagdad, past the closed Dry Creek gas station and by derelict, fenced homes with bullet holes in all their windows. Everywhere there were 'No Trespassing' signs. Bagdad gets an average 2.3 inches of rain each year. I was in the midst of true desert.

South of us was the Marine Corps Air Ground Combat Center, a thousand square miles of flat desert, dry lakebeds and mountains, closed to public access. Now the road got rough, I mean really, truly rough. I bounced and sprung through salt flats, stopping to let Mace out. She raced and tumbled round a solitary, four-foot-tall, grey-white, hoary saltbush, her feet sinking through the thin salt crust to powdery earth below. Soon, and suddenly, we drove through coal-black lava rock. A hub cap flew off, cupboards were thrown open and pots piled out. Tumbleweed rolled, lining the fence separating old US 66 from I-40. Sagebrush and creosote bush burst through cracks in the thin edges of the asphalt.

This was the road less travelled, my only companions my dog and frequent freight trains, with cars marked Kansas City Southern, Burlington Northern & Santa Fe, Canadian National, Canadian Pacific. I counted seven vehicles in the first 50 miles. That's less traffic than in 1925. In World War II, army convoys over a mile long travelled relentlessly through here, from new military bases and manufacturing sites in California, back towards the east for shipments to the European theatre of war.

An oil tanker overtook me, then continued on

the wrong side of the road. I followed suit and it was much smoother. On through Amboy, population 20, where there were vacancies at Roy's Motel. When the AGS *California Guide* was written, Amboy had a population of 95. South of Amboy is Bristol Dry Lake, covered in powdery 'soil' you can sink up to your knees in. To the north, the blue and lavender ranges of the Old Dad and Bristol Mountains were now much closer. A mile past Amboy, past a collection of derelict motor court cottages and boarded buildings, was a hand-painted sign, 'Go back for gas. None for next 70 miles'. From Amboy, the old Atchison, Topeka & Santa Fe railroad parallels old 66. The railroad had watering holes every five miles or so and named them in alphabetical order: Amboy, Bristol, Cadiz, Danby, Essex, Fenner, Goffs, Homer, Ibex, Java, Kleinfelter.

Along a sandy embankment, which for unending miles parallels the northern side of the highway and was built to prevent spring water run-off from the mountains washing over the road, were mile upon mile of stone graffiti: initials, names, crosses in varying sizes of pebbles and stones, some highlighted with turquoise or red paint, all pronouncing 'I am me. I am unique.' In the middle of nowhere, by the dusty, derelict Road Runner Retreat and a neighbouring gas station, both shuttered, I stopped at a 'shoe tree' for lunch. The tree, a spiny blue paloverde in rare leaf, was growing by a culvert, a wash under the road for run-off waters, and from it, weirdly, hung hundreds of athletics shoes.

To the east, cumulus clouds were forming in the sky, the first clouds I'd seen since the Pacific

North-West coast. At Essex where the population has increased from 30 in 1939 to 80 today, the old road curved north, under I-40 towards Goff, and just beyond, in an expansive desert populated by tall yuccas, I stopped for a walk. A long-limbed, black-collared lizard basking on a boulder taunted Mace, who gave chase while I walked along the course of a run-off wash that had cut over two feet into the sand. It all seemed so familiar—the cactuses, the tumbleweed, the pale blue mountains, the bright blue sky, the Mexican maraca sounds. I'd seen it so many times in films and TV, it felt as if I had been here before. Then I wondered about those maracas. I looked down. Ten inches from my left foot was a coiled, diamond-back rattlesnake, angrily shaking its rattle, flicking its tongue, tasting my presence. I slowly backed away, climbed out of the wash, found Mace, forklifted her and carried her back to the GMC. Now snakes don't bother me. I've caught quite a few, mostly garter snakes but also some water snakes, all venomless. As a child I'd just grab garter snakes behind the head. They were good for frightening the girls a few cottages down the lake. Water snakes were more of a challenge. I'd tie frogs by their waists to stumps in frog bog and wait, sometimes all day, for a water snake to attack. Snake on a string.

I grabbed my camera, a forked piece of driftwood I'd collected in Oregon, my large cooking knife and, curiously, now that I think about it, a pair of surgical gloves. That rattle would make a great souvenir.

The rattler was still there, coiled and beautiful, about two feet long. I took pictures of my footprint inches away from its hide, then moved forward with the stick I'd pin it with in one hand and a rock I'd use to smash in its head in my other. I left the knife that I'd use to cut off its rattle on the sand at the top of the wash. The rattler peered from the shadow of the plant it was under. It was exquisite—gorgeous—its silky cream, brown and black skin a perfect camouflage on the desert sand. It rattled again as I approached, but I didn't hear the sound of aggression, I heard fear. That snake wasn't threatening me. I was the one who threatened it. Suddenly I felt a fool. Why on earth did I even think of killing it? I climbed out of the wash, watched it for a few minutes, then retreated, leaving it shaded from the sun on its own land. I felt embarrassed. Still do.

*   *   *

Throughout the night coyotes yipped and howled. A bright full moon silvered the landscape, as Macy and I walked the rocky Arizona desert before dawn. Mace found a shoulder bone and some vertebrae and did her usual gazelle leaps of joy. She nosed around a fox den she discovered under a mesquite bush, where the fox had used sticks and bones to construct a sort of Buckminster Fuller geodesic dome entrance. Hanging from a taller bush by a dry riverbed was an old, cream-coloured enamel plate, pockmarked with dozens of bullet holes.

I had heard large animals near us during the night and judging from the wet patches in the sand, there were possibly antelope nearby. Light broke and I saw the desert had bloomed in yellow blossoms. There was a single, fresh, desert aster standing in full blue bloom a few feet from where I'd parked, although this flower normally blossoms in the spring. Our campsite was surrounded by a landscape of cactuses, chollas, Spanish bayonets and multitudes of fat, fleshy, prickly pears. I carefully picked some of their largest ripe purple fruit, avoiding the tiny, barbed spines, and then dropped them into a saucepan. Peeled with a knife they were so bland and tasteless, I generously added them to Macy's morning meal.

The Arizona morning was crisp, its light orange and iridescent. The boulders were ochre, terracotta and golden, interspersed with surprisingly verdant-green bushes and blue-green cactuses. The sky was impossibly blue. This stretch of old 66 in Arizona, like that in California, is 150 miles long. Once more I was almost alone on a road that was once the most travelled route to the coast, as important to the opening of southern California and Arizona to migration from the east, as was once the Oregon Trail to the Pacific North-West, or the Santa Fe trail from Independence, Missouri, through the Rockies to New Mexico. In the 1940s, '50s and '60s when the automobile became the country's personalised form of mass transit, US 66 was here to channel what, in demographic terms, must have been the greatest movement of people in the history of this country, from the rustbelt of the North-East to the sunbelt of the South-West.

At Valentine, where the Bureau of Indian Affairs building was now boarded shut, I drove under the railroad line onto a rare side road, parked and walked. A black and white bird with a crested head—a roadrunner—walked with its goofy gait, searching among the tumbleweed in the shadows of a low-built derelict building, once an incomer's home. I've read they eat rattlesnakes, grabbing a snake by its tail, cracking its body like a whip against the ground until it's dead.

The family that once occupied this low concrete building were not the only migrants here. The ancestors of the tumbleweed crowding its walls came from the arid steppes of the Ural mountains in Russia. It's said that this ubiquitous weed was transported to America in flax seed, imported into South Dakota by Ukrainian farmers. Within fifteen years, tumbleweed had spread across the Rockies to the Pacific Coast.

Beyond Valentine arose burnished, copper-coloured, flat-topped mesas standing guard like medieval fortresses. As a train, forming a perfect mirror-image question mark, snaked down from a mountain pass, I entered the Hualpai Indian Reserve. At one time the Reserve town of Peach Springs here had motor courts, cafes and tourist businesses. Now there was only desolation. Seligman was more fun. US 66 stimulated a 'Mom and Pop' economy along its entire route—auto courts, restaurants, cafes, gas stations, trading posts, tourist traps, kitschy souvenir shops. The opening of I-40 destroyed that local economy, siphoning the life-blood from places like Peach Springs. Seligman successfully rebelled. Its Main Street, the route of old 66, is lined with gleaming 1950s and '60s cars, retro diners, motels, cafes and gift shops. In an avalanche of kitsch, it throttles the visitor with plastic turquoise and bogus memorabilia. It recycles a quaint iconic image of

THE TURQUOISE TEPEE, WILLIAMS, ARIZONA

old US 66, an image captured in Bobby Troup's cartographic ballad's punch line, 'Get your kicks on Route 66'. I found it enchanting.

Williams, 6762 feet above sea level, was the last Route 66 town bypassed by I-40. In 1984 when the bypass finally opened, Williams's merchants had successfully prepared for their future. Mimicking Seligman, only on a grander scale, it charms with an earnest attempt to be retro. I bought Julia a Navajo silver belt made with 1942, 1943 and 1944 half-dollars and silver dollars. As the southern rim of the Grand Canyon was only an hour away, I left Steinbeck's route and headed to Grand Canyon National Park, stopping on our way for a 90-minute walk with Mace where, among prickly pear cactuses, my dog emerged triumphantly with a snow-white lacy bra dangling from her mouth. Nuts. No sign of its occupant.

At the entrance to the park, there was a ten-minute wait as four lines of cars were processed through. It was even more crowded in Grand Canyon Village—nowhere to park, legally or illegally. Every inch of space was occupied by cars and RVS. I circled the RV lot thrice, then headed east. After the solitude of the desert, I was psychologically unprepared for the congestion of Grand Canyon. Strange, isn't it? One of the most desolate places on earth and you can't move for people.

At Grandview Point the crowds were thinner. There was no space in the parking lot, but I found a safe pull-off where I parked and walked Mace, on her leash, of course, to the rim of the canyon. Throughout my trip people have asked whether I was going to visit the Grand Canyon. To many it's the Holy Grail, the one natural site in America not to be missed. Arriving within a week of visiting Sequoia National Park, where nature proclaims its stunning ability to create beauty, somehow what I saw in front of me seemed truly awful in its destructive immensity. A mile-deep slash, perhaps ten miles wide, in serrated bands of red, ochre, yellow and cream, it was, to my eyes, on this day, the epitome of nature at its most malevolent.

I stopped at each lookout along East Rim Drive. At Moran Point, the father of a Liverpool University veterinary student took photos of Mace and me. At Navajo Point, 7461 feet above sea level, a polite, unassuming Wisconsin dairyman took even better ones.

Beyond the park, past stands selling Navajo pottery, blankets and jewellery—so they said—is the land of the Navajo Nation. And beyond the Painted Desert, past Flagstaff, I returned to the old road through Winslow and Winona, Arizona. Yes, it's sad, but I did pretend I was one of The Eagles and hummed Jackson Browne's 'Take It Easy' as I passed the corner. I didn't see 'a girl My Lord, in a flatbed Ford, slowing down to take a look at me', but did see a whole lot of hokum advertising the song and the intersection.

*   *   *

I hadn't expected to fall in love. These travels were to reacquaint me with the continent where I'd spent the first half of my life, to help me resolve where home was. She's beautiful, elegant, young yet mature, sophisticated and vivacious. I hadn't even expected to meet her. That added a little *frisson* to our short relationship. I'd meant to charge through New Mexico in a day, but was absolutely captivated by her allure and stayed much longer.

The day began eventfully in Arizona. Just after dawn I pulled off the road by two parked 18-wheelers to make breakfast and give Macy some exercise. As I opened the door she sighted a jackrabbit and, once more, hared after it. Its long brown ears bounced as it sped off in high, long leaps, zigging, then zagging as the predator gave chase. Then, inexplicably, it zagged and zagged again. Macy's brain did an instant mathematical calculation. She altered her trajectory and crossed the hare's intended path at the exact millisecond it arrived there. Her mouth widened and she grabbed it by its neck. I saw her jaws give an instantaneous crush and the hare hung lifeless.

I was angry but Macy was exuberant and elated. Her neck arched back to her shoulders, her tail raised high like a victory flag and she pranced in a wide arc over the desert sands, the hare hanging limp from her jaws. Like a Tennessee Walking Horse she high-stepped back to me and past me. I commanded 'Drop' and she did so, releasing a seven to eight-pound, old, male, black-tailed jackrabbit. I examined his warm, flaccid body. The ears were scarred but there were no signs of disease, certainly no eye or nose signs of myxomatosis. Mind you, I didn't even know whether myxomatosis existed here. I looked in his mouth. There was a cheesy substance at the base of a broken incisor. The old hare had a tooth abscess. I assuaged my guilt feelings by telling myself my dog had given the old guy a clean and fast death. 'That's what we need more of in Iraq,' commented one of the truckers, who'd watched the chase from his cab.

Gallup, New Mexico, on a Sunday morning was deserted except for Navajos in jeans and Stetsons and relentless activity in the railway freight yards. The pawn shops offering 'Indian pawn'—old silver jewellery—were all closed. Damn. I'd hoped to see—maybe buy—old Navajo turquoise and silver jewellery, old rugs and saddles. I had to content myself by visiting the few stores open, all selling modern Native American handicrafts, all incongruously operated by Lebanese and subcontinent Indian businessmen. All the rings, belts, earrings and necklaces I looked at were similar and I wondered how many were local and how many imported from Pakistan, Thailand and the Philippines. Native American arts and crafts is a billion-dollar-a-year business. Counterfeiting 'handicrafts' is profitable. In each shop the owner was able to find one or two old pieces—none, I am happy to say, as attractive as the one I'd bought for Julia in Williams. Here, in Gallup, I learned my first fact about New Mexico. I asked a shopkeeper why licence plates say 'New Mexico USA'? Why the 'USA'? He explained that even now, 90 years after achieving statehood, many Americans don't realise that New Mexico is part of their country. The 'USA' on the plates is a state PR exercise aimed at the rest of the country.

Just beyond the Continental Divide, on both sides of the road were occasional circular Navajo hogans, their front doors all facing east to catch the rising sun, each a different size including the very grand, even prefabricated. Ten miles beyond

Grants, I entered irrigated farmland and then a black lava-flow landscape. I stopped at an Indian Trading Post for a Dairy Queen, one for me and one for Mace. At the Laguna Indian Reservation I stopped at the Route 66 Casino, walked over the giant custom-made carpet map of Route 66, inspected some of the 1250 slot machines and then moved on again, listening to Spanish rap on the radio.

Approaching Albuquerque, there was a sign pointing north to Santa Fe. Steinbeck got morose in New Mexico. He camped one night near the Continental Divide, talked with his dog, concluded that he'd 'stopped seeing' and drove on through to Amarillo, to a planned reunion in Texas with his wife—which Julia and I had also arranged to do. I've never been through here and was still hungry 'to see' and the words Santa Fe were alluring. At the unexpectedly artful terracotta- and turquoise-coloured interchange of I-40 and I-25, I headed north towards the state capital.

'Close Los Alamos Nuclear Waste Dump Now' proclaimed a billboard as I headed north. I'd forgotten New Mexico is also Trinity, Alamogordo, 16 July 1945.

It was in Santa Fe, with its narrow red brick cobbled streets and its warm terracotta-coloured buildings that I fell in love with this land. The air was clear and fresh, clean and warm. I parked under mature shade-offering trees by the Santa Fe River, a mere creek of a waterway, walked through streets of pueblo-revival-style shops, past Spanish-speaking men selling necklaces of dried red chillies, and chanced upon the Sunday market in the grounds of nearby Loretto Chapel. Tourists and sellers were relaxed, smiling and talkative. Everyone wanted to talk to and stroke Macy. I left her with a couple selling handmade necklaces and earrings, to visit the severely Gothic interior of the chapel where there is a spiral staircase winding, according to the literature, 'mystically' without support. I returned to a crowd all asking about Macy, wanting to adopt her. We continued walking, past St Francis Cathedral, past the Indian Arts Museum and into Santa Fe Plaza. In front of the Palace of the Governors sat a row of 30 or more leather-faced Navajo women, blankets spread in front of them, selling turquoise, silver and shell bangles.

At the bottom of the plaza is a black granite marker, the end of the Santa Fe Trail. I told Macy to 'Stay' while I took a picture, but before I could do so Rebecca—English, stylish, casual, elegant, and I soon learned unhappy with her husband—left the bench where she was sitting with a girlfriend eating an icecream and took photos of both of us.

Roy, also English—sloppy, articulate and successful—told me how he'd chanced on Santa Fe twenty years ago and now owned the Jaguar dealership. Ernesto, a Spanish-speaking street artist selling vibrant watercolours of his hogs, his chickens and his home, a proud-looking man of my age, with flowing curly grey hair, a full moustache, wearing a Stetson and tinted glasses, stroked stoic, still Macy and told me a story.

'This man. He had a very curious dog, and he would go to people and smell in a certain way that was very embarrassing. So the man was trying to think of a name that he could give to the dog, so he named him Star Trek. You know why? Because in his smelling habits he went far beyond where any dog had gone before.' Ernesto's laugh was so infectious that I almost bought a pig painting. 'It's amazing how every dog has its own personality,' he continued, looking at Macy. 'What type of brand is she?'

Rebecca had asked where I was staying for the night and I explained I was going to head back to an RV site. She suggested if I was staying at one out of town off I-25, I should consider visiting The Inn at Sunrise Springs. 'Nothing quite like it.'

The RV sites looked dull and ugly so I drove on up a narrow road, through barren hills littered with juniper trees, to Sunrise Springs, 'global, ecumenical, peaceful, inspirational, artistic, creative, holistic and celebratory', according to Megan Hill, the owner, in the resort's promotional brochure. I parked my home under shady trees in a corner of the parking lot, exercised Mace, then changed into a clean, buttoned shirt, pressed trousers and leather shoes for what was to be an artistic, creative and almost inspirational meal in the Blue Heron Restaurant.

Apricot-coloured walls, candles, soft chairs, Asian rugs, hand-painted ceramics, soft classical music—it all created a relaxing ambience. Small purple and white orchids on the white tablecloths added a sparkle of gay, living colour. The restaurant was quiet; only a lone woman reading a book while she ate, and an affluent, healthy-looking couple at a corner table. My waiter told me Santa Fe was heaven on earth. I asked how long he'd lived here and he explained he'd arrived from New Orleans three months earlier. I ordered a bottle of white wine—a New Zealand sauvignon, if you want to know—a mozzarella, beetroot, tomato and watercress salad, and duck breast with wild and brown rice, shitake mushrooms and bok choy.

It took only minutes to strike up conversation and join the couple at the corner table: Conrad, a lawyer, and Tina, his vivacious wife, visiting from Telluride, Colorado, to inspect an Audi TT they were thinking of buying. Conrad and Tina were from Greater Los Angeles. They moved to Colorado eight years ago. 'Colorado and New Mexico are today what California was a generation ago. Now the coast's polluted and the quality of life isn't what it should be. The only quest is for riches, not just for security and comfort, but for obscene riches. This land is still pure. People here have their feet on the ground.'

They gave me a little history of Sunrise Springs. 'It doesn't say so in the brochure, but the owner ran this place at a loss for years. Her family in San Francisco supported her. She was a hippy who came here to meditate. Somewhere along the line it turned into an efficient business. There's mindful painting and astrology for transformation and spirit journeys, and a peace lodge where you can sweat and purify yourself but there are also Japanese cooking lessons, yoga, t'ai chi, pottery, even how to learn the Japanese tea ceremony.'

I'd finished my bottle of wine and was sharing their second bottle of red over fig cheesecake dessert and coffee, when talk turned to politics. Conrad's tone changed. 'Mr Bush has embroiled us in a family feud,' he told me. 'He wants to get even on behalf of his father. We're in Iraq because of a grudge, not because Saddam has nuclear bombs.

Who knows whether he has weapons of mass destruction in Iraq. There sure are bombs in Pakistan and those are the ones that'll get into the hands of the fanatics.'

Tina was silent. She neither nodded in agreement nor interjected to oppose, and Conrad continued. 'How do you see America from the outside?' he asked, but before I could answer he went on. 'Mr Bush and Mr Cheney are the vanguard to what is happening here. Do you know what CEOs get paid? A couple of million seems reasonable. Ten million, if you're truly inspirational, seems reasonable. Does any man's worth really justify a hundred million a year? Do you know what it costs to run for office? Only the enormously wealthy seek high office today and even they need the support of industry's CEOs. The system feeds on itself. Look at that Halliburton thing. We're supposed to be the most egalitarian country on earth, but we're not, Bruce. We're gated and we're stratified. At least up here in Colorado and New Mexico you can be part of the community, you can get away from what's gone wrong.'

Through the windows, the soft lights along wooden paths lit the cottonwoods and willows surrounding the pond. The book reader had left. The restaurant was empty. We stepped out into fresh, cool air, they to their newly constructed *casita*, complete they had told me with log fireplace, while I returned to the parking lot. There was no way I was going to drive to a campsite in my state, so there in the car park we slumbered.

My home needed an oil change and that was as good a reason as any to return to Santa Fe. Besides, the place felt homey. I wanted to stay longer. While it was being serviced, Mace and I ambled to the far side of the road to a Starbucks in a mall's car park. I asked a wiry young woman, sitting outside in the refreshing morning sun, whether she would watch Macy while I got a coffee. She did and we struck up a conversation. Charlotte was a massage therapist of which, she told me, there were 3000 in Santa Fe. There are also two healing arts colleges and a healing arts institute although I didn't ask the difference. Charlotte explained that Santa Fe's population was, she thought, around 50,000 with another 200,000 more in the surrounding region.

'People come here to be re-created,' she explained, mysteriously. No, I didn't ask for an explanation. It was just too good a word to be translated. 'Meditation's really big here. That's why I stayed. Doctors at the University of Wisconsin have shown that meditation makes you less anxious. They got EEGs that prove it. They tested a Buddhist lama and after meditating he could control his startle reflex, and that's something doctors say you got no control over. Then they tested ordinary people who were taught to meditate and found that after meditating they had more activity in the front part of the brain where happiness lies.

'You know, lots of people are just negative. They just criticise. They don't enjoy life. They're like—paralysed. They need to drain that poison from their minds before they can be happy. If they'd just sit down and target the weakest points in their lives, they can re-create themselves.'

I asked her what was the best form of meditation and she explained that 'mindfulness meditation' was. Shades of Sunrise Springs! 'You train your mind to be aware of each thought you get, then just let each thought go without making any judgement about it. Don't let your mind wander. It's tough at first, but I did it. You can too. That's why I decided to stay here.' All the time she spoke, Charlotte was applying touch therapy to Macy, whose eyes were closing as she performed canine meditation, thinking only of the moment. I looked at my blonde and thought she was as good a teacher as Charlotte. 'Blessing to you,' Charlotte offered, as she finished her coffee and departed.

I drove back, past the Indian Hospital and Indian School, past the Atcheson Topeka and Santa Fe train station, to the plaza, filling with early morning strollers. I looked at them and it dawned on me I was surrounded by my generation, tree huggers from the sixties, now with surplus income, gone wealthy but not cynical. No one was fat. Not a single solitary one.

People from yesterday remembered Macy by name and said hello to her and to me. Anglo-American vendors, at the north end of the plaza, ate salads with chopsticks as they awaited potential sales. I said 'konichi-wa' to a band of young Japanese and they bowed and giggled and all exuberantly said 'konichi-wa' in return.

I looked around, almost clinically, at the pueblo-revival architecture. Of course you can say it's contrived. After all, it was intentionally

336

formulated, a local design exercise a hundred years ago, an attempt to create a regional vernacular before California Mission-style overwhelmed the state.

It's appealing in many ways. The terracotta-plastered adobe walls are earthy and seemingly natural. So too are the projecting wooden roof beams and longer projecting rainwater gutters. The wooden posts at the portals or supporting the verandahs add to the unfettered, natural look. Flat roofs project an innocent intimacy and the stepped-up roofs of the two-floor buildings maintain a human scale. Driving back into Santa Fe today, I passed new suburbs built in Santa Fe-style. The local ordinance restricting the height and style of buildings in the historic heart of town is now almost 50 years old. It may seem incongruous to view Lithuanian and Polish religious relics through the window of a pueblo-style shop but, believe me, it works. The heart of Santa Fe has avoided the drab sameness of most other American cities.

We wandered through stores filled with top-end Western-style goods: leather beds, suede cowgirl shirts with turquoise buttons, old Navajo blanket-covered armchairs and Navajo belts at three times the price of those offered by the Mancunian dealer at the antique fair near San Francisco. In Pinkoyote, I almost bought Julia a T-shirt only for its engaging coyote logo—pink, of course. In another shop I met a striking blonde Valkyrie of a German. In her snake-skin, beige cowboy boots, sashaying suede skirt, denim shirt and Navajo belt and necklace, at her age she might have looked like mutton dressed as lamb, but her height and her sheer confident presence pulled it off. She was wearing Double D Ranch, Yoakum, Texas, clothing. I made a note of that. I knew the chief would be interested.

Santa Fe is at an elevation of 7000 feet and to the south are the Sandia Mountains. I drove back towards Route 66, past a stand of brilliant-yellow aspens, clones of each other, as coastal redwoods are clones, through hills dotted with dark green squat junipers, stopping to take Macy for a stroll along the appropriately named Perros Canyon Road. The road I was on, Highway 14, was the route through which the Navajo people were marched by Kit Carson into their years of enforced incarceration at Fort Sumner. I stopped in Madrid, once a coal-mining community supplying the Santa Fe railroad, then a ghost town, now a thriving artists' colony. In one shop I met a displaced Irishman, twenty years in New Mexico. 'I tink it's about time to go back home,' he offered, when he learned I was from London.

'How can you give up this sunshine?' I asked.

'I tink now's not the time to go back home,' he continued. I had gone into his shop looking for local turquoise stones and he explained that most turquoise in New Mexico, including what I saw in front of me, was from Tibet and China. 'Look at this carefully,' he explained. 'It's fine turquoise but that black matrix tells you it's from Tibet. You'll see cheap turquoise that's been dyed or treated with resins to seal it or stabilise the colour. Some of it isn't even turquoise, it's fake, chrysocolla. The best turquoise now, that's from Cerrillos. It's mostly green with waxy veins of volcanic rock in it. You can see it at the Casa Grande Trading Post

338

there.'

I backtracked to Cerrillos, pristine in its still authentic grid of dusty dirt roads and nothingness. Once there were 21 saloons and four hotels here. Now there was St Joseph Church and the Casa Grande Trading Post, Petting Zoo & Mining Museum. Macy went for a stroll, meeting a pit bull and Rottweiler, both of whom she greeted warmly, as female dogs are adept at doing. They found the city chick alluring but remained gentlemen. At a dead-end track I visited Casa Grande and, as my Irish friend had assured me, found local green turquoise for sale. The store's owner had arrived 30 years ago and stayed. In town lived two families from Belgium and another from Norway. It was another community of vagabonds, runaways and misfits, much like Stockholm, Wisconsin, only drier and sunnier. I took an instant liking to Cerrillos.

I was enamoured with all of New Mexico and at I-40 and the remnants of Route 66, I decided to deviate from Steinbeck's route, remain in New Mexico and head south towards the Mexican border then east to rejoin his trail in Texas. The road descended through high-rolling prairie dotted with sheep and cattle. On a miles-long stretch where farmed buffalo were grazing, snow fences had been erected beside the barbed wire. A hundred years ago, local Comanche women, when butchering buffalo in hot weather, sliced their meat almost paper-thin, smoked it and dried it in the sun. This they called *charqui*, anglicised now to 'jerky'. This grazing land I was driving through was gradually turning green from the recent rain. Ninety miles south of Santa Fe there were road signs, left to the Billy the Kid Museum and Gift Shop, right to Alamogordo, test site of the first atom bomb.

That word, Alamogordo, sent a shiver through me. I know the history well. Robert Oppenheimer, Director of Los Alamos, the nuclear laboratory built on what in 1942 was an isolated mesa west of Santa Fe, had chosen this site in the aptly named Jornado del Muerto Desert, to test his implosion weapon, the first atom bomb. He named the site Trinity, after a poem by John Donne he had been reading. On 15 July, the day of the test, General Leslie Groves, the military commander of the Los Alamos laboratory, called the governor to alert him that the entire state might have to be evacuated. The nuclear physicist Enrico Fermi was heard taking bets that the bomb would incinerate all of New Mexico.

At 5.30 a.m. the 'gadget', as the device was called, exploded with a force of 21,000 tons of dynamite, evaporating the tower on which it stood, turning the sand beneath to green glass. A searing light, brighter than the midday sun, lit up the surrounding desert and this was followed by a blast of air against which distant observers had to strain to stand, and then a roar—a sustained, awesome, thundering roar. The mushroom cloud ascended twelve kilometres into the sky. Groves's deputy, General Thomas Farrell, thought it 'blasphemous to dare tamper with the force heretofore reserved for the Almighty'. Oppenheimer was reminded of the Sanskrit text from the *Bhagavad Gita*, '*Kalosmi lokaksaya krt pravrdho*'—'I am become Death, the Destroyer of Worlds', and Kenneth Bainbridge, Director of the Project, said simply and honestly,

340

'Now we're all sons-of-bitches.' The military reported it as an accidental explosion at an ammunitions dump.

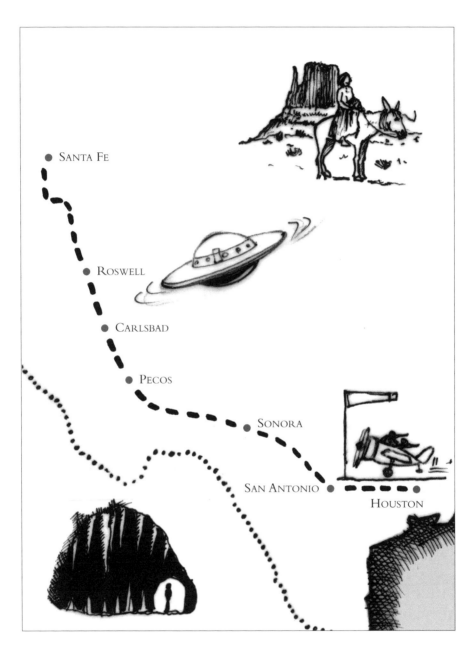

SANTA FE

ROSWELL

CARLSBAD

PECOS

SONORA

SAN ANTONIO

HOUSTON

CHAPTER TEN

INTO TEXAS

 Before the long slog through Texas, I wanted to visit Carlsbad Caverns. Pete, the educator, in California, had suggested this was a geological site I shouldn't miss. Nearing Roswell, New Mexico, I passed a road sign pointing west, 'UFO crash site'. I was near the international home of little green aliens.

Driving into town at 9.30 a.m., there were still seven RVs parked in a corner of the local Wal-Mart parking lot. This was my fail-safe if I couldn't find a place to camp tonight. Further into town I passed big men dressed in green, guys in berets walking briskly towards the turreted New Mexico Military Institute. A weather sign reported it was 56 degrees F. Billboards for motels and restaurants all advertised special AARP (American Association of Retired People) rates. It had been the same throughout the South-West.

Downtown on Main Street I cruised past Earth Station, Not Of This World, Alien Zone, Alien Resistance Headquarters, UFO Museum and Research Center, Zone Two Alien Headquarters. Outside this quaint, quiet town on the northern rim of the Chihuahua Desert was an Army Air Corps base where, say locals, in 1947, a flying saucer crashed. I discussed with my dog the merits of visiting the International UFO Museum and Research Center but, seeing that she refused to lift her head and look, I concluded that we should move on, past irrigated alfalfa fields being harvested and industrial dairy-go-rounds of Holsteins. Just south of Roswell, at a wash under the highway, the roadside barrier above the culvert was impacted by a compression of shrubs, roots and branches. There must have been a very recent and very ferocious flash flood.

Today, water is to this region of America what gold was to the conquistadors, the land's most precious resource. Spanish settlers, on their way north to Santa Fe, found only dry, barren plains. So too did the first Anglo-Americans to reach southern New Mexico. In 1891 Nathan Jaffa, on his land near where I now was, found water: artesian water. Geologists soon investigated and discovered that the entire region, west to the Sacramento Mountains and east into Texas to bluffs beyond the Pecos River, was porous limestone. Water from melting mountain snows or heavy rains, as there had been here perhaps only a day previously, filtered into channels through the limestone to the valley floor. Hydrostatic pressure forces some of this pure, cold water to surface springs. Wells, some of them 700 feet deep, bring more to the surface, providing the life-blood for crop irrigation. Artesia, 40 miles south of Roswell, is aptly named, but in 1923 while drilling for artesian water near here, oil was discovered. I drove through irrigated cotton fields interspersed with nodding donkey oil wells, then, near Bradley Park Lake, I saw a Chevy Border Patrol vehicle. I was nearing Mexico.

Past a sign to Dog Canyon Campgrounds and countless nodding donkeys I entered Walnut Canyon, ascending the five-mile drive to the Carlsbad Caverns Visitors' Center. This was pure, picture-perfect mountainous desert. The Chihuahua Desert is America's largest, over

345

200,000 square miles, although most of it is in Mexico, with slender fingers inching into southern New Mexico and Texas. I was in one of those fingers.

I drove up through creosote bush, four-foot-high slender Christmas chollas, straggly erect ocotillos and profuse prickly pear cactuses to the cavern entrance. A kennel service was available but the weather today, although brightly sunny, was cool. So I opened the windows to draw the fresh breeze through the screens and left Mace with crayons and a colouring book while I took the long walk into the caverns through the Natural Entrance rather than take the elevator down from the Visitors' Center. A sign told me that 'Uninformed Rangers are available to assist you with information and to answer your questions'. I've got to see an optician when I get back to London, I thought. This desert light is playing tricks on my eyes!

Carlsbad Caverns were discovered by early settlers intrigued by the dusk sight of hundreds of thousands of bats rising from the desert and they soon found the entrance to a massive bat cave. Some settlers stayed on, to mine the massive 40-foot-deep deposits of bat dung, a natural fertiliser. Mexican freetail bats still live in the cave and there's a bat-flight viewing amphitheatre to the east of the parking lot. Although it was now late October, the bats had not yet migrated to Mexico where they over-winter. That night they would make another exodus, lasting over an hour, to fill their stomachs several times over with moths and other night-flyers.

A sign at the Natural Entrance said, '750 FEET

DESCENT'. Another, in English and Spanish warned, 'ATTENTION: TO BYPASS BY LEAVING PAVED TRAIL HAS RESULTED IN SERIOUS INJURY AND DEATH'. A third said, 'TO BRUCE'S DAUGHTER EMILY: IF YOU COME HERE DON'T MAKE THIS DESCENT IN YOUR KITTEN HEELS'. OK, only joking. Just two of those three signs are for real.

'Isn't that just like Gaudí's Sagrada in Barcelona?' asked a grey-haired woman, with a Texas accent, of her walking companion as they carefully picked their way down the steep walks into the depths of the caverns. That was no joke and an arresting comment. When, unplanned and unexpected, I stayed in Europe 35 years ago I left behind a naive, unworldly continent. That's no longer true. A retired grass cutter in George Washington National Forest in Virginia had been to 'Piccadilly Square and the white cliffs of Dover'. A fast-food waitress in Maine had fallen in love with Paris. A Wisconsin potter's daughter was studying at Cardiff University. A North Dakota car mechanic was about to visit Germany. An Oregon waitress had trekked the Himalayas. A San Francisco relative was on his way to China.

I read in British papers how parochial, introspective and isolationist, even xenophobic, America has become, but meeting people here and listening to them, I have not come to this conclusion. This Texan woman looked at a stalagmite in a cavern in New Mexico and she saw in it Gaudí's great Catalan cathedral. Is that not wonderful? Is that not hopeful? Does that not encapsulate and articulate a different, less commented-on America with a worldly, knowledgeable maturity?

347

Before leaving on this trip I thought that I'd find the continent embarrassingly parochial. I said, 'I've got the feeling that America doesn't do irony at all, let alone do it well. Will I still feel at home, after living in a hugely ironic culture for over thirty years?' I feel awkward reading that now. It was a glib, uninformed judgement. 'Doesn't do irony?' Shit. Have I been watching *Frasier* for ten years and missing it?

The descent continued for almost two miles, 755 feet down, to be exact, to a rest area, restaurant and gift shop. The temperature there was 56 degrees F and 99 per cent humidity. It felt like home, a typical London day. Greg, our guide from New Zealand, took a group of twenty of us, Americans, Mexicans, Japanese, Polish and me, on the King's Palace guided tour—rooms hundreds of feet long, ceilings hundreds of feet above us, stalactites, stalagmites, columns, cave pools, flowstones, drapery curtains. He was a good guide, a caver, now a bit bored taking tours, longing to get back to exploration.

Macy and I lingered for the afternoon in Walnut Canyon, trekking under the bluest sky through soapbush and juniper covered in copper-coloured berries. Sotol cactuses sprung in profusion from the white limestone hills, their dry, golden flower stems over ten feet tall. Lechuguilla agaves burst from rocky crevices, their thick waxy leaves protecting the precious moisture within. Prickly pear cactuses were in abundance, the palest of green. Each prickly pad was almost the size of a baseball catcher's glove, grander in scale than any I had seen in the Mojave Desert, their orange-purple fruit littering the ground. Down in a wash

348

MACY AMONGST THE SOTOL CACTUSES, CARLSBAD,
NEW MEXICO

grew scrubby, honey mesquite. Their bean pods littered the white gravelly sand. There were coyote footprints in the softest sand.

*   *   *

Pecos, Texas, has a Wal-Mart, a JC Penney Catalog Store, a Beall's Department Store, a Dollar General Store and an Alco Discount Store. Like dominoes dropped in dirt they sit, flat-topped, isolated, surrounded by salt-crusted flat scrubland. The earth was soft from recent rain and Macy's feet left perfect brown images compressed into the sugar and cinnamon surface of the field beside the Wal-Mart where we camped overnight.

Both my RV neighbours, one pulling a trailer, the other in a bus conversion, had fired up their generators, and I did too, making coffee and toast for breakfast. Mace gambolled with the trailer's hound, I chatted with my fellow overnighters.

The AGS *Texas Guide* describes Pecos as 'much like a cowboy in store-bought clothes', but that romantic notion has given way to the uniformity of the rest of the regions of America I'd passed through. Texas likes to think it's a whole lot different from the rest of the United States. Not any more. Since I left, like the rest of the continent, the Lone Star State has been homogenised. 'Don't mess with Texas', threaten the road signs, but now they're part of the state's anti-litter campaign.

To the west was the low blue line of the Guadalupe and Delaware Mountains, the southern remnants of the Rockies. To the south-east, where I was heading into golden morning sunlight, was a high plateau of rolling hills sweeping to the horizon. Even in the sharpness of early morning light, it was a blend of anonymous neutral tones. An Oasis Christian Fellowship Chevy van tested divine intervention by passing me with a stream of oncoming 18-wheelers on the other side of the road. I slammed on my brakes and he cut in, as an oncoming semi hit the far soft shoulder. At Fort Stockton I joined I-10 heading back east, through semi-arid cattle land with scant vegetation, a land interspersed with irrigated fields of alfalfa, pecans and cotton. One pecan grove had been freshly flooded, the trunks of its mature trees mirrored in the still water below. More fields of green grass turned the vista into symmetrical parkland. A herd of Appaloosas calmly grazed.

In Sonora, bypassed by the interstate, I stopped for lunch. The wide, empty streets, lined with now unwanted, false-fronted old businesses, sang of a forgotten West. Rings of yellow ribbons had been wound like individual golden arm bands around the trunk and every branch of the tallest pecan on the green lawn of the town hall. Sonora was settled in 1889, a dry town, where property deeds carried a stipulation that liquor could not be sold on the premises. A local politician was influenced to omit the clause accidentally from a deed for a city lot and the Maud S saloon opened.

I asked the waitress at a busy local diner I visited if she knew where the saloon was, but she had never heard of it. Over a truly disgusting turkey sandwich—it was made of blanched, still-frozen turkey slices and iceberg lettuce in toasted white bread spread with a glutinous yellow something— accompanied by a Coke—more fizz than flavour—

351

and shoestring fries—more palm oil than potato—
I showed her the AGS *Texas Guide* where it
explained that a few years after Sonora was
founded, it was discovered that the town was not
on state land but on private property already
owned by a New York firm. The townsfolk not only
had to buy their land once more, but now also their
own homes.

'Far out. Where'd you get this book?' she asked,
and called her boss over, who also read the
paragraph and was surprised by the history of her
town.

Further east the hills became gentler and
greener, covered in fresh-scented cedar trees. I
had entered the Texas hill country, old-fashioned
American hunting and fishing land, first settled
160 years ago by northern European immigrants—
Germans, Poles, English. I stopped at a rest area
and Mace rolled in green grass for the first time in
weeks, surrounded by monarch butterflies floating
in the air around her. I was heading for Kerrville.
Pete had told me the cowboy artists' museum was
worth a visit.

Straddling the banks of the Guadalupe River,
the town appeared relaxed and vacation-oriented.
I looked for the Chamber of Commerce, my sure
way throughout this trip to get local information. I
cruised the compact old business section and up
and down the multiples strip but couldn't find it, so
I went to my own personal chamber of commerce:
the nearest veterinary clinic.

On the main road out of town, next to a
carwash, was the Ark Veterinary Clinic. Now that
must be the most common and banal, but
pragmatic and useful name given to veterinary

clinics throughout the English-speaking world. 'Ark'. What does that do for you? Noah? Caring? Inclusive? Capable? Traditional? Can handle anything? First letter of the alphabet? First name in the *Yellow Pages*? Who was I going to meet?

I introduced myself as a vet to the receptionist, asked where the cowboy museum was, and she said, 'Let me call Dr Bennett.' Dr Bennett was her husband. It was a Mom and Pop veterinary clinic with petite, blonde Joanna on reception and jovial, rounded Joel behind the examination table. I instantly liked them—not unexpectedly, after all, we did share a profession, and possibly a certain view on life. The Bennetts bartered a deal. They'd give me the information I wanted, on condition that I joined them for dinner.

I found Kerrville-Schreiner State Park on the banks of the Guadalupe River. The AGS *Texas Guide* told me that the Schreiner part was once a private game reserve sheltering herds of buffalo and antelope.

Joel and Joanna took me to the Cowboy Steak House for dinner—mesquite sirloin steak and a baked sweet potato. Joel thought my longhorns were real class and, twinkle in eye, said if I wanted to pass as a local, I should mount them on the front bumper rather than leave them stashed where they were on the top of the vehicle.

At the restaurant I absently commented on Joel's school ring, a typical American gold monster. He raised his hand and said, 'Everything on this ring has a purpose. Everything's symbolic. See, here on top, those thirteen stripes symbolise the thirteen original states, and see these five stars, they stand for development of the mind, the body, integrity of character, emotional poise and spiritual life. The eagle behind the shield, he stands for agility and grace and your ability to fly to great heights of achievement and ambition. Here, on this side, is the Star of Texas and the olive branch of peace. Those live-oak leaves mean strength to fight when you have to, and the ribbon on the bottom, it says you gotta join your ambition with your need to serve. And here, on the other side, that cannon, it symbolises that the citizens of Texas had to fight for their freedom, and the crossed flags they remind us we have our duties to the state and to the country. You see these indentations all round the bottom, all these little pits like little donut holes? Each one stands for one of the bums you went to university with. See how they're worn down between my fingers, how they're disappearing? That represents they weren't such big bums after all.'

I guess that's something we all learn eventually. I took my kids to Alberta once, to a twentieth-anniversary class reunion. I met classmates I couldn't stand while at college and now saw only good people, good parents with polite kids.

We shop-talked. Joel explained there was a local rabies problem. 'Game farmers exported grey foxes from west of here to Georgia for fox-hunting. A dog died there from rabies and when they rounded up and killed those foxes they found most of them had rabies. A local man imported a sheepdog from Scotland. It cost him four and a half grand and it died from rabies because he wanted to save himself the cost of a vaccination. We've had it around here in a bobcat and mountain lion—confirmed cases.'

354

I know a thing or two about rabies. In 1963, my class of veterinary students were human guinea pigs, testing a new form of rabies vaccine. Until then, vaccine had been made as Louis Pasteur had first done in 1885, from animal nerve tissue. These old vaccines offered moderate protection, but were locally painful, with frequent and serious side effects. Occasionally Pasteur's vaccine stimulated the immune system to attack the body's own nervous system. Around one in every 3000 people developed a condition in which nerves lost their fatty coating, their myelin. By the late 1950s newer methods of vaccine manufacture had been developed. The vaccine we were injected with had been grown in embryonated duck eggs, inactivated with a chemical called beta-propriolactone then mixed with a little antibiotic. I had a mild local allergic reaction, swelling and skin reddening, but the vaccine induced a good, measurable antigenic response. (The rabies vaccine I had given to Macy before bringing her to America was far more sophisticated and rarely causes even the mildest unpleasant reaction.)

Rabies in wildlife has a cyclical ebb and flow. In Ontario, the red fox and the skunk are its natural reserve, and the number of cases flows to a peak every eleven years, infecting and killing so many animals it loses too many potential hosts and ebbs away, only to arise gradually once more. By the 1980s, as more and more people visited areas of the province where rabies was endemic, the provincial Ministry of Resources took action. Its vets were aware of successful oral vaccination of foxes pioneered, curiously, by the Swiss of all people, who began the programme by tossing chicken heads containing oral rabies vaccine out of helicopter windows. German vets improved both the palatability of the baits and the accuracy of baiting and, along with the French and Belgians, perfected the concept of vaccinating wildlife from low-flying aircraft.

'Don't you have racoon rabies in Canada?' Joel asked. 'We got grey fox rabies. It started near Sonora and stretches mostly north and east back here. Dogs, cats, cows, goats, they all got it. Texas National Guard flies bright yellow Twin Otters they borrow from Ontario. They fly just above the trees and drop millions of baits, fishmeal for coyotes, sugar-coated dog food with vanilla for the foxes.'

Joel was right about racoon rabies. It didn't exist in Ontario when I lived there but when racoons for hunting were moved from the south to West Virginia, the 'coons spread north producing what may be the greatest rabies epidemic ever. The cases I was told about in the private RV grounds in West Virginia and at the New York State Park on Lake Ontario's shore were racoon rabies. The first case in Ontario was seen in 1999 in the Thousand Islands of the St Lawrence River separating Ontario from New York. A classmate at the vet school tells me they were prepared. A Racoon Rabies Task Force had already been set up, including one of my old room-mates. They created an aerial vaccine buffer zone, a trap, vaccinate and release zone and, by the American border, a kill-a-lot-of-wildlife zone. It worked. There hasn't been an explosion of rabies in Ontario as there has been in upstate New York, where I had to show Macy's rabies vaccination certificate.

Into the evening we swapped vet stories. I really liked Joel's about Guiseppe, a blind fifteen-year-old Yorkie let out one night into his own back yard for a final pee, who got stomped on by a deer. Guiseppe's distraught owner brought Guiseppe's limp body to Joel to see what could be done. 'Isn't there anything you can do?' And Joel turned and looked at his shotgun. Guiseppe's owner shot that deer.

We steered away from politics, but before Joel and Joanna drove me back to our campsite, Joel did say, 'Bruce, this is Texas. There's a fine tradition of corruption here. We all know it. We know they get kickbacks. That's why you go into politics. We know we're lied to. Look at Waco. Mr Bush, he's a Texas politician. We know we're being lied to. Right now, we just don't know what to believe and what not to believe.'

*   *   *

There was an article once, I think it was in the magazine *Science*, in which a scientist wrote that it seemed to him his beard grew heavier when he knew he'd soon be having a conjugal visit from his girlfriend, or wife—I can't remember which and it doesn't really matter. So this scientist, being a cause and effect man, a guy who likes facts, started weighing the whiskers he shaved off each day and, sure enough, as the day of the womanly visit approached, his shavings grew heavier.

In the morning, when I looked in the sink I just couldn't believe how littered in chin whiskers it was. Julia was arriving in Houston the next evening and it was time to get ready. First, I visited the

357

National Center for American Western Art. The Texan and American flags, flaring from a flagpole against a sky an identical blue to the flags, were perhaps more memorable than the art gallery itself. Somehow I had expected a museum of Remington bronzes, artwork by turn of the century cowboys. It was a pleasant enough but uninspiring display of the West seen through the eyes of Western-living fantasists and realists. A white Stetson, sitting on the dashboard of a car parked in the adjacent lot, was as interesting.

I picked up a local tourist guide at the centre and saw that both Kerrville and nearby Bandera were home to 'exotic game' ranches. So this was where the bastards were.

I learned about these ranches while advising a superb film-maker, Antony Thomas, for a TV programme on our relationship with animals. His documentary *Man and Animal* is the best intelligent discussion of animal welfare I have ever seen.

There are probably 1000 'exotic game ranches' in the States where, on a 'no kill—no fee' basis, you shoot tame exotic animals. You shoot with guns, you shoot with crossbows, or you shoot with a simple bow and arrow. To make sure you don't damage its head, you shoot it first to maim it. You don't want your trophy head with a hole in it. And what do you kill? Well, almost anything as long as it's exotic, harmless and beautiful—axis deer, blackbuck antelope, impala, oryx, springbok, gazelles. If you're cheap and still want to kill something, then for a few hundred bucks they'll line up a sheep for you to assassinate, a mouflon or aoudad, a Corsican or Hawaiian. For years now, the Humane Society of the United States has tried

358

unsuccessfully to convince the federal government to pass a Captive Exotic Animal Protection Act. Fat chance when the vice-president shoots tame birds.

I'm not against all hunting. I've got no problem with hunting for consumption where there's a surplus of game, and that applies to most parts of North America and Scandinavia. I don't have objections to regular fishing. It's the unnaturalness of exotic hunting that I find so repellent. It's the antithesis of good sportsmanship. In my AGS guides are always listed the states' fish and game laws. Even 60 years ago they said, 'no spotlighting deer', 'no leaving hooks unattended', 'no hunting from motorised vehicles'. Killing an exotic animal that's been habituated to humans, that has no chance of escape, is as sportsmanlike as shooting your own cat.

I returned to a laundromat on the multiples strip to wash my clothes and bedding. 'Self-operating. That's what I like to see in a young man,' said Granny, watching me fold my clothes as hers tumble-dried. Back beside Joel's veterinary clinic, a team of Mexican kids set to work washing and waxing my home, and while they did so, I caught up on a little writing, then went with Joel, Joanna and client friends to Mamalitas, a Tex-Mex restaurant for lunch. I didn't want to tell my hosts that the food looked and tasted like grasshopper juice, that the Monterey Jack cheese was like bleached rubber, though they'll find out if they read this book. Joel's client, a restaurant owner from nearby Bandera, told me how, when his Yorkshire terrier's windpipe collapsed, Joel accompanied him to the surgical specialist in San

Antonio. Having got a handle on Joel the previous evening, that didn't surprise me. He's the type of vet who surrounds himself with injured wild birds and nurses them to recovery. That tracheal collapse must have been well inside the chest cavity, for nothing could be done. The man confided to me that, a year on, he still couldn't think of getting another dog.

*   *   *

I set up camp at Palmetto State Park for the night, deserted but for two other vehicles, a pick-up and trailer and an RV towing a pristine green Morris Mini estate. I first thought the sign at the entrance to the park said 'Sam Marcus River'. After all, I'd been through Seligman, Arizona, and past Nathan Jaffa's ranch near Artesia, New Mexico, but it was, in fact, the San Marcos River that I camped near on this last night before the chief's arrival.

On a trail was a wooden sign: 'Watch for Snakes'. The AGS *Texas Guide* had already warned me:

> Rattlesnakes are common throughout the State. Suction kits for first aid are available at most drug stores. Copperheads and cottonmouth water moccasins are usually found along streams. The most dangerous of Texas' four poisonous reptiles, the coral, is encountered less often.

I reined in Macy, lashed her to me and we walked paths laid by Civilian Conservation Corps men in the late 1930s, through groves of palmetto and pine. It was as if we were in southern Florida. Signs explained that this was but an island remnant of palmetto that once spread along the Gulf of Mexico coast from Florida almost to Mexico. A spectacular red, black and yellow snake crossed our path and then, hearing shuffling off the trail among the palmettos, I saw a foraging nine-banded armadillo, armour-plated, ten inches long, with another ten inches of Cheshire cat-like ringed tail. It seemed oblivious to us, probably habituated by frequent proximity to park visitors, and it continued nosing and digging in the forest leaf and dirt, looking for insects and worms.

After dinner I met one of the two other campers, a retired drama teacher from a local university, an elderly Vincent Price lookalike with a snow-white Van Dyck beard, walking with his wife. I asked him about Woman Hollering Creek, which I'd passed near the turnoff to the park and he explained that its name derived from an old Spanish story 'La Lorona',—the weeping woman. 'You hear the same dramatic morality tale throughout the world in all languages. The essence of each story is the same, but the circumstances are different. The essence is that a woman drowns her baby. The variations come in the circumstances: to revenge the father who has run off with another woman, to unburden herself so she can run off with another man, because she is unmarried and will be disgraced, because she's a fool and doesn't think she can handle raising a child. The essence then returns to the story with the denouement— her remorseless regret, her weeping, wailing, sobbing, or in this instance, hollering.'

I'd chanced on another Pete, another Grandpa

Bill, another walking encyclopaedia, so I asked about the snake I'd seen. 'Was it red on yellow?' he asked, but I couldn't remember. 'If it was black, red and yellow, it was a coral snake. They're more common around San Antonio than elsewhere. I've personally never seen one.'

I asked why the exact colour banding was important.

'Red on black, poison lack. Red on yellow, kill a fellow. Mind you, I've also heard, red on black, friend of Jack. Curious that one, isn't it? The Mexican milk snake is red on black on yellow.'

By now it was dark. Mosquitoes were abundant, but my academic friend enjoyed talking and his wife enjoyed that he enjoyed talking, and, eventually, we drifted into politics.

'I'm a lifelong Democrat,' he explained, 'and I'm out on a limb on this one. I avoid the subject but there's no doubt in my mind that this government has used the surge of patriotism after 9/11 to fulfil policies it would not otherwise have been able to contemplate. I won't even talk about this with my friends because it's considered unpatriotic to disagree with Bush policy. This is about settling old scores and expanding the American oil-industry control abroad, to ensure a constant cheap and safe source of oil. That may or may not be good for America. What's not good for us is to do so with the type of arrogance and moral clarity we are showing the rest of the world. Too much moral clarity is a dangerous thing. It makes killing too easy. Bush declares that we are serving God's will, that our cause is right. Can he not see that he is using the same type of moral clarity that Bin Laden is using? I served my country in Korea. This

362

is an exceptional country, but that doesn't mean we are more virtuous or honest or truthful than Canada or Germany, or any other country that chose not to join this escapade. If we could not persuade our closest friends of the virtue of this endeavour, could this administration not see that the course was wrong? There was time to reconsider. Bush and his cohorts are making problems for our children and our children's children.'

Now the mosquitoes were miserable. So was I, for I could find nothing in his argument I disagreed with.

*   *   *

'My daddy shot heroin and my mommy shot heroin, but then my daddy shot my mommy, then he shot his self, and I was orphaned but that was good because a church-going family, believers, adopted me, and I went to Sunday school and discovered Jesus, and now I pray to God and sing songs for you on the radio and . . .', and, well, I think I'm going to go shoot heroin if I keep listening to these western ballads on local Texas radio.

I set off for Houston, kamikaze butterflies and other insects aiming accurately at my just-cleaned GMC. My drama professor told me he was pretty sure there was a Double D Ranch outlet store somewhere along I-10. Yoakum was certainly less than an hour's drive away and that would be an ideal place to pick up something for the chief, but if it was there I missed it. I started rehearsing Macy for her reunion and we reviewed our ten-point plan.

1. Practise obedience. Pretend you never lost it.
2. Groom yourself. Pretend you are always pristine clean.
3. Run to greet her.
4. Be enthusiastic. Tell her you're amazed she's still alive.
5. Dance and wag with your entire body.
6. Be loyal to her. Stay close by her, not me.
7. Take any gift she may bring with gentle grace. Carry, don't chew.
8. Let her touch you all over.
9. When she greets you, nuzzle her to remind her of your faithfulness.
10. Groan with pleasure.

Mace told me I should practise what I preach.

Traffic was chaotic and I reached the airport later than I planned. I passed Halliburton's offices, ironically, or otherwise, just across the road from Bush International Airport, parked far away in a long-term car park where there was room for my home and took Mace to the terminal.

'I'm sorry but dogs aren't allowed on the bus,' intoned the driver.

'This is a trained seeing-eye dog. I'm taking her to meet her helpless, elderly, blind, frail, female owner arriving from London.'

'Ah, let him on,' suggested a businessman passenger behind the driver, and we boarded the bus.

Julia had already passed through baggage and customs and was in the main terminal.

'Here I am,' she cried. I ran to her. She threw her arms around Macy, who followed the rehearsed plan and went berserk with cries and whines, and leg-leans and body-rubs. Julia did the same to her, then pulled one of Mace's favourite toys, a cuddly soft shark, out of her handbag and gave it to her dog, who carried it triumphantly around the terminal hall, much as she had done with a jackrabbit a few days earlier—tail erect, head back, high-stepping. Their uncomplicated, unalloyed, honest greeting brought smiles to the faces of everyone around, but Julia was now concentrating on me and probably missed that.

We took the packed bus back to the car park where Julia inspected her new home, instantly approved, and we departed for Lake Houston State Park, where I'd planned we'd spend the first night.

All the park's campsites had been taken by a Happy Hollow Elementary School weekend camping trip, but the volunteer park ranger offered us an isolated pull-off in a shady corner. This was ideal. We were more on our own here than we would have been in a regulated site and were visited only by occasional dads sneaking off from their kids for fags in the forest.

The air was buzzing with mosquitoes. Mosquitoes and Julia don't mix. She's known for years that American mosquitoes find her sweet English blood particularly appealing and their anticoagulant causes her to suffer flamboyant allergic reactions. And besides, having lost her spleen, somehow, a few years back, her natural defences against mosquito-spread diseases, especially malaria, are severely compromised. Julia stayed on the inside of the screened door while the park ranger and I talked snakes.

'Lots of 'em here. Look for Hershey's Kisses on their sides. They're copperheads. Look like hourglasses from above. They're the most common biters. Not scared off easy. A man tripped and landed on one recently. Had some fool woman here a few years ago. Went for a barefoot moonlit walk and regretted it.'

It was 8.00 p.m. and dusk had just turned to night, but it was 2.00 a.m. by Julia's small but still well-formed little body, so all three of us went to bed.

Next morning, Macy and I were off before dawn for an hour's walk along humid trails, while Julia slept. We returned and I prepared dog food for Mace and maple syrup-cured Canadian bacon, sliced Sara Lee brown toast with unsalted butter and fresh-squeezed orange juice for Julia: breakfast in bed. I had a toasted wholewheat bagel, Maine blueberry jam, bacon and a quad espresso. This is a good way to start the day.

Julia dressed and called Mace for a cuddle, kissing her on her head. 'What's this?' she asked, but she knew that what she had almost kissed was a tick walking through the golden hairs on her dog's head. She grabbed it and her jaws clenched as she squeezed it and presented it to the vet. 'Haven't you been treating her?'

I had, but what can you say? We now had a woman with us. Mace and I were going to have to sharpen up.

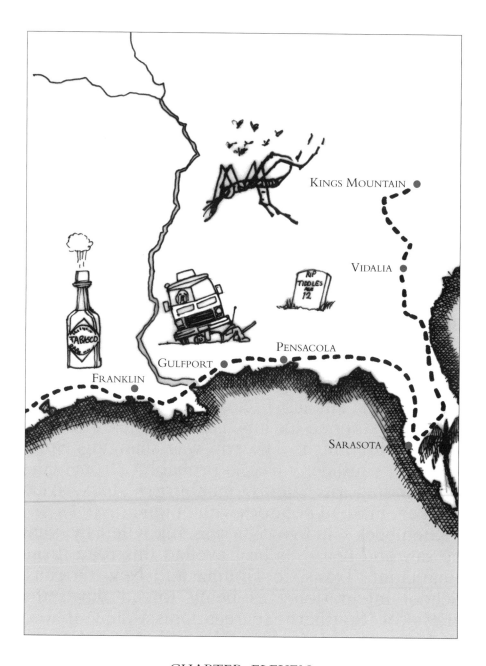

CHAPTER ELEVEN
THE DEEP SOUTH

 Let me be frank. If I had not been following Steinbeck's route I would have avoided this part of America. Louisiana, Mississippi, Alabama, Georgia—the indelible image of the Deep South in my unreconstructed, northern, 1960s mind is peaceful, rightful, protest marches; Sheriff Bull Connor; snapping German shepherd dogs, water cannon, police batons; dynamited churches; putrefying bodies in shallow graves. But here I was completing Steinbeck's circuit, with two attractive females, the passenger seat occupied for the first time since visiting my family in Ontario.

After exercising both blondes on a side road near China, Texas, we crossed the state line into Louisiana. *'Bienvenue en Louisiane'*, said the road sign, the first and last French I read or heard in the state. We stopped for lunch at a Creole buffet. We stopped for lunch! The trip was changing. Spicy Creole sausage, rice, probably from the surrounding rice fields, hamburger steak, fried chicken, mashed potatoes with onion gravy.

Steinbeck's indignation was rekindled by what he saw and heard as he travelled this road, from Beaumont, Texas, to Houma and New Orleans. School integration was being forced down the craws of Southern segregationists and it was sticking in their rancid gullets. Steinbeck recounted stopping for gas in Beaumont and the attendant seeing Charley in the back.

'Hey, it's a dog! I thought you had a Nigger in

there.' And he laughed delightedly. It was the first of many repetitions. At least twenty times I heard it—'Thought you had a Nigger in there.' It was an unusual joke—always fresh—and never Negro or even Nigra, always Nigger or rather Niggah. That word seemed terribly important, a kind of safety word to cling to lest some structure collapse.

I was reminded of Southern cops when driving through Lafayette, I saw billboards promoting someone named Armbuster for sheriff. Julia told me to look again. It was Armbruster. Drats.

The dashboard air conditioner had stopped working, an unexpected glitch, and it was hot and humid, but there was a breeze coming through the screen windows, so I didn't power up the generator to run the two roof units. The flat, developed landscape was uninspiring, tacky casinos everywhere—in gas stations, in bars, or standing lonesome and bleached beside the old road. We drove through New Iberia, Jeanerette and Baldwin, deep into bayou country. The names on businesses and mail boxes I passed were all familiar: Thibodeau, Rousseau, Broussard, Arceneaux, La Biche; similar to those I'd seen in Vermont and, of course, in New Brunswick and Quebec.

Broussard. That was certainly familiar. It was a Joseph Broussard who organised the greatest single exodus of Acadians, in 1764, from Halifax to Santa Domingo in the Caribbean, then French-owned and called Saint Domingue. Finding Acadians already there in a distressed state, he took his refugees on to Louisiana, settling in the winter of 1765 in the land we were driving through. Like Chanel's owner in New Brunswick, the man who talked through a toothpick in his mouth, these local Louisiana Cajuns have their roots in Nova Scotia's Acadian dispersal, but here they form a powerful foundation to Louisiana's culture, so much so that Kathleen Blanco, running for governor as I drove through, emphasised her old Louisiana connections by including her maiden name in her political posters: 'Vote for Kathleen Babineaux Blanco'.

Louisiana's capsule history is this: discovered by Spain, claimed by France, dumped by France and reluctantly accepted back by Spain; owned by Spain during the 30-year period from 1760 to 1790 when the Acadians arrived, then secretly transferred back to France in 1801, just in time for France to sell the territory for around $15 million to the United States in 1803. Some Congressmen were steadfastly opposed to a land of 'foreigners of doubtful allegiance' being admitted to the Union, but in 1812 Louisiana was granted statehood.

It looked like bad timing. America had just declared war on Britain and had invaded Ontario, expecting the Canadians to welcome their neighbours as liberators freeing them from the yoke of British oppression. They'd forgotten that of the 100,000 inhabitants of Ontario—called Upper Canada at the time—four out of five were American-born or the children of families American-born. More than Americans care to admit, their Revolutionary War was really America's first civil war. In the War of Independence, 'Loyalist' corps, individuals opposed to secession, were raised in every colony, from Georgia to Massachusetts; Americans fighting Americans. Over 100,000 of the losers had their property confiscated. Most moved to Canada, the so-called United Empire Loyalists.

These resettled people were not just vanquished Brits, they were a microcosm of the whole European mix in the colonies they vacated, in what was now the United States of America. United Empire Loyalists' records in Toronto show that 38 per cent of Loyalists had their national origins in Great Britain, 23 per cent in Germany, 5 per cent in Holland and 4 per cent in France. Chanel's owner's family fought with the British against the Americans, only to find themselves forcefully ejected from their land to make way for English-speaking Loyalists.

In January 1815, after a peace treaty between the United States and Great Britain had been signed, a British naval force, unaware of that treaty, attempted to reach New Orleans. It was driven back by a combined force of Americans, Spanish-speaking Louisianians, French-speaking Creoles and Cajuns, Choctaw Indians, coastal Baratarian pirates and 'free Negroes'. A war against Canada unwittingly had accelerated the integration of Louisiana into the Union.

The flat road we traversed paralleled Bayou Teche, through unending fields of eight- to twelve-foot-high green sugar cane in various stages of growth. Double-length trailer trucks lumbered down this narrow road, bits of sugar cane debris flying from their loads, their tyres leaving cakes of mud the size of footballs scattered over the road. This is Louisiana's Sugar Bowl, the state's most fertile land.

We arrived in attractive Franklin, a town that oozes Southern charm. Settled by Pennsylvanians, Franklin residents opposed secession from the Union and in 1861 immediately capitulated to Federal forces. During the Civil War, all sugar cane grown in this parish made its way up north. The consequence of their action, well, really their inaction, is that the town was left unscathed by the war. Good for tourism on the 200th anniversary of the Louisiana Purchase. Today Franklin has over 400 homes on the Historic Homes Register. Main Street was closed to traffic, awash with people enjoying a Saturday street party. Perfect, I thought. A great place and ideal circumstances for Macy and me, accompanied by the chief, to meet folks. I stopped and parked on a side street, then looked at Julia and realised it was not the ideal time to park and party. It was afternoon for me but beyond the point of no return for her. Her body was still back in Britain. It was best to move on.

We moved on, at least I tried to. I turned the GMC's ignition and nothing happened. Zip. There was what you could call a look of tension in Julia's eyes as I turned the key again. Nothing. Then again. And again. Then I remembered the auxiliary battery button on the dash. This is a clever gadget that GMC dreamed up 30 years ago. Let's say you're in the desert, leave the lights on all night and drain the battery. No problem. Just depress the rocker switch on the dashboard, which hooks the starter motor to an auxiliary battery, and, presto, your life's saved. Holding that button down with one hand, I turned the ignition with the other and the engine started. Somehow the main battery had gone dead. Stone flat dead. That's why

I'd lost the air conditioner an hour back.

I don't know why but I thought it would be better to return to US 90. It could be that I thought there'd be more help there, but as I did so, the engine spluttered as if the gas was contaminated with moisture. I played tremolo on the pedal, trying to keep the engine going, but we slowed and burped along the rumble strip rather than the road itself, slowing even more. On an approach to a long bridge the engine backfired, and *pfut*, it died. I coasted to a stop, tried the auxiliary battery, but there was no response. Juiced out. *Kaput*. Surrounded by swampy bayou, the air filling with mosquitoes screaming, 'Suck the strangers dry!', the sun about to set—no power. 'Is this what you call an adventure?' a tired Julia asked plaintively.

*   *   *

Before leaving on our trip I'd joined the RV scheme of the AAA, the American Automobile Association. I have enough trouble changing a tyre on my Saab. Changing one on a six-wheeled 12,000-pound vehicle was something I thought best left to others. While Julia tried to relax, I telephoned their Emergency Road Service and was told they'd send a mechanic who'd try to jump-start me, but if he couldn't he'd tow me up to 100 miles, to a destination of my choosing. Where, I thought, would I like to be towed to in Louisiana's Cajun country? New Orleans was well within 100 miles and I assumed there would be a GMC service centre there that could help. Then I remembered, the 'Black List'.

Before leaving England, I downloaded into my

373

laptop computer the 'GMC Motorhome Assist List, aka the Black List'. It's a list of GMC owners throughout the United States and Canada, initiated by a GMCer named Black, willing to help fellow GMCers with advice, overnight hook-ups and repairs. I found the list and checked for GMCers in Louisiana. One in Baton Rouge had hand tools, a floor jack, jack stand, bearing tools and GMC maintenance manuals. Another in Monroe, in north-east Louisiana, was willing to travel up to 50 miles to help. The GMCer in New Orleans could 'direct fellow GMCers to local entertainment hot spots and give crawfish-eating, oyster-shucking and beer-drinking lessons'. One in Franklin had 'hand tools and coffee. Know where parts houses are. Internet access. Space in the driveway for one coach with electricity only'. Franklin! That's where we were!

I phoned and spoke to Carol Scott who passed me on to her husband Al, aka Scotty. I explained to Scotty what had happened and asked his advice on where we should get towed to if we needed repairs.

'Cancel triple A. I'll pick up a friend and be with you in fifteen minutes.' I was the accident waiting to happen.

A Harley Davidson biker pulled up and asked if he could help. I explained that the cavalry was coming and, while Julia remained in her new home, I took Macy for a walk by the edge of a paralleling train track. Returning to the road, I saw a Harrier jump jet hovering over my home. Two ropes dropped from the cockpit and down abseiled Al Scott and his friend Bob Hustler, USAF flight engineers (retired). OK, this time you know, I lie!

Actually, the pair of healthy-looking, grey-haired septuagenarians arrived in a clean white Chevy Sonoma pick-up. Equipped with tool kits and flashlights, they embarked on a joint operation, something I learned later in the evening they had done a thousand times before while serving full time in the air force.

Bob made an immediate diagnosis of a broken battery cable. The battery had never been fixed in its box and, bouncing over the 10,000 miles I had already covered, eventually caused the cable to fray and crack. Bob visited Wal-Mart for parts for a temporary fix, but there was still no juice. Scotty switched the cables so that the starter motor now ran off the auxiliary battery. That gave us headlights but not enough juice to turn over the engine.

They were stymied. Scotty turned to me, grinned and said, 'You're in the cult now.'

It was dark. Julia and Macy were screened inside. The generator wasn't firing up, so there was no air conditioning. Three guys, two knowledgeable, one nodding in assent, were being consumed by the most carnivorous mosquitoes I'd ever chanced upon. Searching under the chassis, Bob found a frayed alternator belt and finally made his diagnosis. 'That's a real can o' worms.'

Julia and I were now removed from the equation. Bystanders. Bob and Scotty discussed the dilemma. Then Bob three-point-turned his pick-up to face the GMC head on, jump-started my home and, riding shotgun behind us lest the vestigial power from the auxiliary battery fade and we lose our headlights, Al barrelled us back to his place at a speed I never knew my little home was capable of. We parked in the entrance to his daughter's adjacent drive, leading down to their home on a Bayou Teche canal.

Scotty's wife Carol made us coffee and offered me a meal. Julia had heard the cacophony of face- and arm-slapping going on as we stared at the battery and knew that in the presence of such self-abuse tonight was not a night to leave her screened security. She and Macy remained in the GMC on the driveway. A couple of hours later, when I returned to my home, Julia warily unlocked the door and let me in. I didn't know it locked. Not a happy bunny. I'd expected her to be asleep, but the thought of spending the night in someone's drive kept her too alert to slumber.

*   *   *

I was awakened at dawn by the hollering of frogs, crickets and birds singing a seven-note song in an adjacent golden rain tree covered in hundreds of autumn's red-pink papery seed pods. The noises were all coming from a single source, a mockingbird, a colourless, formless, nondescript blathermouth. It was nondescript but it was memorable. Its song matched perfectly the rhythm of that old ballad 'Listen to the Mocking Bird'. That was exciting, it really was. Leaving Julia to catch up on her sleep, I walked Macy, trying to keep my dog from investigating each home's backyard and, as I did, an early morning single-engined crop-duster dive-bombed the cane fields on the far side of the canal. Scotty explained later that sugar cane is sprayed with Monsanto's weedkiller Roundup—a glyphosate—to kill off

376

new shoots. That increases the sugar yield. A hawk floated in circles above us, probably conditioned through experience that when the cutters move into the fields, critters rush out.

Carol made breakfast for her husband and me, grinding her own hazelnuts for the coffee. Bob arrived and joined us. The Scotts and Bob, I learned, were part of the 'New South'. Originally from the North-East, the Scotts retired to Louisiana when their son-in-law was employed by the Chitimacha Indian Tribe to head security at their nearby Cypress Bayou Casino.

The Chitimacha were once a large coastal tribe, probably numbering 20,000 in 1500, but half that by 1700. Historically, the tribe had a nobility structure. The nobility were restricted to marriage within their caste and, as numbers dropped, the range of socially acceptable partners diminished. Marriage to African-Americans was forbidden but marriage to Caucasians was allowed, and there was ample intermarriage with Cajun families, conversion to Catholicism and adoption of French as their language. By 1784 numbers of full-blood Chitimacha had dropped to 184, by 1880 only six families remained. The 1910 census listed 69 Chitimacha, only three of whom were full-bloods. Recovery began after the federal government granted to this vestige of a tribe a reservation. When attorney bills were about to claim most of this, a Miss Sarah Avery McIlhenny purchased the land at a sheriff's sale and ceded it to the federal government who put it in trust for the tribe. The casino is on this land.

I've checked on the Internet and, if I've got this right, Miss McIlhenny's mother's family owned

377

Avery Island, a 180-foot-high salt mound in the marshes south of nearby New Iberia, while it was her father, Edmund McIlhenny, who 130 years ago dreamed up the recipe for Tabasco sauce. Avery Island still has an active salt mine and is home to *Capsicum frutescens* pepper fields. If you're a Tabasco junkie, you can make a peppery pilgrimage to the bottling plant and see how the peppers are ground into mash, mixed with Avery Island salt, then aged for three years in white oak barrels before being blended with vinegar.

Here's something you don't want to know. Does your dog eat the cat's poo from the litter tray? If it does, Tabasco sauce is the answer. The best aversion therapy I know is to inject, with a needle and syringe provided by your vet, a little Tabasco sauce into a piece of poo and leave it for your dog to find and eat. Other than a few chilli-loving Labradors, it cures them all.

Julia awoke refreshed. She was still deeply, deeply British, but with a little sleep and a bit more to eat, she intuitively understood the spontaneity of what was happening; that this was how, over the past months, her husband and her dog had been living. She saw that Scotty and Bob had been waiting for us to come along for, what, five years?

Al showed me inside his GMC. 'Not enough information with GMC's dash,' he explained, as I looked bug-eyed at the *Starship Enterprise* array of working dials he'd added to his dashboard. Al moved his GMC out of his drive, jump-started mine and moved it to pole position, nose to garage door, facing a fully equipped, pristine workshop. Hospitals should be this immaculate and organised. Scotty had everything a GMC would need, from bearing tools to a jeweller's magnifying loop.

Diagnostics began. Scotty explained that the GMC has a sunken manifold, so gas pools easily. My pumping the pedal had flooded the manifold and that caused it to sputter and stall. While Scotty recharged my battery, Bob visited the local Auto Zone for a new battery cable to replace the previous night's temporary repair. In a relationship that has endured for over 40 years—Bob moved to nearby Charenton, after the Scotts moved to Franklin—these two buddies played mental mechanical softball with each other and came up with this scenario. My battery had started shorting out. The battery's aberrant behaviour increased the strain on the alternator. This led to the alternator belt fraying and finally tearing away. That probably happened somewhere between Beaumont, Texas, and Lafayette, where I lost the air conditioning. I looked up the GMC manual to get the code number of the alternator belt, but Scotty, a true GMC anorak, and I'd learned by now that to maintain one of these old beauts you have to be an anorak, explained that when belt manufacture went from Imperial measure to metric, that code number was assigned to a belt with a very slightly different size. All three of us returned to Auto Zone where Scotty bought a differently coded belt, still measured in inches rather than centimetres.

Without so much as a nod or flip of a coin or my-back's-killing-me, Bob slipped under the vehicle to inspect 'the can o' worms'. He'd spent his working life crawling inside the wings of C124s to carry out in-flight repairs, so he might have felt at home under the GMC, his nose blackened by grease, his mouth sprinkled with flaking rust as he removed first the power-steering belt, then the air-conditioning belt to get to where he would install the new alternator belt.

'You'd think an aircraft designer designed this dang thing,' he muttered.

Scotty explained that aircraft are designed wholly for dynamics. It is the flight engineer's enduring challenge, not just to diagnose a problem but to figure out how to get at it to repair it. By 1.00 p.m. my flight engineers, happily back on active duty and working as a well-oiled team, had fitted a battery cable, had inventively installed bolts over the battery to keep it sound in its box and, most important, had replaced the alternator cable—one bear of a job. They had done this work on a driveway, without a pit to work from and, I'm sure, did it more efficiently, more accurately and faster than it could have been done at a GMC dealer in New Orleans. Scotty checked my battery, saw it still wasn't taking the charge, and concluded that the final item I needed was a new battery. 'Check the alternator belt each day,' Bob advised. 'It'll need to be tightened.'

I asked Carol where we could take our saviours for lunch on a Sunday. She suggested Cypress Bayou Casino. Macy stayed with the Scotts' daughter. She told us later that when Macy was let out to wee, she ran straight to the GMC and just sat beside it looking anxious. That was only the second time in over two months she'd been parted from both me and her home.

With a son-in-law as head of security, we were pretty much assured a fast table and a short history of the casino. In the late 1980s, Carol explained, the Chitimacha started Bayou Teche Bingo. In the early 1990s they changed the name, added slot machines, and eventually dropped bingo. By the late 1990s there were 135,000 square feet of casino, three restaurants and massive parking lots and bus bays for day-trippers from Texas. Lunch was enormous.

Back to the Scotts' and I made one final trip in Bob's Sonoma, this time to Wal-Mart for the battery. It was quickly installed. We rendered our profuse, really profuse, obsequiously profuse thank yous and departed, over the Atchafalaya River, where we'd broken down 24 hours earlier, through fields of sugar cane and forests of cypress, tupelo, gum and water oak, past massive oil business activities, and then along Bayou Boeuf, a tributary of the Atchafalaya, covered in a profusion of water hyacinths, to Linda's RV park—a great location for a trailer trash film.

*   *   *

'Schooling rat Dan,' Linda offered, as I swung through the screen door to the front office of her RV site. 'Smatty fan,' she continued, nodding her head towards Julia and the GMC. Whoa! I'd finally met a native and couldn't understand a single word she was saying.

'We'd like to stay tonight. Have you got thirty-amp hook-ups?'

'Cher dew. Sand is here an Jess Fallabilly. Sat ate een.'

Linda's home by the road, wooden, single-storey, painted white once, wasn't very wide but

EXHAUSTED IN LOUISIANA

took up almost the entire width of her property, a pencil of grass extending from the road back to an overgrown canal. Fences and mature trees lined the sides. Linda was a peroxide blonde, blowsy and just that wee bit sinister-looking. She was so happy to have passing trade, she gave me a discount on what she told me was her normal fee for 'Fan sea Arvys'. I walked through her office to the back porch where Billy, beer-bellied in bib overalls, was sitting on a rocker by a rusty old electric soda cooler. Beside him, Bette Davis stared unblinking from a wicker wheelchair, butcher's knives in both hands. Just kidding. Billy heaved himself onto a golf cart and guided us the 30 feet to site 18, our hook-up for the night. I plugged in and turned on the air conditioners. Linda was right. It was cooling right down, but even so my mighty fine home felt a lot fresher with double AC booming away.

Mosquitoes the size of dragonflies greeted Macy and me on our morning ramble round the distant recesses of Linda's RV site. Julia remained incarcerated in her home, happy as a Labrador pup, with her now standard bacon, eggs sunny side up, toast and freshly squeezed orange juice breakfast in bed. We left early, heading for Houma. This road, State 182, must have originally been a *cordelle*, a tow path for horses to pull barges up the canal. If so, it's one of the oldest roads in the state. Sugar was first refined here in 1794 and the elegant, white, antebellum plantation homes that we passed whispered of former grandeur. I stopped by a small, low-built, white clapboard church and adjacent cane field where Macy disappeared among the cane stocks, then raced around the cemetery. The burials were all above ground, in stone coffins, a sure sign of how low lies the land of Terrebonne Parish. Steinbeck thought that Houma was one of the pleasantest places in the world, so we did a circuit round the business centre and residential areas of town but, with marauding mosquitoes in mind, headed on towards New Orleans, stopping to buy sweet green satsumas from a couple of grizzled men, in bib overalls, parked by the roadside in a battered, sun-bleached, old pick-up.

There's something about grown men in bib overalls that frankly I find a bit worrying. I raised my kids in bib overalls—Dr Dentons. There were two reasons. The first was that they were practical, and because they were hard to get in London, a real fashion icon there. The second was that my cousin Elliot manufactured them. In fact, back in 1973, Elliot bought one of the first GMCs off the production line. He used it as his mobile office while his chauffeur Sam, a World War II tailgunner, drove him and two other Dr Denton execs from their homes in Memphis, Tennessee, to the Dr Denton factory in New Albany, Mississippi, 90 miles away. That GMC was multi-purposed. Elliot married an orthodox Jewish girl and when he developed a deep need for a Chinese take-away, he ate his non-kosher meal in the GMC parked on his driveway.

It was already 85 degrees. We had no generator to run the main air-conditioning units while driving, so decided to skip New Orleans and drive on towards Florida. We cruised through low, flat country of bayous and cypress swamps. Grey Spanish moss—it's not really a moss but rather a flowering bromeliad—dripped from live oaks and cypress trees, adding a sombre, almost funereal tone to the livelier greens of saw palmetto and pine. In my lifetime, Spanish moss was still stripped from trees, from here to Florida, cured by drying on racks in the sun for six months and run through a 'gin' to remove the rotted outer husk, leaving resilient fibres looking much like horsehair only stronger. It was used as stuffing for mattresses and cushions.

The highway coursed on stilts over treeless salt marsh and cypress swamp, sometimes at grass level, sometimes at mid-tree level, sometimes at tree-top level. We drove on to Mississippi.

*   *   *

The air was fresher on the Mississippi coast; there was a slight breeze, and the blindingly white beach, extending east to the horizon, was virtually empty. I knew this sand. This is the motherlode for the sand on the barrier islands by Sarasota, Florida, the sand of Crescent Beach on Siesta Key, where my parents have wintered for 30 years and where we were heading. This is almost pure quartz, cool on your feet even on the hottest summer day. In another 'x' thousand years, Gulf currents will have moved this sand east to the Florida panhandle, south down the coast, eventually dumping it all in the Caribbean. Macy gambolled on the beach, racing in and out of the Gulf. I did too. Julia ventured just outside her front door; no further lest the mosquitoes zap her. The south's first yacht club was organised here at Pass Christian in 1849, where we were, and Beach Boulevard—US 90— rimming the water, is lined with elegant, old, two-storeyed homes, all with verandahs or balconies, or both, all robed in mature gardens of palm trees, camellias, roses, oleanders, honeysuckle and wisteria. Until recently they looked onto the turquoise waters of the Gulf of Mexico. Now they are all within sight of the massive casinos that have sprouted waterside.

Julia had been in the States for three days now and hadn't experienced the predatory thrill of bargain-shopping, so in Gulfport I headed up to a Premium Outlets Mall for her to stalk fashion, while I went to Wal-Mart and bought some 12-volt wire and alligator clips to make a jump for the circuit board. It worked. I could park, pull out the generator drawer, fix my alligator-clip bypass wire to two points on the circuit board—Scotty showed me which ones—and turn on the generator. We now had main air conditioning when we stopped. Driving back to meet Julia, I stopped at a Krispy Kreme. Mace hadn't had a warm, sickly-sweet donut for weeks. Three original Krispy Kreme donuts, I calculated, contain roughly the same number of calories as a standard tin of dog food.

At Shepard State Park, near Gautier, Peggy, at the Park Ranger Station, greeted us in full warpaint—silvery lipstick highlighted with burgundy lip-liner, mascara you could tar a shack with, flowery dress, fire-engine-red hair. Park rangers usually wear Smoky the Bear uniforms. Mississippi sure is reinventing itself, I thought, then Peggy explained she was from Vancouver, Washington, an incomer, a new resident of the Deep South, part of the 'New South'. She drove a massive Pace Arrow RV and because the park was too small to warrant a team of full-time park rangers, Peggy was paid $5.25 an hour to work as park hostess. 'All the locals find work at the casinos,' she explained.

I used up the last of my Wisconsin blue cheese in a salad for dinner and my remaining wood from Ontario, Wisconsin and California for a campfire which Julia viewed safely through her home's front window. Mace spent the evening treeing feral cats that swung back and forth, like inverted metronomes, from the tops of thin trees. Cats were everywhere, seemingly the most common wildlife in the park.

If I were a feral cat, I'd like to live here on the Gulf Coast. There are over 65 million pet cats in the United States, cats that own people, but just as many, probably more, feral ones, individuals that survive by finding their own meals. This coast must be great hunting territory for cats, ideal because it's good basking country and well populated with us. We're important because we produce superb garbage. And the place is rife with wildlife: mice, squirrels, rabbits, geckos, lizards, snakes, birds. Cats are superb at how they modify their eating habits according to what's available. Of course, bird lovers hate cats. One report, in English newspapers, estimated that a million birds a year are killed by free-ranging cats. Another report from Wisconsin estimated that cats kill almost eight million birds each year, in that state alone.

Like it or not, cats, be they feral (that's unowned) or free-ranging (that's owned but allowed to wander freely outdoors), have become part of the world's natural ecosystem. Some people say they're not a part of the 'natural' ecosystem, but that's not true. They're not part of the 'original' ecosystem, in the same sense that many of the wild flowers of Ontario are not a part of that region's original ecosystem. Cats, horses, house sparrows, tumbleweed and West Nile virus, none of these were part of America's original ecosystem, but they're are all here to stay. They won't go away. There's no doubt that cats are refined killing machines, that a free-ranging house cat kills simply for pleasure.

In a Michigan study, a well-fed farm cat killed 1600 small mammals and 60 birds in an 18-month period. Feral cats, however, are not as profligate. They are more inclined to kill to eat, hunting primarily when hungry. The curious consequence of these differing behaviours is that our free-ranging pets are more likely to unleash environmental destruction than cats like the one Macy chased up the tree. Mind you, those cats may well have been pets once. I've been told more than once by park rangers of the problems they have with campers bringing their cats to state parks and releasing them, in the misguided notion that this was 'best for the cat'.

*   *   *

Entering Alabama, I stopped at their state Welcome Center. I wanted to find someone who could tell me where I could find out who Robert E. Coxe was. In 1992, at an auction in Chichester, Sussex, I bought Robert E. Coxe's passport, the eighteenth passport issued by the Confederate States of America, signed at Montgomery, Alabama, on the 26 April 1861. The passport, issued to 'Robert E. Coxe, his wife and child going to Europe', described him as 45 years old, five feet ten inches tall, with a high forehead, dark eyes, aquiline nose, small mouth, round chin, dark hair, dark complexion and dark face. The auction catalogue stated the passport was signed by R. Cromby. That was wrong. It was signed by Robert Toombs, the Confederate States of America's first Secretary of State.

I showed the passport to the woman on duty—blue-eyed, grey-haired, carefully and conservatively dressed. She was fascinated by it and called over her colleague, younger, darker haired and as generously warm in appearance.

'Look a' this.' They read it slowly, carefully, word for word.

'He must a' been a black man,' my welcomer stated and her colleague agreed.

'What would a black man be doin' goin' to Europe?' asked the younger.

'He had dark hair and a dark face,' said the first woman, reinforcing her opinion, then she turned to me and asked, 'What does agraline mean?'

'That says aquiline,' I explained.

'What does that mean?'

'Hooked, like an eagle's beak,' I answered.

'Black men usually have broad noses. This is wonderful. Thank you for showing it to me. I'm specially interested because I'm a Daughter of the Confederacy.'

'So am I,' offered the younger woman.

I wondered whether being a blood-descendant of someone who fought for the Confederacy was a minimum requirement to work in an Alabama Welcome Center, but saw there was an African-American woman cleaning the floors, so I knew I was wrong.

'How racist is the south today?' I wanted to ask, but Julia was beside me and I didn't want to embarrass her. Carol and Scotty told me that under the veneer of acceptance it was still in the bone, that 300 years of culture can't be eliminated by a piece of legislation.

A phone call to a local historian told me I'd get more information about who Robert E. Coxe might be off the Internet, from genealogy sites, than from visiting any archives in Montgomery, so I continued east, through Mobile into Florida. We'd passed through four states in 24 hours.

*   *   *

My family's been visiting Florida for four generations, for almost 100 years. With Julia on board, I'd planned from the outset to abandon Steinbeck's route up through Mississippi and to drive down to the family condo in Sarasota. As was my visit to Toronto and Lake Chemong, this was a trip back home.

We headed east through the Florida panhandle, Julia, trapped by mosquitoes, happily trapped, as she'd fallen in love with her new home. I decided to barrel ahead to cover the next 500 miles as quickly as possible. Somehow I was getting the feeling that my journey had changed. Throughout my travels I'd dictated observations and comments into a tiny digital recorder about the size of a Stabilo highlighter pen. It had hung from my neck, sat in my pocket or been clipped onto the seat, while I travelled. I'd used it anywhere from 30 to 60 times a day. Now, with Julia beside me, I talked with her more and observed less. The day before, I didn't use it at all. Somehow travel was no longer an adventure, an experience, a quest. It had become a family holiday.

To break the journey, east of Pensacola, just past a dead brown bear on the highway, in a land of milk chocolate and black coffee-coloured rivers, I turned off to De Funiak Springs, parked under shady live oaks and took Macy for a walk around the one-mile circumference of the perfectly round lake. Christmas lights had just been installed on the trunks of palm trees and carefully garlanded over shrubs. There were free-standing lighted mangers, stars, flowers, Christmas trees and signs: 'Merry Christmas', 'Peace on Earth'.

'Bullet, turn that pink flamingo a little towards me,' I heard someone say. I turned to look but Macy was already greeting Bullet, dressed in grey and white prison stripes, with 'Walton County Jail' written on his back. The man giving instructions, wearing light denim bib overalls and a burgundy baseball cap, was a local retiree, John Simms. John had travelled abroad, seen how Christmas lights can give vitality to a community and, in active retirement, decided that De Funiak Springs needed a unique selling point.

'We'ah now in our sixth yeah and they'ahs two to three million lights. The city gave ten thasand dallahs and the county another twenty-five thasand. I used that to buy thasands of used lights and wooden shapes. We sand-blasted and repainted the plywood. I call it "Holiday Reflections" because all of the lights get reflected off the lake. You stayin'?'

I explained we were only passing through and

391

asked about the men helping.

'We get lots of community help. Bullet, he helps each yeah. Most of the othahs have helped in the past, one way or the othah. Last year a truck drivah from Houston turned off I-10 when he saw the sign and was so impressed that he returned the followin' weekend with his wife to show her the lights. We had forty thasand come last year.'

Bullet was my age—rumble-faced, a bit of a Walter Matthau lookalike. He smiled a lot, stroked Macy a lot, and was quiet. One of his jailmates was baby-faced, wearing glasses, almost academic in appearance, and another, in his late thirties, tanned, wearing a backwards baseball cap, was sharper-looking—a chancer. I asked him what Walton County Jail was like.

'The prison is only capacitated for a hundred, but it's so crowded they fill the exercise yard with an extra holding for the women. On weekends they got over two hundred in there. I'm sleeping on the floor. My boss-man, he came and sat there all day yesterday to get me out, but there was no one to process me.'

All the while, he tickled Mace behind her ears. Her new friend was in jail for driving while his licence was suspended for a previous drink-drive offence. He was eligible for parole, but the jail was short on administrative staff, so he was in the park positioning snowmen and reindeer for John.

I asked what other type of crimes got you in prison stripes at Walton County Jail.

'The sheriff, he just arrested a woman and her husband in south Walton County. They was abusing little doggies. She had nigh on a hundred of 'em, little York-shire terriers, all in tiny cages. I

392

heard tell they was all mangy and covered in shit. Some of 'em died. The sheriff, he had to give her and her husband extra protection at the jail. They just posted bond and they gone now.'

Macy's new friend was probably describing a puppy mill, a breeding factory for whatever breeds happen to be fashionable. American pet stores sell up to half a million pups each year, mostly sourced from thousands of places like this one in Walton County. In theory, the Department of Agriculture's Animal Welfare Act, passed around the time I graduated, protects animals from this form of abuse, but a black hole in interpreting the act allows puppy-mill owners to get away, quite literally, with murder.

Macy and I continued our walk around the lake, returned to our parked home where Julia was reading, and drove her around to the far side.

'There are no mosquitoes and I'd like you to meet some friends we just met.'

My wife is an actress. I mean that, literally. She was a stage, screen and television actress. I wish she could have seen the double-take she did, when she saw the guys in stripes I was taking her to meet. Academy Award-winning. A little more British reserve gently dripped away.

*   *   *

At Suwannee River State Park I paid Macy's Florida two-dollar per night, per animal camping fee, and for the first time since New York State I was asked to show her up-to-date rabies vaccination certificate.

On our regular early morning stroll next day, I

lost sight of Macy. That's not uncommon. But when I heard a loud splash from under the large branches of a cypress that had fallen into the Suwannee River, I gulped hard. There are alligators here. Mace came charging back through the underbrush and I realised that the noise was from fast-flowing water eddying under the tree's trunk and that she wasn't meals on wheels for a resident reptile. It was just beautiful, watching dawn break over the Suwannee River, standing on its limestone banks studded with bald cypress trees, with their curious upright 'knees' protruding from the sand or river shallows. I'm told these knees were once harvested to make table-lamp bases. Park information told me that Stephen Foster, who wrote 'Old Folks at Home' ('Way Down Upon the Suwannee River'), had never visited this river but that didn't stop me from singing the refrain to Mace, as I took pictures to show Julia. Back home I made her a final bacon breakfast, then headed south for Sarasota. Julia picked another tick off Macy's head as I drove.

I'd been through this part of Florida several times before and each time find it more tedious than the last. The monotony was relieved in Marion Country where I passed the Animal Center's 'Neuter Commuter', a converted 45-foot-long bus in which, for $25 or $5 with proof of low income or government assistance, dogs and cats are neutered, vaccinated against rabies, given microchip implants and county licences. 'Please Don't Litter', pleads the Marion County Animal Center. There's a similar service in Palm Beach County called the 'Spay Shuttle'. The 'Neuter Commuter' was parked opposite a pro-life billboard proclaiming, 'Life starts at conception'.

At home in Sarasota, Julia was finally able to emerge from the GMC. For the next week Macy beachcombed on the intercoastal and gulf beaches, foraged behind the strip mall, met the local cops, met morning fishermen who wriggled fresh-caught fish in front of her nose, pounced on geckos, chased rabbits, slept on carpet, or simply lay on the grass outside our front door. Julia and I met up with friends, shopped, ate out lots, house-cleaned. I booked an SUV to carry us and our transport kennel from Charlotte to Newark, confirmed that Julia and I would have seats together for the flight home, and got instructions from Continental Airlines on how my longhorns should be packaged to be carried as my additional piece of baggage. All the time I was treading water. I was enjoying what we were doing, and thrilled that my dog was actually walking on 'my' beach, but the fizz was absent, the expectation missing, the excitement gone. For months I'd got up, made breakfast then winged it. Now that spontaneity was replaced by planning; who to see, where to eat. At the start of our travels it had taken weeks for me to shed my feelings of guilt over being away, over relinquishing responsibility. I must have been inordinately successful because now it was a bit of a bummer coming back to reality. My folks used to bring us kids back all sorts of treats from their annual winter vacation in Florida—Hawaiian shirts, coconuts, orange-blossom honey, sticks of sugar cane, Ju Jube candy, Hershey Bars and sweet onions. Yes, friends, my parents brought their kids back onions, sugary-sweet onions that made hamburgers taste like they were prepared in

395

heaven. The onions were so sweet you could bite into them like fruit. They came from somewhere off US 1, in the heart of Georgia.

We camped at Georgia's Crooked River State Park, next to the Kings Bay Strategic Weapons Facility on the Atlantic, and I took Mace for her regular evening walk. Although sunny during the week in Florida, it was humid, grey and threatening here. 'Ah see you let him off his leash agin and you boat attah heah, you heah me?' challenged the charming park ranger. Welcome to Georgia.

Overnight, Julia got eaten by no-see-ums. They're small enough to get through the screens, so we left early without eating breakfast, joined US 1 and headed north past the Okefenokee Swamp. I stopped to exercise Macy on solid, sandy pine lands of saw palmetto and sedges. Holly with round spineless leaves, more like live oak than English holly, its berries still green, grew in abundance by the roadside. Eighteen-wheelers rocked Julia, cosseted in her home, as they roared by on their way north.

Southern Georgia doesn't seem to be touched much by the magical renewal that I've read has transformed the northern part of the state into one of the greatest growth regions of America. The land looked sad. Perhaps it was just me. I was heading north, to Charlotte, to abandon my home and fly back to London. My mood was as grey as the day.

We drove into cotton country, past collapsed wooden structures that must have been old cotton gins. The word 'gin' was but a southern corruption of the word 'engine'. Eli Whitney's cotton gins, the machines that separated cotton from its hull and seeds, existed near almost every town in this part of Georgia. Using rollers or saws, the white lint was separated from the seed, and while the clean lint was compressed for packing in jute bags, the seeds were blown through pipes to a seed house and then sold on to refineries for processing into cotton-seed oil for cooking. The hulls, the 'cake' left after oil was removed, were used in cattle feed or fertiliser.

Due west of Hilton Head, South Carolina, as Julia picked four more fresh little ticks off Macy, dropping one on my leg, I turned off US 1 towards Vidalia. I had three reasons to visit. I was quite certain the alternator belt was still tight, but wanted a professional opinion on it. I wanted the brakes bled and the oil changed once more, before leaving my home with Buddy. And I wanted to visit the native home of the sweet onions my parents used to bring back for me.

Sweet onions have been grown on a small scale in Toombs County, the region surrounding Vidalia—named after the man who signed the Confederate passport I was carrying with me— since the 1930s. By the 1950s some of these farmers, no doubt wearing bib overalls, were setting up roadside stands on busy US 1, selling their sweet onions to tourists like my folks on their way to or from Florida.

This part of Georgia was notorious for its tourist speed traps. After each trip to Florida, my parents told me that year's horror story of being stopped by a local sheriff for allegedly speeding on US 1 through here, being taken to a remote farmhouse, where the judge, once in his pyjamas, declared them guilty and collected a cash fine. My father took to carrying a ten-dollar bill and a photo of his lookalike cousin Barney, a member of the Royal Canadian Mounted Police, with his licence. If one item didn't work, the other did. 'I understand, Officer. You're only doing your duty,' he'd say, back erect, assuming a military posture. Even so, he drove slow, slow enough to see the onion stands.

I can buy just about any variety of fruit or vegetable in London, but no wholesaler has yet realised what a treat a sweet onion is. I've looked everywhere but can't find any. Other than folks like my parents who travelled through Georgia each spring, most North Americans didn't know about Vidalia onions either until the early 1980s, when Willard Scott, the congenial weather guy on NBC's *Today Show*, held cook-offs each spring comparing his sweet Vidalias to others, invited chefs to cook on air with Vidalias, even flew down to Georgia to check how the crop was growing. The Georgia State Legislative acted fast. They passed legislation defining what a 'Vidalia onion' was, expanding its recognised production range to cover a twenty-county region. In 1990, this noble onion was elevated to the status of 'Official State Vegetable'. Don't smirk. If Wales can have its leek, why can't Georgia have its onion?

Today, one in ten onions sold in the US is a Vidalia. Adopting technology from the apple business, wholesalers store them at 34 degrees F, in a controlled atmosphere of mostly nitrogen with a little carbon-dioxide and oxygen. That keeps Vidalias in food stores through until this time of year: November. I went looking for some,

398

unsuccessfully. When I asked, I was told they'd all gone to the 'big cities'.

*   *   *

A glowing, volcanic red dawn broke over the Clarks Hill Lake. Macy and I walked the beach where waves from previous storms had eroded the terracotta earth from the roots of the overhanging pine trees. The ground was spongy-soft, covered in a blanket of long pine needles. Orange light reflected off the damp tree trunks. It was a monochromic wonder, a world washed in an almost fluorescent, orange miasmic glow.

We were on what once was the Little River. Strom Thurmond Dam, only a few miles away on the Savannah River, had created Clarks Hill Lake. Strom Thurmond. Damn. Now he was a truly successful bigot. Lived so long he finally got called a statesman. We had the park virtually to ourselves. I had parked on a pencil-thin peninsula protruding into the lake. On the far shore, my *Georgia Guide* told me, was an old farmhouse and barn. When the guide was written in 1940, the then owner of that farm had just discovered in his attic an early model of Eli Whitney's cotton gin. He also found parts of other models in the surrounding fields. Fifty feet from the house was Eli Whitney's workshop, in which he perfected the cotton gin.

The story of the cotton gin goes something like this. With a pot of gold waiting at the end of the trail for the person who mechanised the separation of cotton from its seeds, countless inventors entered a race to see if it were possible to build such an 'engine'. Suspicious that spies would steal

399

his ideas, Eli covered the windows of his workshop with narrow iron grates, but believing women incapable of understanding what he was doing (he was a Yale graduate), he allowed them to enter his workshop. It's said that Edward Lyon, dressed as a woman, gained entry, described to his brother John the processes he had seen, and improving on these John Lyon built a successful cotton gin. It was only after tedious, prolonged litigation that Whitney's prior claim was recognised. Georgia planters, however, were angered by Whitney's 33⅓ per cent royalty charge for using his gin and preferred to get theirs from those who had stolen his ideas.

Here's another bit of trivia from the guide. A mile east of this farm is the grave of a Jewish revolutionary soldier, Abraham Simons who, in compliance with his request, was buried in a standing position, musket at his side. His widow married a local Baptist minister, Jesse Mercer, and used her inheritance to fund the establishment of Mercer University.

During our morning walk Mace and I met the neighbours who had arrived in their 40-foot RV after dusk. It made our home look like a dinky toy. Julia had breakfast, played with Macy, and I asked her if she'd like to meet the neighbours. She inhaled, held her breath and took a step back, but I grabbed her hand and walked her uphill to meet a couple in their 60s, farmers from upstate New York who had sold their farm and were now living permanently on the road.

Everywhere in North America there are literally millions of Ozzies and Harriets, free-spirited, nomadic, wholly white, all-American, easy-going, cliché-spinning grandparents, permanently on the road, visiting the kids, picking up mail then moving on.

Travelling the highways for leisure, not for needs, has been part of American culture since the Tin Can Tourists formed their club in the 1920s. The original Tin Canners were snowbirds, using their Model T Fords and trailers to escape to Florida for the winter, setting up camp in city parks from Tampa to Sarasota. The phenomenon took its name from their typical cuisine, canned food, and from the tin cans they fastened to their radiator caps, to signal others of similar ilk. That was their secret handshake, admittance to the club.

By the early 1960s, when Steinbeck travelled with Charley, trailers were being superseded by custom-built camping units bolted on flatbed truck chassis. In the early 1970s, GMC produced its motorhome of the future, a taste of what could be, and by the 1980s, firms were converting coaches into motorhomes, now relabelled recreational vehicles or RVs. These were truly mobile homes, not just with AC, fridges, freezers and cookers but with dishwashers, ice-makers, washer/dryers, TV, VCR, DVD, solar panels, full stereo sound systems. By the 1990s, living permanently on the road had become a mass movement.

Today there are more RVs in North America than there are inhabitants of Sweden, almost nine million. One RV club alone, the Good Sam Club (Good Sam stands for Good Samaritan), has over a million members and it estimates that three million people, almost all over 55 years old, live permanently on the road—nomads—full-timers—Geritol gypsies. That's equivalent to almost the entire population of Norway—man, woman and child—ebbing south in the autumn and then north in the spring, forever chasing the best weather, the perfect, fresh, sunny, 80-degree day.

Wherever I've travelled I've met these healthy, wholesome nomads. Beneath their Eisenhower-generation conformity—the garden gnomes, pink flamingos, howling coyotes, plastic flowers, satellite dishes, fairy lights around their campsites, AstroTurf, barbecues and bicycles—beyond their homespun exteriors is a trend-setting, quietly rebellious people perpetuating that libertarian American tradition of freely arriving then moving on. They've become invisible to state or federal authorities, dropping off electoral registers, renewing their licences and RV insurance using addresses of convenience, often in states with no sales tax on RVs or low insurance rates. They seek independence, freedom, mobility and contentment and find it in their massive, moving American dreams.

Ozzie and Harriet's enjoyment showing Julia around peeled away a little more of the chief's inherent British wrapping. Mrs Retired Farmer was sitting in the sun on a deckchair, drinking tea, gazing over the mercury-smooth lake. Mr Retired Farmer was tinkering. I don't know what with, but he was tinkering. Mrs Farmer was more than delighted to show us around her home. The bed was made and decorative pillows fluffed. A vase of wild flowers sat on the dining room table. The bathroom was sparkling, with fresh towels fluffed and folded. It looked like a superior hotel suite just prepared for the next guests.

Mr Farmer joined us. He explained the

automatic levelling system, the CCTV screen he watched when reversing, the two-way walkie-talkies that came as standard equipment so that the passenger could help direct the driver into tight spaces, the eighteen-speaker stereo system, the flat screen TVs, one in the living room, one in the bedroom. He demonstrated the slides that extended the width of his RV to sixteen feet. That's as wide as my Victorian terraced home!

'You're told they're reliable and the engines generally are, but there's too much that can go wrong. She's a complicated beast, a real woman. What with the electrical circuits, the plumbing, air conditioning, furnace, sewage and motors working the slides, she's a full-time job keeping her on the road but something any farmer can do himself.' Mrs Farmer nodded in agreement. Mr Farmer knew how to handle cantankerous beasts.

I asked how long they planned to spend in this part of Georgia and Mrs Farmer explained they were visiting their daughter who had moved to nearby Thomson a few years previously, another emigrant to the New South. She looked out over the placid lake. 'I think we'll just stay here 'til we feel the urge to move on. It's retirement serenity.'

I didn't want to leave either. The green hills, the island-studded mirror-like lake, the now golden forest, its ground covered in pine needles and autumn leaves, the silence—this is what's burned my heart with memories of what I love about North America, what I hadn't realised I miss so.

*   *   *

Washington, Georgia, is an elegant little town of

narrow, tree-shaded streets and charming old homes. The main street is called Robert Toombs Avenue. We walked along the tree-shaded sidewalk, past a row of Greek Revival, Doric-columned, white clapboard homes to Robert Toombs's House, now maintained by Georgia State Parks & Historic Sites. Outside his home is an official plaque that reads, 'This was the home of Robert Toombs, racist, bigot, alcoholic, pompous egomaniac bastard and lifelong shit'.

Well, actually, it says, 'This was the home of Robert Toombs—planter, lawyer, and distinguished Southern statesman'. So let's just look at what this 'distinguished statesman' said and did.

Toombs voted against American ownership of the Oregon Territory: 'I don't care a fig about and of Oregon . . . The country is too large now, and I don't want a foot of Oregon, or an acre of any other country, especially without niggers.'

Toombs voted against the admission of the State of California.

When South Carolina seceded from the Union, Toombs recommended that Georgia also secede. ' "Defend yourselves; the enemy is at your door . . .!" thundered Toombs from the Senate floor,' quotes the brochure I was given at Robert Toombs's House. It fails to mention that he continued, 'We want no negro equality, no negro citizenship; we want no mongrel race to degrade our own.'

In February 1861 Toombs was sworn into office as Secretary of State for the Confederate States of America. On 26 April he signed Robert E. Coxe's passport. In July he resigned.

Toombs then became one of the worst brigadier

generals in the Confederate Army. A typical comment from another general. 'Toombs is drinking like a fish and making an ass of himself. His disobedience of orders is notorious and his disposition, to shirk all positions of danger.' In 1862 he was arrested for disobeying orders. He resigned his command, annoyed, in his self-regarding way, that the President had not promoted him

By early 1865, the secession states had been all but defeated. Union forces came to arrest Toombs, but rather than surrender with dignity he disappeared out the back door, leaving his wife and pregnant daughter to cope. In 1867, after first ascertaining that he would not be arrested, he returned to Washington, resumed his law practice and rebuilt his wealth.

The leaflet I was given at his home says, 'His last service to Georgia citizens was helping create the Constitution of 1877, which was not amended until 1945.' It does not say he told a Georgia crowd, 'I can make you a constitution by which the people will rule and the nigger will never be heard of.'

Marica at Robert Toombs House State Historic Site gave me her card with her job title 'Interpreter'. At first I thought she was there to translate local vernacular into English I could understand and regretted she wasn't with us back at Linda's RV site in Louisiana, but she was in fact our guide and took us on an extended tour of the cool, high-ceilinged rooms. She was a wealth of information and confided that when offered the job, it was problematic for her to 'interpret' a home that could be seen to venerate a bigot. Marica's conclusion was that it was 'history', it

405

happened, and people were interested in visiting sites that personalised the Civil War. I wondered if the State of Georgia would ever have the integrity to be honest about a man it calls 'its distinguished statesman'.

*   *   *

I was now only a hundred miles from Charlotte, North Carolina, end of the road for my home. We drove through the wooded, hilly, industrial north-west corner of South Carolina, past road signs advertising peaches and fireworks, and a BMW plant whose presence advertised the regeneration of this once poor mills-and-stills region of the state. Kings Mountain State Park was heaving with activity; most of the sites were occupied, many dressed in strings of multicoloured lights. With no park rangers evident, I stopped at an occupied site and Elinor told me to park where I pleased. Park rangers, she explained, would come through tomorrow collecting fees. I found an isolated pull-off and took Mace for a dusk walk through walnut woods, the ground pebbled with large fresh nuts. I filled my pockets.

The evening cooled. I'd used up my remaining firewood so Mace and I visited Elinor to ask where we could buy some.

'Don't you go worrying about that, honey. You jes come with me.' And she took me to her neighbour, a minister, who gave her some split logs, then we returned to her trailer where we picked up some more logs and paper. 'You evah light a fire with green pine, honey?' she asked.

We three returned to our campsite and Elinor

set to work. She collected twigs, wrapped and twisted newspaper, laid her own green pine logs on the pyre and lit a match.

'I can light a fire with jes about anythin', but there's nothin' so good as green pine.' The campfire virtually exploded into flames. 'This'll see you through the night, but if you need more wood, you jes come and ask me.' And she walked off to her light-festooned site, just visible through the trees.

Macy and I had dinner by the fire. The chief took a few photos of us. We both lapsed into fire-gazing, Macy mesmerically, me contemplatively. Another night in the woods. Sleeping under the stars in the desert was exciting. It was a new experience, with fresh sounds and unexpectedly enchanting sights. It was a wonderful experience, but I love the woods. Early learning, I guess. At the cottage, even at college, I knew there was always solitude nearby. I miss that, living now in southern England. That's probably why I so much enjoy accompanying Julia on her frequent trips to Sweden.

The following morning, before leaving, I walked over to Elinor's campsite to thank her for her help and generosity.

'Never you mind,' she replied. 'It's just Southern hospitality. How do you like the South?'

That was a loaded question. I don't care what you say, white guys in bib overalls, driving old pick-up trucks with Mississippi or Alabama or Georgia licence plates, just give me the heebie-jeebies. I explained forthrightly to Elinor that growing up in the fifties and sixties, gaining my impression of the Deep South from what I read in the papers and what I saw on television, this was one part of America I didn't want to visit.

'Honey, this was one part of America I didn't want to *live* in, let alone visit. But I did. Gulfport, Mississippi. Bad things happened here, yes, bad things. But it's changed a lot. Not all, but a lot. This is the New South. I sure hope you like it.'

Hearing this from a black woman, probably older than me—I couldn't tell because her complexion was so fresh—gave me pause. Over the past days I'd been irritable. I've been thinking of the Deep South as it was when I moved to Europe 35 years ago. And like other places I'd visited, here too has changed. Population has shifted from the North-East down to the Deep South as well as westward to Arizona and New Mexico. This land of destitute cotton mill towns now makes BMWs goddamit! A foreigner's car.

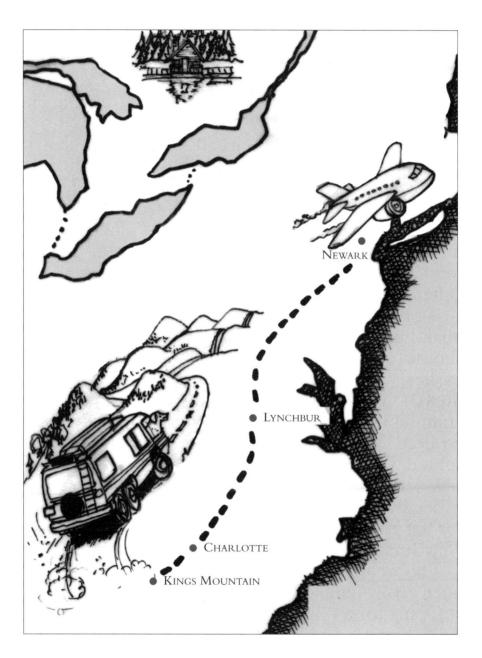

NEWARK

LYNCHBUR

CHARLOTTE

● KINGS MOUNTAIN

CHAPTER TWELVE

GOING HOME

 Charlotte was the beginning of the road home. I wasted an entire day at the local Onan-Cummins generator place, where engineers tried to work out what burned out the $500-circuit board. They saw it had been wired in backwards by their California repairman, but were sure there was a deeper problem. By the end of the day, frazzled and more in debt for the additional hours invested in unsuccessful diagnosis, I gave up. Later in the week, it took Buddy fifteen minutes to repair the generator.

At the Holiday Inn, there were no fireflies at dusk but Mace knew where the rabbits were and shot through the woods as she had done ten weeks earlier. Julia and I visited the local Outback Steakhouse for supper, and next morning, after completing paperwork with Buddy and arranging covered storage for my home, we packed the rented SUV, visited the vet where Macy got more tick-prevention treatment—this time applied officially to conform with her needed paperwork for her return to the UK—and headed for Newark, New Jersey, and our flight back to London.

The weather throughout the entire journey had been truly mellow. We headed into Virginia, stopping for a take-away meal near Lynchburg. My AGS *Virginia Guide* explained that nearby was the home of Colonel Charles Lynch whose harsh activities during the American Revolution are said to be the origin of Lynch Law and lynching. There's something I've never thought of before, naming activities after people. Lynching—Mesmerising—Spoonerism—Caesarian—Fogling. The last one means bunking off with your dog.

On the first day I travelled in the GMC, I drove along the more southerly heights of the Appalachians, along the Blue Ridge Parkway. There the ridge was high and broad, a land of rolling uplands, deep ravines and distinctive peaks. Further north, here on Skyline Drive in Shenandoah National Park, the ridge is often crisply sharp, to the west, right below me, the valley of the Shenandoah River, and to the east the rolling flats of the lower Piedmont country. As Arthur explained on my second day of travelling, the Civilian Conservation Corps built all the facilities here—Skyline Drive, the overlooks, the trails, the shelters. They finished in 1939. We stopped at South River Overlook. The distant mountains were truly all hues of blues, midnight, powder, lavender. On we drove, past Lewis Mountain and Bearface Mountain, their slopes covered in a final defiant blast of autumn colour.

The sun was setting as we approached Naked Creek Overlook. I pulled over to watch the end of our last day in America. Another car was parked at the overlook and a couple in their thirties were sitting cross-legged on the stone wall. They too had stopped to watch the day disappear. I asked Dennis and Peggy if they minded Macy cavorting on the slopes below, which they didn't. Julia sat on the stone wall while Mace and I marched off through the sloping elk meadow.

As we walked, the air filled with music. Harmonica, guitar and voice. I looked back. As the sun was sinking over the blue horizon, Neil Young,

411

standing on the stone wall, was singing 'Heart of Gold'. He turned to Peggy.

'This song's for you, Peggy. I love you and want to marry you. Why won't you marry me?' And he sang 'If I Only Had a Brain' from *The Wizard of Oz*, then segued into a magical 'Shenandoah'. Then The Beatles' 'Norwegian Wood'.

It wasn't Neil Young, but Dennis was good, really good, a classic American troubadour. I don't know if Peggy was moved by what Dennis sang, but Julia and I were enchanted.

The colour of the nearest mountain range turned dark, while the more distant ranges unfolded in mauve and pale blue against the radiance of a shocking-pink horizon. And then, in an instant, the entire sky exploded into a luminescent orange brilliance. Even Macy stopped her investigations, lay down with a plastic Coke bottle she'd found and faced the dying day while Dennis serenaded us into the twilight.

It was dark when we arrived at Big Meadows Lodge. I checked in and when asked who I was travelling with, explained I had my wife and dog with me.

'I'm terribly sorry but dogs aren't allowed.'

'She'll sleep in the car,' I lied.

'I'm really sorry but that's not allowed either.'

I tried a 'last night in America' gambit, she checked with her manager but, once I'd mentioned Mace, there was no way they'd allow us to stay. The receptionist told me there were motels outside the park, about 45 minutes away.

We drove on. Around each bend in the road were dozens of luminous reflecting eyes, white tail deer as abundant here as around the Langfords' ranch in Montana. They were habituated to tourists and didn't move when I slowed, stopped and took pictures. The Drive twisted and turned, ascending to another lodge, Skyland, at 3680 feet the highest point on Skyland Drive. I checked in, not mentioning Macy, asking for a remote room.

Julia reverted to British. 'You can't do that. It's not allowed.'

But Mace and I overruled her. I wasn't going to drive out of the park and stay in some crappy motel on my last night in America. Besides, this was the last weekend of the season. In two days all the facilities would close down for winter. I drove around to our lodge cabin where Julia wanted me to throw a blanket over Mace. She knew there were dog spies everywhere, ready to report us to the dog police. All I saw were fellow guests and a zillion white tails grazing on the grass right in front of the cabins. Door-to-door does. I did throw a blanket over Mace after all and carried her inside.

Next morning, with deer still outside our balcony, I drove a few miles away to the Stony Man Horse Trail and the Appalachian Trail itself for our last morning walk, through forests of hickory, oak and pine. Around us on the heights, the poplar, dogwood and locust had lost their autumn leaves, while in the valley below, in the light of the rising sun, maple and beech trees were still luxuriating in their final display of autumn colour. Two more hawks floated overhead. I've been surprised by how many raptors I've seen throughout America. Mace disappeared into the woods for just over half an hour, but I stood my ground and eventually she returned.

We packed and descended the twisting road off

THE LAST TRUCK STOP IN VIRGINIA

the mountains towards Washington. Traffic oozed slowly through the capital's suburbs and eventually I was back on I-95, and then the New Jersey Turnpike. And you know what zapped through my mind? Simon and Garfunkel, counting cars on the New Jersey Turnpike, all looking for America.

I had come to look for America. I hated the New Jersey Turnpike, but loved almost everything else I found. I returned to America knowing I'd gone native in Britain, that I felt 'British', but the further I travelled the more I realised that this enormous continent was still my home, that this expansive, open culture still felt like family. Tom Wolfe says you can never return home, but he's wrong. You can't turn back the clock to what once was, but home remains, not just in the mothballs of memory but in everyday deeds, in the way people treat you, in what they think about tomorrow, in what their aspirations are. Arnold Toynbee said something like, 'America is a large friendly dog in a small room. Every time it wags its tail it knocks over a chair.' In the rural heartlands, that warmth, that friendliness still exist. I loved being knocked over by such good neighbourliness.

We stopped at a Newark park and as the sun set Mace had a final burst of exultant squirrel chasing. She was truly back in the familiar—a city park, mowed grass, mature trees and plenty of tree rats to chase.

It took longer than I expected to find Continental Cargo. That caused a little consternation to the humans, but on the other hand it meant a shorter time for Macy to be in her crate. She got weighed, paperwork was completed and she was sealed into her transport crate two

415

MACY WAS FINALLY ON HER WAY HOME

hours before departure. I knew there was a little extra to pay, but hadn't expected the vast number of digits on the credit card slip. Dumb. I'd thought when I'd booked our return flights that I'd paid for both of us. Wrong. Continental probably wanted to ease my cash flow so they'd charged only for the outward part of her flight and were now collecting for the return portion.

We returned the car, unloaded our three suitcases and boxed longhorns, and checked in. There'd been a glitch in our seat assignments so we wouldn't be sitting together.

'That will be $350 for the long box please,' the woman at check-in explained, eyeing the seven-foot-long boxed longhorns.

'I phoned from Sarasota and was told that as long as I had no more than two items of baggage and boxed this according to your instructions, it would be treated like skis.'

'Do you have proof of your phone call?'

'Look, I booked our flights through your European public relations office. Here's their phone number.'

The attendant went off to consult her superior.

'I've checked with a Red Coat who says he's sorry, but Continental's European public relations is a different office and has nothing to do with American public relations. He said if you can bend the box in half or cut off part of it, it can travel as regular baggage, but as it's longer than standard we have to charge you.'

I really don't know why I bought those longhorns in the first place. I certainly don't have a wall at home long enough to hang them on and, come to think of it, why on earth would I ever want to hang a steer's horns in my home even if I had a massive empty wall? My mind flitted to poor Macy, sealed in a container, being trundled by another Michael Schumacher on a forklift to a truck, for transport to the airport. I was unhappy to be leaving, unhappy I was separated from Macy; I was just pissed. 'They're yours,' I told the check-in woman.

In the line beside me was another pissed-off customer. Steve's flight to Milan had been oversold, he'd been bumped and was trying to get on another flight. Steve had been listening. 'Would you like the longhorns?' Julia offered.

'Lemme make a phone call to my wife.

'Ya, still here. Are you near the airport? Come on back. I've got something for you to pick up. Don't ask. I'll meet you outside.'

The flight home was short and uneventful. Our daughter Tamara met us at Gatwick and, after a two-hour bureaucratic delay during which Julia burned an extraordinarily large gastric ulcer, we got Mace back and drove to London. I took her to Hyde Park where the late autumn colours were identical to those in Newark twelve hours previously. She sniffed and ran and squirrelled, back on her own turf, oblivious to where she'd been. At least one of the travellers was back home.

MACY'S SOUVENIRS

EPILOGUE

'You've got a letter from the Prime Minister's office!' the chief cried, as I walked through the door after a day at the veterinary clinic. Julia's eyes sparkled as she mischievously wafted a white envelope in front of my eyes.

I'd been back from America for four weeks, back to the satisfying familiarity of days spent meeting and examining animals, to the warmth of the people I work with, but already I was booked to return to Toronto. My father, conscientiously, I'd like to think, had postponed a decline in his health until I'd completed my travels. Now, sudden frailty had forced his urgent hospitalisation. In the following weeks, although I didn't know it at the time, I'd become an Atlantic commuter, visiting my parents for a long weekend every two weeks.

'I didn't open it,' Julia proudly proclaimed, 'but I don't know how I kept myself from doing so.'

The envelope said:

On Her Majesty's Service
<u>URGENT</u>
<u>PERSONAL</u>
PRIME MINISTER

The letter read:

Dear Dr Fogle

The Prime Minister has asked me to inform you, in strict confidence, that he has it in mind, on the occasion of the forthcoming list of New Years Honours, to submit your name to The Queen, with a recommendation that Her Majesty may be graciously pleased . . .

I'd been nominated for a little medal, a royal 'thank you' for some charitable work I do.

Although he was only three years old when his family migrated from Glasgow to Ottawa, my dad remained, throughout his life, culturally British. I took the Prime Minister's letter to him, leaving it with a copy of his grandson Ben's just-published first book, *The Teatime Islands*. On subsequent visits every doctor, nurse, hospital auxiliary and volunteer tugged his or her forelock as I approached. No one had passed his room without being beckoned in by a proud father, to learn that his son was to be awarded a medal by the Queen herself.

My father died before that happened, but those visits to snowy Toronto were doubly comforting. First of all, I could slake my addiction to Tim Hortons breakfasts—coffee, a pecan butter tart and a sesame bagel with cream cheese. These early breakfasts allowed me to continue meeting people, as I'd become accustomed during the preceding months.

'Mind my asking where you got those boots?' was a common opener. The L.L. Bean pull-on waterproofs I'd worn during my travels with Macy were ideal for a Canadian winter and their practicality didn't go unnoticed by other butter-tart eaters.

I struck up a bi-monthly friendship with Peter, a computer software engineer by trade, a photographer by passion. Peter's firm creates software for call centres and was responsible for the Republican Party's Presidential Election fund-raising call centre.

'The American public would probably find it faintly ironic,' he commented, 'that the "jobs-for-Americans" Republican Party's call centre is in Mumbai. They sent linguists to India who trained the locals how to speak with perfect Texas accents when answering phone calls and soliciting donations for Bush's re-election. You'd swear you were talking to some home-boy in Crawford.'

Secondly, I was able, probably for the first time in my life, to have a one-to-one with the guy who gave me half my genes.

'How are you feeling?' I'd foolishly ask.

'Even its tail is a burden to a tired old horse,' he'd answer. I hadn't known that my father could think that way. After he died and I was tidying up his papers, I was bemused—dumbfounded really—to see the notes he kept in his wallet.

Do all the good you can
In all the ways you can
In all the places you can
In all the times you can
To all the people you can
As long as ever you can.

I ask for grace enough to listen to the tales of others' pains. Help me endure them with patience, but seal my lips of my own aches and pains.

Marriage is a legal, religious alliance entered

into by a man who can't sleep with the window open and a woman who can't sleep with the window shut.

When you question your wife's judgement, remember she married you.

I attribute the harmony in my marriage to my growing loss of hearing.

Stories flowed during my visits. Some were figments of his declining mind, like the repetitive fiction that he'd just interceded to help a woman and got coshed on his head by the baddie. Others were based on fact. I learned exactly where he was born: Ibrox Park Road, Glasgow. I heard stories of summers in Britannia Heights outside Ottawa, of tussles with other boys, of escapades, of shenanigans. More unexpectedly, I learned what he truly thought of his wife and children and these were satisfying moments. There's a Talmudic saying, 'When a father helps his son, both smile. But when a son must help his father, both cry.'

That's not true. I trimmed my father's moustache and sideburns, neatened his hair, unruly at the back of his neck exactly as mine is, and we both grinned and chuckled at the reversal. I helped him with his body functions and was content that such a private man, at least on some occasions, did not have to rely upon strangers. He declined rapidly and, for all of us, it was a not unreasonable way for a 97-year-old to die.

*   *   *

Those frequent returns to North America allowed me to wind down slowly after such an enjoyable venture. Bunking off with my dog had been a small event in a grand landscape. I learned, to my surprise, that for all my acclimation to European values and culture I still felt fully at ease— content—with people throughout North America.

Those few months' travel in North America answered some questions but raised others. The British government frequently reminds me that I'm European. I've visited many European cities, but other than in Sweden I've spent little time in the European countryside. With the European Union expanding east, into the lands of my forebears, would I feel as 'European' there as I felt 'American' in America? Travelling with my dog, would I meet with the same warmth I encountered in North America? Would language be an insurmountable obstacle? Is it even remotely possible for an 'Anglo' to feel as at home in Europe as I did in the United States?

If I were to travel from London, England, through Belgium, the Netherlands, Germany, Denmark and Sweden to Finland, then down through Estonia, Latvia, Lithuania, Poland, the Czech Republic, Slovakia and Hungary to Slovenia, then across Italy, France and Spain to Portugal, and back north through Spain and France to London, the distance travelled in that diamond would be less than the distance Macy and I traversed around the rectangular periphery of the United States. Europe is surprisingly small compared with North America.

And Macy? Dogs may live for the moment but they learn from the past and Mace sure learned during her travels. For several months I let her act like a dog. I eased up on the control panel. I let her make her own decisions rather than, as I should have done, channel her behaviour into what I felt were suitable activities.

It started with squirrel chasing, a fruitless activity she's indulged in her entire life. She graduated to white tail deer chasing, a new and futile experience. Her predatory behaviour culminated in successful jackrabbit chasing. Before this trip she charged at anything that moved. She was a clumsy hunter, Macy the klutz. No more. During her months in America she added skills. She improved her intuitive understanding of movement and motion. She refined her ability to predict the behaviour of other animals according to their actions. She began to develop a more sophisticated ability to mentally map large territories. She perfected her ability to investigate a territory systematically. She cultivated the wolf in her. She became a killer.

Prior to her travels, Macy had chased but never caught wildlife. Her success in the Mojave Desert changed that. Returning to Sussex, I didn't see the rabbits in the hedgerows and the first ones she caught probably didn't see her either, their eyes blinded by the purulent discharge of myxomatosis infection. I only knew she had killed when I saw her trotting, head high, through the wheat field rather than running as she usually did. She killed instantly, then brought her kill to me, dropping the pathetic, warm bodies at my feet.

Soon she graduated to successful squirrel chasing. She understood that some squirrels don't run to the nearest tree but, rather, to the largest. I intervened when she took on foxes.

A fox in the open runs for cover, and what was worrying, but I also have to admit admirable, was Macy's understanding that a direct chase was futile. Running the shortest route to the same cover the fox was running towards was more likely to be successful, and on more than one occasion she came within a stride of success.

I needed help so I drafted in an experienced and reliable dog trainer—the chief. I admit it. I'm putty in my dog's paws. Julia takes no nonsense. It was back to boot camp—sit—stay—walk—down. At the merest glint in Macy's eyes, Julia barks and my dog responds.

A month after my father died, Julia and I and two of our children, Ben and Tamara, had our visit to Buckingham Palace for the investiture. Britain does these stylised 'thank yous' brilliantly. Ten years earlier I'd received the next level down form of acknowledgement, an invitation to one of the July garden parties, to tea with the Queen in the gardens of Buckingham Palace, together with thousands of others. Now, with military precision, and with surprisingly relaxed, good humour, the royal courtiers rehearsed me and explained that when my name was called, to walk forward and meet Queen Elizabeth and that when she raised her hand to shake mine, that was the cue to move on.

My turn came—I think the man in front of me got his gong for selling oil tankers to Lower Slobovia—the Queen pinned the medal on my jacket and we talked—and talked—and talked some more. We talked about training dogs. We talked about Macy in Montana and Macy in

Mississippi. My hunch is that she found dog talk more to her liking than oil tanker talk. In the audience Julia and the kids squirmed. They thought I was refusing to leave, but I'd been told to wait for that handshake. Eventually it came, not a limp-wristed grasp but the firm sort that provokes sensation.

Over lunch Ben leaned over and said, 'Dad, you can't deny it. It's less than twenty years since you got your British passport but you're now part of the Establishment, honoured by the Queen.' Then he lapsed into his plan for us to go off on an adventure together.

'We can retrace the route Grandpa took almost a hundred years ago to Canada. Pick up a sailing boat on the Clyde, sail through the Western Isles, because they're so beautiful, then out to St Kilda, across the North Atlantic to Newfoundland, up the St Lawrence River to Montreal, then the Ottawa River to Ottawa. What do you think?'

'Sounds like fun, Ben,' I replied. 'But if I'm going to live in a confined space for several months with anyone, I think I'm going to stick with Macy.'

BIBLIOGRAPHY

Travels with Charley—In Search of America. John Steinbeck, The Viking Press, New York, 1962

Delaware—A Guide to the First State. Compiled and written by the Federal Writers' Project of the Works Progress Administration for the State of Delaware, The Viking Press, New York, 1938

Virginia—A Guide to the Old Dominion. Compiled by workers of the Writers' Program of the Work Projects Administration in the State of Virginia, American Guide Series, Oxford University Press, New York, 1940

West Virginia—A Guide to the Mountain State. Compiled by workers of the Writers' Program of the Work Projects Administration in the State of West Virginia, American Guide Series, Oxford University Press, New York, 1941

Pennsylvania—A Guide to the Keystone State. Compiled by workers of the Writers' Program of the Work Projects Administration in the State of Pennsylvania, American Guide Series, Oxford University Press, New York, 1940

New York—A Guide to the Empire State. Compiled by workers of the Writers' Program of the Work Projects Administration in the State of New York, American Guide Series, Oxford University Press, New York, 1940

Massachusetts—A Guide to its Places and People. Written and compiled by the Federal Writers' Project of the Work Projects Administration for the State of Massachusetts, American Guide Series, Houghton Mifflin Company, Boston,

1937

New Hampshire—A Guide to the Granite State. Written by workers of the Federal Writers' Project of the Works Progress Administration for the State of New Hampshire, American Guide Series, Houghton Mifflin Company, Boston, 1938

Maine—A Guide 'Down East'. Written by workers of the Federal Writers' Project of the Works Progress Administration for the State of Maine, American Guide Series, Houghton Mifflin Company, Boston, 1937

Vermont—A Guide to the Green Mountain State. Written by workers of the Federal Writers' Project of the Works Progress Administration for the State of Vermont, American Guide Series, Houghton Mifflin Company, Boston, 1937

The Great Lakes Guidebooks. George Cantor, The University of Michigan Press, Ann Arbor, 1979

Ontario Wildflowers. Linda Kershaw, Lone Pine Publishing, Edmonton, Alberta, 2002

Bugs of Ontario. John Acorn and Ian Sheldon, Lone Pine Publishing, Edmonton, Alberta, 2003

Michigan—A Guide to the Wolverine State. Compiled by workers of the Writers' Program of the Work Projects Administration in the State of Michigan, American Guide Series, Oxford University Press, New York, 1941

Wisconsin—A Guide to the Badger State. Compiled by workers of the Writers' Program of the Work Projects Administration in the State of Wisconsin, American Guide Series, Duell, Sloan and Pearce, New York, 1941

Minnesota—A State Guide. Compiled and written

by the Federal Writers' Project of the Works Progress Administration, American Guide Series, Viking, New York, 1938

North Dakota—A Guide to the Northern Prairie State. Compiled by workers of the Federal Writers' Project of the Works Progress Administration for the State of North Dakota, American Guide Series, Oxford University Press, 1950 (1938)

Montana—A State Guide Book. Compiled and written by the Federal Writers' Project of the Work Projects Administration for the State of Montana, American Guide Series, Department of Agriculture, Labor and Industry, State of Montana, 1939

Trout and Salmon of North America. Robert J. Behnke, illustrated by Joseph R. Tomelleri, The Free Press, New York, 2002

Idaho—A Guide in Word and Picture. Prepared by the Federal Writers' Project of the Works Progress Administration, American Guide Series, Oxford University Press, 1950 (1937)

The New Washington—A Guide to the Evergreen State. Compiled by workers of the Writers' Program of the Work Projects Administration in the State of Washington, American Guide Series, Binfords & Mort, Portland, Oregon, 1941

Oregon—End of the Trail. Compiled by workers of the Writers' Program of the Work Projects Administration in the State of Oregon, American Guide Series, Binfords & Mort, Portland, Oregon, 1940

California—A Guide to the Golden State. Compiled and written by the Federal Writers' Project of the Works Progress Administration for the State of California, American Guide Series, Hastings House, New York, 1939

Arizona—A Guide to the Youngest State. Compiled by workers of the Writers' Program of the Work Projects Administration in the State of Arizona, American Guide Series, Hastings House, New York, 1940

New Mexico—A Guide to the Colorful State. Compiled by workers of the Writers' Program of the Work Projects Administration in the State of New Mexico, American Guide Series, Hastings House, New York, 1940

Texas—A Guide to the Lone Star State. Compiled by workers of the Writers' Program of the Work Projects Administration in the State of Texas, American Guide Series, Hastings House, New York, 1940

Adventures with a Texas Naturalist. Roy Bedichek, Doubleday & Co., Garden City, New York, 1947

Louisiana—A Guide to the State. Compiled by workers of the Writers' Program of the Work Projects Administration in the State of Louisiana, American Guide Series, Hastings House, New York, 1941

Mississippi—A Guide to the Magnolia State. Compiled and written by the Federal Writers' Project of the Works Progress Administration, American Guide Series, Hastings House, New York, 1938

Alabama—A Guide to the Deep South. Compiled by workers of the Writers' Program of the Work Projects Administration in the State of Alabama, American Guide Series, Richard R. Smith, New York, 1941

Florida—A Guide to the Southernmost State. Compiled and written by the Federal Writers' Project of the Work Projects Administration for the State of Florida, American Guide Series, Oxford University, New York, 1939

Georgia—A Guide to its Towns and Countryside. Compiled and written by workers of the Writers' Program of the Work Projects Administration in the State of Georgia, American Guide Series, The University of Georgia Press, Athens, 1940

South Carolina—A Guide to the Palmetto State. Compiled by workers of the Writers' Program of the Work Projects Administration in the State of South Carolina, American Guide Series, Oxford University Press, New York, 1941

North Carolina—A Guide to the Old North State. Compiled and written by the Federal Writers' Project of the Work Projects Administration for the State of North Carolina, American Guide Series, The University of North Carolina Press, Chapel Hill, 1939

U.S. One—Maine to Florida. Compiled and written by the Federal Writers' Project of the Works Progress Administration, American Guide Series, Modern Age Books, New York, 1938

Lake Ontario. Arthur Pound, The American Lakes Series, The Bobbs-Merrill Company, Indianapolis, 1946

National Audobon Society Pocket Guide. Familiar Animal Tracks of North America. John Farrand, Alfred A. Knopf, New York, 1993

National Audobon Society Pocket Guide. Familiar Trees of North America—East and West. Ann H. Whitman, Editor, Alfred A. Knopf, New York, 1986

432

National Audobon Society Pocket Guide. Familiar Birds of North America—East and West. Ann H. Whitman, Editor, Alfred A. Knopf, New York, 1986